Tragedy
Since 9/11

RELATED TITLES

A Cultural History of Tragedy: Volumes 1–6
Edited by Rebecca Bushnell
978-1-4742-8814-9

Contemporary Adaptations of Greek Tragedy: Auteurship and Directorial Visions
Edited by George Rodosthenous
978-1-4725-9152-4

English Renaissance Tragedy: Ideas of Freedom
Edited by Peter Holbrook
978-1-4725-7280-6

Reader in Tragedy: An Anthology of Classical Criticism to Contemporary Theory
Edited by Marcus Nevitt and Tanya Pollard
978-1-4742-7042-7

Visions of Tragedy in Modern American Drama
Edited by David Palmer
978-1-4742-7693-1

Tragedy
Since 9/11

Reading a World Out of Joint

Jennifer Wallace

BLOOMSBURY ACADEMIC
LONDON • NEW YORK • OXFORD • NEW DELHI • SYDNEY

BLOOMSBURY ACADEMIC
Bloomsbury Publishing Plc
50 Bedford Square, London, WC1B 3DP, UK
1385 Broadway, New York, NY 10018, USA

BLOOMSBURY, BLOOMSBURY ACADEMIC and the Diana
logo are trademarks of Bloomsbury Publishing Plc

First published in Great Britain 2020

Cover design: Louise Dugdale
Cover image: Roberto Schmidt/AFP/Getty Images
Back cover image: Jean-Marc Bouju/AP/Shutterstock

A catalogue record for this book is available from the British Library.

Library of Congress Cataloging-in-Publication Data
Names: Wallace, Jennifer, author.
Title: Tragedy since 9/11 : reading a world out of joint / Jennifer Wallace.
Description: London ; New York, NY : Methuen Drama, 2019. | Includes
bibliographical references and index.
Identifiers: LCCN 2018056541 (print) | LCCN 2019006502 (ebook) | ISBN
9781350035638 (epub) | ISBN 9781350035645 (epdf) | ISBN 9781350035621 (pb)
| ISBN 9781350035614 (hb)
Subjects: LCSH: Tragedy. | Tragedy–History and criticism. | Tragic, The, in literature. |
European drama (Tragedy)–History and criticism.
Classification: LCC PN1892 (ebook) | LCC PN1892 .W29 2019 (print) |
DDC 809/.9162–dc23
LC record available at https://lccn.loc.gov/2018056541

ISBN: HB: 978-1-350-03561-4
         PB: 978-1-350-03562-1
         ePDF: 978-1-350-03564-5
         eBook: 978-1-350-03563-8

Typeset by Integra Software Services Pvt. Ltd.
Printed and bound in Great Britain

To find out more about our authors and books visit www.bloomsbury.com
and sign up for our newsletters.

The arc of the moral universe is long but it bends towards justice.

MARTIN LUTHER KING, JR.

The time is out of joint. O cursèd spite
That ever I was born to set it right!

HAMLET

To Robert, for all those 'why?'s

CONTENTS

LIST OF FIGURES

1

Tragic Events and the Idea of Tragedy

Probably every age has its fair share of tragic events. After all, as the great critic Raymond Williams once said, we come to tragedy by many roads but the ultimate destination of all our journeys is death. Each individual has to cope with living (and sometimes partly living), loving and losing, suffering and surviving, hoping and declining. Such are the ordinary vicissitudes of life when some fortunes rise and some slip a little downwards, and sorrow, daily injustice and infidelity are unremarkable.

However, it seems as if this age, the first two decades of the twenty-first century, is especially an age of tragedy. We have witnessed a growing fundamentalism and the clash of cultures in which the polarization between friends and enemies is starker than ever. We have felt optimism as revolutions have swept through the Middle East, apparently liberating a people based on their own aspirations and efforts, only to see those new regimes fall into chaos, old systems re-imposed and all principles of political belief interrogated and set at naught. Wars have been waged on a questionable mandate, hundreds of thousands of lives have been lost and billions of dollars spent, and the situation now seems more violent and disordered than before the wars. Perhaps no other age has had such an acute sense of futility and powerlessness. We watch an economic world of growing inequality between rich and poor, in which international corporations seem to be above the law and beyond democratic accountability and the individual questions his relationship with the collective and with the state. We live lives of credit and debt, where the bonds of trust and reciprocation have been turned into servitude and slavish dependency. Meanwhile, the coral reefs die and animal species become extinct at an exponential rate as the planet warms and the scientists warn us in vain about a dire future for the world. Instead of heeding their warning, with hubris we take advantage of the melting Arctic to drill for more of the oil that caused the warming and the melting in the first place. Then when the global south seeks refuge from the droughts and famine produced by our warming planet, as well as from the wars and violence caused by our interventions in their states, we put up fences to keep them out. So the victims of our arrogant complacency die in their thousands at our borders, drowning at our coastlines and rivers, crushed beneath the wheels of First World prosperity.

Such is the modern world of which I speak in this book on tragedy. It is strikingly the case that tragedies on the stage flourish in periods of great transition. Greek tragedy arose when a religious, mythical sensibility gave way to a secular, logical and democratic outlook and the clash of values led to uncertainty and conflict. Shakespeare was writing during the Reformation when beliefs in purgatory, confession and the miracle of the Eucharist were overturned and kingship lost its divine right. We are undoubtedly experiencing a similar period of cultural transition now. So, is there a similar flourishing of tragic expression? Writers, artists and film-makers certainly respond to our turmoil and confusion and try to make sense of it all in their work, and I consider a number of these plays, novels, movies and art pieces in this book alongside my primary focus upon tragic events. What are the new forms of tragedy that are being produced to respond to the specific novel characteristics of our contemporary world? Writers and theatre directors are also returning to the old classic tragedies, performing them anew as they seem to speak urgently to the questions that arise now. This has been a golden age for the innovative re-performance of Greek and Shakespearean tragedy and other works in the canonical tragic tradition: Marlowe and Webster, Buchner, Ibsen, Brecht, Miller, Beckett.

The defining moment of the last twenty years was 9/11, when two planes flew into the World Trade Center and everything seemed to change. On a literal level, the event ushered in heightened security at home and two wars abroad: the immediate revenge bombardment of Afghanistan for a missing target, since Osama bin Laden had already fled, and then the subsequent campaign in

Iraq whose connection with al-Qaeda and 9/11 was non-existent but frequently erroneously repeated. President George W. Bush announced his global War on Terror, telling the world that 'you are either with us or against us', while Tony Blair also saw the attack on September 11 as a turning point in world affairs. His speech just a month later, at the British Labour Party conference, declared his ambition to 're-order the world':

> So I believe this is a fight for freedom. And I want to make it a fight for justice too .... The starving, the wretched, the dispossessed, the ignorant, those living in want and squalor from the deserts of North Africa to the slums of Gaza, to the mountain ranges of Afghanistan: They too are our cause. This is a moment to seize. The Kaleidoscope has been shaken. The pieces are in flux. Soon they will settle again. Before they do, let us re-order this world around us.[1]

This speech presaged the British close alliance with America and the commitment to the War on Terror. The significance of Blair's idealistic or arrogant vision (depending on your perspective) was not lost on commentators. Here was an attempt to impose one moral code upon the rest of the world, the ambition of which was like the 'hubris' of the ancient tragic hero, rivaling the gods in its aspiration, going beyond the boundary of acceptable, mortal limitations. Hubris, of course, always deserved to be punished by the gods. 'Nothing in excess' was, by contrast, the wise advice carved in stone at Delphi.

The shaking of the 'kaleidoscope' meant that New Yorkers, Americans, the Western world, felt immediately more vulnerable. There was a sense the metaphorical boundary separating them from the struggles of the rest of the world had been ruptured. Now they were opened up, dependent, precarious. And so, after the initial shock and disorientation of the event, there was a possibility, according to some commentators, that we could be entering a new age of sympathy and tolerance. 9/11 could have resulted in the 'good work of compassion', as the philosopher Martha Nussbaum has argued, when Americans made 'real to themselves the sufferings of so many people whom they never would have otherwise have thought about'.[2] In realizing the precarious nature of their nation, which previously had seemed impregnable and supremely powerful, Americans were newly able to appreciate the vulnerability of others and thus potentially to develop what one commentator, Judith Butler, called a 'fundamental dependency and ethical responsibility'.[3] We could, she said, 'imagine community' differently.

Yet alongside the newly awakened compassion, 9/11 also ushered in an era of fear and intolerance, when the boundaries between 'us' and 'them', friends and enemies, were delineated more sharply. According to Slovenian cult philosopher Slavoj Žižek, the event was not actually a surprise or shock, as the common consensus would have it, but was in fact presaged by decades of paranoid fantasies of catastrophe and threat, and appropriated to justify and confirm long-established ideological responses, like increased bombing abroad and heightened security measures at home.[4] In other words, Americans had been imagining themselves under attack for years, in numerous Hollywood movies and popular fiction, and this fear justified their violent response, increased military spending and heightened domestic surveillance. 9/11 was, for Žižek, a throwback to an old mythology: domestic bravery and external threat. Certainly, rather than Butler's ethics of 'common human vulnerability', the discourse of the War on Terror reached for much older ideological terms: hero, sacrifice, crusade, good and evil. September 11 is the paradigmatic tragedy of the twenty-first century, and so I cannot avoid returning to it again and again, like some unresolved trauma, throughout this book. It can be considered a tragedy on many different levels, from the simple statistics of the loss of life and the subsequent far greater loss of lives in its name, to the traditional tragic emotions – pity and fear – which it provoked, to the potential forms of tragic recognition to which it could have led (the possibilities of compassion and shared precariousness) to the hardening of ideological positions and growing violence and division for which it was taken as justification.

But what does it mean to call an event a tragedy? It might seem self-evident that an experience which is devastating and maybe fatal to those involved, which defies expectation and full comprehension and which has consequences in the future for the community is tragic without any further analysis needed. But in fact, philosophers and literary critics have spilt much ink pondering the nature of tragedy and coming up with strict definitions based upon aesthetic, political theories. Readers might find it strange to learn that, within the academic sphere, there is often a sharp division drawn between tragedy in literature or philosophy or the theatre and tragedy in the form of terrible events in the world.[5] In fact, academics often preface their analysis by noting that their serious and carefully considered use of the term 'tragedy' is far removed from the supposedly glib way that journalists liberally scatter the word. Perhaps reflecting this academic tradition, when ordinary people are asked to think about the word 'tragedy', they will often start talking anxiously about the 'rules', based on a dim memory of school Shakespeare classes and some misrepresentations of Aristotle. Tragedy, they often think, must be limited to the fortunes of an individual. They might mutter something about 'hamartia' or a moment of choice. Isn't each hero supposed to suffer from a 'fatal flaw'? Tragedy, bizarrely, becomes a precious commodity, jealously guarded by the scholars in their libraries and not shared with those who cannot understand Aristotle and Hegel and Nietzsche or afford a theatre ticket, but who might indeed have some first-hand knowledge of injustice, depravation and despair.

Indeed, this book on tragic events in the modern world is highly controversial in some circles in academia, hard to fathom though that may appear. Delineating the fateful, tragic decision of Eteocles to meet his brother in battle in Aeschylus's play, *Seven against Thebes*, is quite acceptable; interpreting the resolution of Mohamed Atta to fly American Airlines Flight 11 into the North Tower of the World Trade Center as tragic is provocative and, for some scholars, impermissible. But these divisions between literature and life do not explain why playwrights compose tragic dramas in the first place nor why we are drawn to see them performed century after century, nor indeed what the purpose or relevance of art and culture to our modern world is at all. What's more, as Raymond Williams argued, ultimately it is not possible to 'distinguish between an event and the response to an event in any absolute way' and by extension to distinguish between a 'real' and a 'mediated' event.[6] Any event is inevitably mediated by narrative report and interpretation. We transition from a position of spectator, when, according to Adrian Poole in the context of watching Shakespeare, 'there is a more-or-less clear line of demarcation separating [us] from what [we] are looking at', to that of witness, 'when [we] are on the edge of an action from which [we] are not clearly separated, when a decision is required from "us"'.[7] And the story or 'event' is as much about those decisions as the original incident. In traditional tragic drama, whether by Sophocles or Shakespeare, minor characters who find themselves drawn into the action become as much a focus of audience attention as the heroes since they signal the compulsions and challenges of witnessing tragedy, which we share. So, by extension, the responses to a crisis become part of its causes and effects, its consequences and explanations, the whole narrative arc. To witness devastating, painful events, with all the accompanying challenges of complicity and compassion, is to find oneself, in some way, a participant in the tragedy.[8]

Tragedy – if we are to attempt a definition – is born out of the connection, as Raymond Williams once observed, between 'event and experience and idea'. The event produces a feeling or prompts a moment of decision, experienced by the participants and witnesses in diverse and varying ways. These feelings and decisive acts are born out of the gap between hope and despair, between expectation and reality, between question and answer, prompted by the event which tests deeply our resources for confronting these things and shatters the security of easy theories or explanations. The thoughts and emotions are usually – but not always – communicable, since they emerge from the structures of feelings shared by the wider community, whether that be grief or anger, despair or loss, or even the empty guffaw of bleak futility. But these feelings in turn are shaped by the idea that this is how one *should* feel or respond or represent one's experience. So the idea of the tragic shapes the feeling and the feeling shapes the idea, and both become filtered by layers of tradition and representation and cultural practice. Thus the process of recognition is often a vital component of tragedy. Setting an event and experience in context, as part of a pattern of human activity and understanding and in conformity with a history of tragic tradition, forms the process of recognition which helps to shape a tragedy and, often, to make it bearable – and sharable.

But all this is to describe tragedy in very abstract, theoretical and generic terms, which actually runs counter to the proper force of tragedies. For tragedies happen in the particular, not the abstract. They don't cause their victims to break down in sorrow because a set of theoretical criteria has been met. Anger, grief and despair do not obey rules but defy them. They erupt unexpectedly and maybe are only regulated with recognition subsequently. Consequently, all we can do is examine each event or each experience on a case-by-case basis, just as we respond again and again to different productions of Shakespeare or Sophocles in the theatre, and seek to understand it by setting it within the larger patterns of tragic practice. We can calibrate events and movements in the modern world with narratives and practices in culture, and consequently find that people today react to events in ways which can be traced back to customs in Greek tragedy and that, conversely, an awareness of the tradition of tragedy can help us to make sense of the world now.

In my endeavour to seek out the traditional patterns of culture in the modern world and to understand our current predicament along familiar tragic lines, however, I have found that one philosopher in particular has proved very helpful. Born in 384 BC and active in the same years that Alexander the Great was conquering most of the known world, Aristotle might not seem the most obvious or relevant guide to the crisis of our modern situation. And yet his writings on tragedy, fragmentary and cryptic as they are, have proved a rich and apt resource to which I have returned again and again. One reason Aristotle is still so richly capacious is that he apparently incorporates diverse interpretations or definitions of tragedy into his account. Contrary to popular belief, there are no strict, clear Aristotelian 'rules' of tragedy. Instead he allows the force of tragedy to be located both in the play's formal content and in the audience response to that, or in other words, both in the event and in the experience. He argues, on the one hand, that tragedy is about action, that it is inherent in the plot, and that it is enough just to hear the details of the story to be moved. Tragedy, he wrote, is the 'representation of an action which is complete, whole and of a certain magnitude', with a clear and naturally connected 'beginning, middle and end'. Tragic plots 'ought not to begin or finish at arbitrary points'.[9] Effectively what Aristotle was doing was trying to find the intelligible logic of tragedy's artful patterning of events. Tragic drama was a way of shaping our experience into a neat form that made incidents seem necessary and explicable. It was about the relation of history to narrative and to what philosophers and critics would call the 'aesthetic'. This notion of life as a logical pattern is also what lies behind Hegel's influential theories in the early nineteenth century – that tragedy occurs when there are collisions of values and perspectives but that these are resolved in the forward march of history. Tragedy, in other words, leads ultimately to harmony and righteousness, according to Hegel, and we can be better 'reconciled' to individual suffering when it is set in the larger context of teleological history and the 'glimpse of eternal justice'.[10] And this belief is there implicitly in Martin Luther King's famous declaration, which forms one of the two prefatory quotations of this book: 'The arc of the moral universe is long but it bends towards justice.' There has long been thought to be a correlation between narrative pattern and moral order or between the conclusion of a story and the hope of justice. We can therefore supposedly hope to *read* that 'world out of joint' if we have the right tragic grammar and vocabulary.

On the other hand, Aristotle also argued that tragedy is about the feeling of pity and fear experienced when seeing an individual – the hero of the story – suffer and undergo a change of fortune. The spectator's *experience* of tragedy is where its significance lies, rather than in the plot or action. But what exactly that experience might be and what its function is remain very ambiguous. This is where Aristotle's famous theory of catharsis comes in. Tragedy, he claimed, washes our emotions or washes us free of our emotions (depending on how the Greek is translated) by allowing us to feel pity and fear while viewing the sufferings of others.[11] If we are washed free of our emotions, then the purpose of watching tragedy is to purge ourselves of uncontrollable passions and to gain relief, in a licensed space, so that the city can function more effectively.[12] Tragedy distracts us from confronting the real problems in the world. If, alternatively, tragedy washes our emotions, then its effect is to make us more attentive in the future, more sensitive to the psychological pressures of difficult choices, better witnesses each time. Watching tragic drama might make us better at watching it again in the future (a rather solipsistic conclusion, one might think), but it might also make us better witnesses to injustice, vengeance and expressions of grief in the wider world.

Pity, or what the philosopher Martha Nussbaum prefers to call compassion, has a moral force.[13] It is often thought to be the starting point for radical social change. Action begins with emotion, and the feeling 'directed at the serious suffering of another creature or creatures' is powerful, especially if the suffering is deemed to be undeserved and potentially close to our own predicament.[14] This is why literature can be considered useful in eliciting and cultivating capacities for this kind of feeling. Aristotle indicates this with his 'washing the emotions' comment. And one of the aims of this book is to read our 'world out of joint' in the light of our sensibilities and the emotional intelligence learned from watching tragedy in the theatre. But compassion is frequently and confusingly conflated with empathy which is far more ambiguous. Empathy involves the ability to enter into another's way of thinking. It necessitates an imaginative leap into another perspective. Of course, this can make us extraordinarily sympathetic if we share another's pain. It can broaden our horizons if we genuinely imagine the viewpoint of distant strangers. But empathy can allow the unscrupulous to get inside the mind of another to manipulate him. Iago, for example, understands Othello's vulnerabilities possibly even better than he does himself but this does not lead to kindness or mutual support.[15] What's more, empathy without rational thought can produce distortions and superficial sentimentality. According to the psychologist Paul Bloom, in his recent book *Against Empathy*, 'The problems we face as a society and as individuals are rarely due to lack of empathy. Actually, they are often due to too much of it.'[16] Empathy is myopic, innumerate and biased, causing people to value the single case over the many, the familiar over the strange. We pour out public feeling about the latest sad story on the news while neglecting whole sections of society who need help but whose claims might be more complicated and less reducible to simple emotions. Instead Bloom makes a case for 'the value of conscious, deliberative reasoning in everyday life'. This is actually similar to the 'dialogue' that Nussbaum calls for 'between vivid imagining and impartial principle'.[17] Compassion or empathy only have a public function if they involve making the imaginative leap from the single case to the general principle and if they result in action of some sort. The shooting of Malala Yousafzai in 2012 is just such a moment of shocking tragedy that provoked widespread compassion and brought the struggles of girls demanding the right to be educated to international attention.

Watching tragedy raises important questions about what is the appropriate response to the suffering of others and who is entitled to express it. The debate about compassion and empathy suggests that imaginative access to the feelings of others, near or distant, is possible. But often traditional tragedies explore the limits of our understanding as much as its reach. The novelist George Eliot claimed that it was enough 'to conceive with that distinctness which is no longer reflection but feeling' that somebody else had 'an equivalent centre of self, whence the lights and shadows must always fall with a certain difference'.[18] In other words, one does not need to know *what* the other person is feeling or thinking but simply to recognize that he or she might feel or think differently. It is sufficient for moral understanding to recognize the limits of our empathetic knowledge. Tragedy, by opening us up to a recognition of the precarious situation of others, whether or not we can explain it or justify it on a rational basis, produces bonds of interdependence and reciprocity.

So, recognition is a complex activity, in the theatre, in philosophy and in our daily ethical, political life. And reflecting those complications, different terms can be used for the process, from appreciation and respect to knowledge and acknowledgement to bearing witness. At one end of the spectrum, the act of recognition establishes the separate identity and what is known as the independent 'sovereignty' of another.[19] At the other end, it involves self-recognition too, an acknowledgement – through the encounter with others – of one's own situation and cognitive limitations.[20] Tragic recognition entails a reciprocal process of understanding, sharing in each other's vulnerability and limitedness. In this way, gain paradoxically comes from loss. At one point in Aeschylus's *Oresteia*, the chorus sing of wisdom coming through suffering: Παθει μαθος (*pathei mathos*, literally 'learning through suffering') is the phrase in Greek.[21] The connection between these two words is ambiguous. How does learning come through suffering? What kind of learning or wisdom is it? Does tragic knowledge entail taking on something of the suffering which one acknowledges in viewing the experience of others? Seeing and suffering have long been connected in our minds. The word for 'witness' in Greek – μαρτυς (*martys*) – is also the origin of our word *martyr*. And so it is that witnessing and bearing witness to tragedy have a double sense: viewing events but also participating in the experience, sharing the burden of that tragic acknowledgement.

Besides pity, of course, there is also fear, the other emotion identified by Aristotle as central to tragedy. Fear, he thought, was 'a pain or disturbance arising from a mental image of impending evil of a destructive or painful sort' which can be provoked when we realize that we are watching 'a man like ourselves', subject to similar human fallibilities.[22] So, as I have said, tragedies can have a positive moral effect, jolting those experiencing them, including the bystanders and witnesses, into opening themselves up into a richer imagination of the lives of others. But fear can overwhelm pity, close down our capacity for compassion and encourage us to respond to the threat of assimilation by creating greater distance and distinction than was originally there. According to Aristotle, under the influence of fear we structure the world into friends and enemies, deciding where the boundaries of identification and compassion lie. It is tragic fear that has riveted the structure of feeling underlying the War on Terror, polarizing the world into those who are 'with us' and those who are 'against us'. The feeling is one of defensiveness and threat; the enemy's supposed purpose is to destroy the 'American way of life' or 'British values'. And the response is so often also one familiar from the classic tradition of tragedy: revenge.[23] The attack on the Twin Towers was followed by the speedy bombardment of Afghanistan, while the supposed threat to the 'Western' values of justice, tolerance and the rule of law was answered by Guantanamo Bay, which operated outside the law and continues to fail to bring its last inmates to a fair trial.[24] 'Freedom isn't free' is a much-repeated popular slogan in America, but its curt paradox cuts much deeper than those who mouth the words probably realize. In a revenge culture, values and principles become corrupted by violence and the distinctions between the morally self-justified and the bad are blurred. So Hamlet famously notes that the 'world is out of joint. O cursed spite / That ever I was born to set it right!' and arguably kills more people in his 'righting' of wrongs than his uncle, Claudius, had done originally. America's 'freedom' is cancelled out by the avenging action carried out in its name, restricting the liberties of its citizens for national security and taking away the lives and livelihoods of its enemies in order to protect a value which has been negated by that very operation.

This book traces the arc of pity and fear, and the consequential acts of recognition or misrecognition, over the last two decades. There have, of course, been many tragic events during this time that I was not able to include in the book. Some of the most devastating ones, such as Hurricane Katrina in 2005 or London's Grenfell Tower in 2017, while having a 'natural' or trivial cause, exposed the underlying systemic structures of social inequality, poverty and neglect which exacerbated the number of fatalities. The decisions taken or not taken – to raise the sea levee in order to protect the wealthy New Orleans neighbourhoods or to skimp on more expensive fireproof external cladding in the Borough of

Kensington – were influenced by the desire for private profit and the callous disregard for the poor and were tragic in their consequences. Other tragedies over the period which I could have written about here include the opioid crisis ravaging America fuelled by big pharmaceutical companies, the continuing occupation of the West Bank and the siege and bombardment of Gaza or the rise and fall of the reputation of Aung San Suu Kyi in Burma. Indeed, it is the sad nature of a book of this kind that the possible material to be covered seems endless and ever growing in extent. But instead, I have focused on the events that occurred as a consequence of 9/11, the terror and revenge and turmoil unleashed apparently relentlessly and with fearful necessity in response to the attack upon America. The effect is thus to see the last eighteen years as one long narrative plot, an arc of history rather than a series of isolated events, one chapter following another with apparent tragic inevitability.

A book of this sort is, of course, faced with the challenge of distinguishing between significant and insignificant events, especially difficult when they have all happened so recently and before they have necessarily had time to settle into the public memory. When do events become history, once described by a historian as a 'meaningless succession of events' amounting to 'one damned thing after another'?[25] And when does that history become narrative or indeed amenable to being read as tragedy? In considering these questions, I have partly taken my cue from the Romantic poet Percy Bysshe Shelley, who was writing just after the euphoria of the French Revolution had finally been completely dashed with the defeat of Napoleon and the restoration of the Bourbon monarchy in 1815. Shelley had lived through, and continued to experience, the political rollercoaster of that turbulent period from day to day, and yet he professed a capacity to get the measure of his times. He read the narrative pattern of the age in a way that seems to anticipate Martin Luther King's bending arc:

> There is a reflux in the tide of human things which bears the shipwrecked hopes of men into a secure haven after the storms are past. Methinks, those who now live have survived an age of despair.[26]

This was written when life for radicals like Shelley had been made so difficult by the repressive post-war government in Britain that he was about to leave the country forever, and only five years later he drowned off the coast of Italy.

The patterns of tragedy lie deeply embedded in the structures of our contemporary crisis. What does it mean to be a citizen in the modern world? How does the individual fit into the collective? By what ideals are we to live and are we powerful enough to bring them into fruition? What are the choices between the courses of action that face us? Traditionally, tragic drama is deeply rooted in the idea of the polis, the community, the political clash of competing values. And tragic events can bring people together, working in adversity with compassion and altruistic action. But this strengthening of the bonds of community is often achieved at the expense of outsiders, those who are different, the enemy. The ancient Greeks invented the word 'xenophobia', and their tragic dramas reflect the deep division in their minds between Greeks and 'barbarians' (also a Greek word), us and them. The plays both reinforced this division and also challenged it, exploring the anxiety over the boundaries we set around our sense of identity. As more migration happens across the globe, with the growing economic division between north and south and the violent turmoil caused by war, climate change, intervention and exploitation, the question of who forms our community – with its tragic implications – becomes ever more pressing. Night after night, on the Mediterranean coastline or Mexican–US security fence, border guards, police and humanitarian workers try to implement or alleviate the impact of an immigration policy which stems from the same impulses that are calibrated in the tragic tradition.

Along with plot, pity and fear, the location of tragedy has traditionally been highly significant in drama, from the boundary between city and wilderness or the threshold between palace sanctuary and the outer world which frequently formed the sites of ancient plays to the blasted heath, the battlefield or the bedroom in Shakespeare. These settings were chosen because they were contested places – between men and women, rulers and citizens, between the sane and the mad – and so were fraught with powerful tensions and conflict. The sites which have the strongest impact upon our feelings today are either ones in which terrible loss or catastrophe has occurred – I think again of Ground Zero in New York which has become a semi-sacred site despite the fact that its memorial competes for attention with both mass tourism and the needs of commerce – or they are places of contestation. The Old

City of Jerusalem, and in particular the area of the Temple Mount, is probably the most disputed and tense one square kilometre in the world. Jews and Muslims lay claim to the same piece of rock, the supposed site of the first and second Jewish temples and the ground from which Muhammad ascended into heaven. Men have lost their lives on both sides in their efforts to worship at the small piece of ground that is sacred to them. Archaeology, religion and politics come together in a toxic combination which breeds passionate beliefs, fervent hatreds, fear and violence.[27]

The fundamental beliefs around the Temple Mount remind us how closely connected religion and tragedy have always been and how the language and tenets of faith underpin our contemporary crisis. Traditional tragedies often involved sacrifices, either the sacrifice of others or self-sacrifice for a greater cause. And the ideology of sacrifice – soldiers paying the 'ultimate sacrifice for their country' or suicide bombers prepared to go through 'martyrdom' for the jihad – has shaped the discourse of the first two decades of the twenty-first century. Sacrifice supposedly tests and confirms the values by which we live, the principles for which we are prepared to die. It brings people together and renews their commitment to the collectively agreed ethics, even while an individual has to suffer death to facilitate this. As the classical scholar Helene Foley noted about sacrifice in ancient tragic drama, it restores 'communal order and shared standards of behaviour'.[28] But as sacrifice has been practised and co-opted in popular discourse both in the West and within radical Islam, the 'restoration' of 'order' is used aggressively to disorder the enemy. Iphigenia justifies her act of self-sacrifice in Euripides' *Iphigenia in Aulis* by saying 'Through my death ... my fame as the liberator of Greece will be forever blessed' and that 'it is right that the Greeks should rule barbarians, and not barbarians Greeks. For they are slaves and we are free', without realizing the irony of the very compulsions that drive her to her death.[29] Freedom is not free in ancient Greece, despite this strict dichotomy articulated here. And similar ironies run like a fault line through our contemporary understanding of heroism and sacrifice, martyrdom and atonement in the field of conflict and international relations.

These traditional patterns and concerns of tragedy, then, lie deeply embedded in the critical, harrowing predicaments of our time. The relationship between the individual and the collective, the response of pity and fear when witnessing suffering, the ambiguous implications of viewing the pain of others, the importance of recognition and the act of revenge, the restrictions and possibilities of a unity of place and time, the role of religion and sacrifice: all these are the core elements of what we think of as traditional tragedy and continue to structure the feelings and dilemmas of our contemporary situation. Understanding those core aesthetic and philosophical concerns can allow us to begin to make sense of our modern world or at least to apprehend precisely its lapses of sense, its tragic *aporia*.

The medium of tragedy, however, is changing all the time. Photography and film have of course been used to report violent conflict and suffering around the world for the last century, and the appeal to pity and fear is frequently governed by what we can see, what we choose to look at and what we are shown.[30] But now our contemporary world is dominated by the visual image on a different scale. We live in an age of spectacle, a culture that is saturated by an overabundance of photographs, selfies, YouTube videos. Tragic events around the world are witnessed, rather than simply reported, with ambiguous consequences. On the one hand, viewing pictures of suffering makes it palpable to us and provokes a response, just as the ancient Greeks realized when they rolled the dead bodies out into the theatre for the chorus and the audience to see and lament. Abstract ideas about human rights and justice are harder to ignore when they become embodied in individual cases to which our attention is drawn by photographs. This visual recognition forms the foundation of our ethics, compelling us to acknowledge our relationship with others and fostering tolerance. But on the other hand, a plethora of visual images can also lead to mere spectacle. Are we losing our capacity to respond because of the excessive number of images? Are we in danger of suffering from what has been termed 'compassion fatigue'? Actually these very anxieties, about the effect of witnessing suffering, lie embedded in the structure of traditional tragedy. Euripides was provoking similar dilemmas back in 415 BC with the *Trojan Women*, when captive women competed with each other over who could offer the most grievable spectacle of suffering while the callous gods departed, indifferent to the scene.

Increasingly now the medium for reporting and accessing the news is the internet, social media and news websites rather than traditional mainstream media. This has had the effect of democratizing communication, allowing for grassroots political organizing and the dissemination of truths the establishment might have wanted to repress in the past. It is hard to imagine the rebellions of the Arab Spring or Occupy without the technology of the internet. But those truths have given rise to the notion of post-truth, in which nothing can be trusted or believed and objective integrity and justice are undermined by a cynical appeal to a false relativism. In some ways the tragic effects of social media, phones and their false witness are not so different from the ones arising from new technologies which have been explored in traditional tragic drama. I'm thinking in particular of the ambiguous significance of writing which occurs in various ancient Greek plays, such as Euripides' *Hippolytus*.[31] There Phaedra kills herself, hanging a written tablet around her neck falsely accusing her stepson of rape. Her husband believes the charge because of the written statement, backed up by the powerful image of her dead body, and curses his son. This is fake news ancient-style. Of course, Greek tragedy takes place under the gaze of the chorus and the audience; there is full disclosure. By contrast, the lies peddled on social media are clandestine and private, metaphorically whispered in each individual ear and therefore even less open for scrutiny and rebuttal. Details of how social media has been harnessed to manipulate democratic elections, through the use of data mining and targeted messaging by companies like Cambridge Analytica, are still coming to light as I write. 'We just put information into the bloodstream of the internet and then watch it grow', according to the former CEO of Cambridge Analytica, Alexander Nix.[32] As lies are figured as a virus and false belief as an infection, democracy and all that goes with it – justice, responsibility, collective consensus and debate – are undermined from within. Trying to read between competing accounts and to make judgements with critical acumen will probably become increasingly important for civic life if the technological opportunities afforded by the internet continue to be exploited still further in the future.[33]

So, ultimately, I am making a plea for the important place of the literary, critical imagination in today's crisis. Reading and thinking about tragedies are vitally relevant to our modern predicament. Writers have a moral responsibility to engage with the world in the best way that they can, by writing, speaking out and drawing public attention to an issue through culture. In this regard, Susan Sontag has set a great precedent. Her production of Beckett's *Waiting for Godot* in 1993 in the besieged city of Sarajevo has become a *cause célèbre* for the controversial place of theatre and the arts in a conflict zone. Bringing together a cast of actors that included Croats, Muslims and Serbs, even while the Serbs were bombarding the city for months and attempting to inculcate racial division, Sontag directed the play which became the 'cultural frontline'. The performers would be digging trenches or carrying rifles earlier in the day and then would put down their guns to act, while the audience, who were as hungry and worn down by the siege as the cast, sat on filled sacks and watched the play by candlelight. As they felt surrounded by the enemy and abandoned by the West, they watched as Vladimir and Estragon were told, having waited for Godot all day, that he wasn't coming that day but maybe tomorrow. Meanwhile they could hear the sound of mortar fire outside.

Sontag's production provoked a certain amount of criticism and derision in various quarters. The right-wing, anti-intellectual press scorned her supposed naivety and irrelevance. Why would anyone, in the middle of a desperate war, need a production of Beckett? There were a few unjustified comments about narcissism too. But more interesting and substantial was the critique by the philosopher Jean Baudrillard that *Waiting for Godot* in Sarajevo was actually paradoxically facilitating the West's betrayal of the Bosnians. European policy, he argued, was to tacitly allow the Muslims to be slaughtered but this harsh agenda was being whitewashed by a *faux* pity exemplified by the theatre performance. Sontag was replacing what should have been a tough political oppositional campaign with an emotional response, based upon the power of compassion and symbolism. And this act of compassion, he maintained, was for the benefit of the West rather than for those at the war's front line. Those actually caught up in the conflict found that life became more urgent and precious, according to Baudrillard, and they became all the stronger as a result. They did not think of themselves as pitiable. And those in the West strangely envied them that strength and sense of purpose. 'We feel the need to salvage the reality of war in our own eyes and to impose this reality (to be pitiable) upon those who suffer from it but do not really believe in it' was Baudrillard's harsh comment. 'All the corridors, opened by us to funnel ... our "culture", are in fact our lifelines along which we suck their moral strength and the energy of their distress.'[34]

Baudrillard's criticism of Sontag's well-intentioned efforts in Sarajevo goes right to the heart of what is at stake in attempting to make tragic drama relevant to tragic events in the world or to think about the ethical responsibility of culture. The exercise of emotional feeling is fraught with misunderstanding and frequently open to ridicule and attack. Western colonial privilege, bolstered by its traditional canon of literature, expressing pity for other parts of the world thrown into turmoil partly by the legacy of our military interventions, is a cheap but valid charge. But Susan Sontag rebutted this criticism triumphantly. On a tangible level, the production was a success in that the local people of Sarajevo felt hugely boosted by the event. They applauded Sontag's 'bravery – coming here, living and working with us' and the city's mayor bestowed honorary citizenship upon her. In the years since her death, the Beckett production is still remembered and the central city square, where *Godot* was staged, has been renamed Sontag Square. The theatre performance arguably drew international attention to the plight of the city, in a way that the documentary dispatches from international reporters and photojournalists had not quite managed to do and helped to change public attitudes to the war. But on a less tangible level, she re-established the principle that writers and creative artists should engage with the world and are vitally needed to do so. The impact of the production was partly based upon the fact that Sontag had been prepared to risk her life to go to Sarajevo. For a few weeks, she made herself as vulnerable as the Bosnians, which gave her work an urgency and authenticity. Reflecting afterwards, she compared the gesture to the Spanish Civil War, which attracted writers like Hemingway, Orwell and Simone Weil. 'They went as an act of solidarity and from that act grew some of the finest literature of their time.'[35] The risks taken to stage *Godot* were not only for the benefit of Sontag and a greater version of Beckett, despite Baudrillard's remarks, but were the chief source of strength for the people of Sarajevo, because of the symbolic value of an outsider witnessing and sharing their experience. But the impact was also based upon the production's 'defiance of fascism and barbarism'. And this defiance came precisely from the 'normality' of a theatre production. It was the very fact that acting and theatre were not strictly about survival in an extreme situation but about courageously engaging in an activity normally associated with times of peace and security that made it so powerful. Baudrillard had observed, in his attack on the event, that 'to do something for the sole reason that one cannot do nothing never has been a valid principle for action', presumably in answer to Sontag's sense that as a creative artist one should try and do *something* in a crisis rather than abrogate responsibility. But the subtle effects and powerful symbolism of the Beckett production, which continue to resonate in the civic memory of Sarajevo, beg the question of what exactly the 'thing' is which is being done. It is hard to plumb the depths precisely and with reductive literalism when analysing the structures of feeling and the effects of culture. One cannot always quantify results or 'outcomes' of artistic endeavours in the way expected by modern economic discourse. 'Something is taking its course', as one character, Clov, says in Beckett's play *Endgame*.

Susan Sontag showed how writers, theatre practitioners and artists could make their work directly relevant to the world around them and she was not cowed by accusations of elitism or other-worldliness. And by extension, literary criticism can be, and indeed should be, engaged in the contemporary crisis as well. There is, it seems to me, something grotesque in an academic climate that encourages critics to seal themselves off in libraries and offices in order to worry about footnotes and labyrinths of self-reflecting theories while the world metaphorically – and sometimes literally – burns. But there is also something blinkered and foolhardy in a culture which separates itself from the insights of critical attention, takes no heed to what goes on in the theatre or the academy and which sees no relevance in a sophisticated analysis of tragic crisis or spectacle when responding to the predicaments of our modern world. Literary criticism should be reinvested with an ethical, political, moral relevance. We are living through an age of radical crisis. A critical attention which is shaped by centuries of witnessing tragedies and which is accustomed to pondering the limits of our understanding and sympathies as well as their potential is vitally necessary for the complicated, war-torn and riven world of the twenty-first century.

2

Lamenting 9/11

We could begin the narrative like this. At 7.35 am, in Boston's Logan airport, Mohamed Atta boards American Airlines Flight 11 bound for Los Angeles, along with four conspirators. Thirty-nine minutes later, a second plane, United Airlines Flight 175, takes off from Logan airport, also bound for Los Angeles and also carrying five hijackers led by Marwan al-Shehhi. Meanwhile, in Washington Dulles airport, at 8.20 am, American Airlines Flight 77 leaves for Los Angeles, with Hani Hanjour and four accomplices on board. United Airlines Flight 93 takes off from Newark airport 40 minutes late, at 8.42 am, with four hijackers, bound for San Francisco. By 8.14 am Flight 11 has been hijacked, and at 8.46 Mohamed Atta flies it into the North Tower of the World Trade Center, between floors 93 and 99. At 9.03 am, the South Tower is hit by Flight 175, flying about 950 km/h. Flight 77 smashes into the Pentagon building in Washington, DC, at 9.37, causing the deaths of 189 people. At 9.58, the World Trade Center's South Tower collapses after burning uncontrollably for 55 minutes. Thirty minutes later, the North Tower falls. Meanwhile, Flight 93 crashes in Pennsylvania, brought down by the passengers fighting the hijackers. All flights are cancelled over American airspace for two days.

Or it could be told another way. Tuesday September 11 dawned a perfect New York late summer morning, blue skies and a balmy 70 degrees. Just at the time when most workers had settled into their desks at the two 100-storey towers of the World Trade Center in Lower Manhattan and were checking their first emails, lattes in hand, a commercial airliner transformed into a guided missile by a hijacking pilot crashed into the building. Those on the lower floors began to evacuate the building but above the fireball people tried to reach the roof for a rescue that never came. The terror of being trapped in a burning inferno only increased when the second tower was hit less than 20 minutes later with an even greater fireball. Some became so desperate, trapped by fire and smoke, that they jumped the hundred floors to their deaths. Most died, however, when the two towers collapsed from the intense heat of the fire, a terrifying storm cloud of grey ash, rubble, flames and toxic fumes. In all, including the fatalities in Washington and Pennsylvania, around 3,000 people died that day, in less than two hours.

Or we could focus on an individual. Carlos Segarra and his wife had just recently bought a bigger house in Brooklyn so that their newly married son and his wife could live with them along with his son's wife's mother. Mr Segarra worked on the forty-sixth floor of the South Tower, more than twenty floors below where Flight 175 hit the building. But he stopped to help an asthmatic colleague make his way down the emergency stairs to evacuate the building. The two of them had just reached the entrance lobby when the tower collapsed. His son commented that his father's act of selfless attention shown to the colleague, which cost him his life, was typical of him. 'His final actions sum it all up', he said. 'He was very kind'.

Or we could tell it the way most people witnessed the incident. I woke up on the morning of September 11 in London feeling mildly depressed. I can't remember now the reason for my melancholy but it resulted in my telephoning a friend and arranging to meet for a drink that evening. Around two hours before we were due to meet, she called me to check that I was OK, given the desperate nature of the news. I knew nothing about it but switched on the television, then around 4 pm, to find that everything had already happened, the planes crashing, the fireballs erupting into the sky and the two towers collapsing apocalyptically. The footage was played repeatedly on the television, a circulating loop, and I was held by it, fixated by the destruction and obsessively trying to fathom an explanation by watching the violent episode again and again. Later that evening, I met my friend in a bar and we viewed the spectacle together on a big screen; I saw it repeatedly in the days and weeks and months to come.

The traumatic event of September 11, 2001, became the tragedy of 9/11 through a process of endless retellings, ritual lament, public commemoration and various imaginative or artistic interventions which were absolutely in accordance with classical tragic tradition. Traumas rupture the psyche. They 'are not fully grasped as they occur' and resist the healing process of cognitive apprehension, reflection and memory, only to cause the subject to return to the original shattering scene in 'repeated flashbacks and nightmares'.[1] These flashbacks are often exceptionally vivid but recur repeatedly precisely because the victim cannot know or understand the original event. He or she can only 'act-out' the experience. Tragedy, by contrast, has traditionally offered the opportunity to resolve trauma by means of narrative 'working through', by performing it on stage and thereby 'turning what is essentially unpleasurable into something to be remembered and to be processed in the psyche'.[2] Tragedy transforms the clotted impasse of trauma into linear narrative; it seeks to make what cannot be assimilated nevertheless intelligible to rational or at least emotional cognition, 'modified by interpretation'.[3] A private, unshareable wounding becomes mitigated and managed as a publicly witnessed experience, remembered communally rather than endlessly experienced as violent flashback.[4] Or at least this might be considered one of the premises of tragedy, even if frequently such resolution, healing and intelligibility are not actually possible, and tragic dramas merely re-stage and rehearse the traumatic and the intractable in a series of irresolvable and repeated narratives.[5] My four attempts to 'tell the story' of 9/11 at the beginning of this chapter are one such failed effort at tragic 'working through'.

Dating right back to the fifth-century Greek dramatists, who were writing in the shadow of Homer's fictional Trojan War and during the contemporary Peloponnesian War, and evident also in plays like Shakespeare's *Hamlet*, composed when plagues were ravaging London, lamentation is traditionally one of the chief modes of tragedy. Grieving for individuals, whether on the stage or in our public acts of commemoration, gives their lives significance, their loss meaning and their legacy a lasting memory. In this way, the initial trauma is worked through, acknowledged and absorbed. But not all laments nor all tragedies succeed in transcending their original traumatic effect. How far did the task of tragedy manage to transform the events of September 11?

Event, trauma and tragedy

According to the philosopher Slavoj Žižek, an Event (which he elevates with a capital letter) is an 'effect that seems to exceed its causes'.[6] It erupts suddenly without explanation, defies our understanding and transforms the context in which it occurred. According to this somewhat apocalyptic line of thinking, the event shatters the humdrum nature of normal daily life, erases all existing assumptions and even necessitates novel modes of conceptualizing thought itself.[7] How do you represent a catastrophic event when it seems to blow apart the very notion of representation?

The attack on the Twin Towers in New York on September 11, 2001, is this kind of Event, disrupting even 'the conditions of analysis', according to the philosopher Jean Baudrillard.[8] He meant that what has become known as 9/11 not only overturned the settled sense of geopolitical world order in the post-Soviet era, the state of affairs that Francis Fukyama famously termed 'the end of history', and punctured America's complacency about its own invulnerability and hegemony, but it also shattered established concepts of symbolism, fantasy, logic and political interpretation.[9] The violence, speed and unexpectedness of the attacks were partly behind this sense of their unthinkability, as were the colossal nature of the statistics: nearly 3,000 people killed in the period of less than two hours; two 417-metre tall matching skyscrapers collapsing in the heart of one of the world's most densely populated cities; 1.5 million tons of wreckage shipped to the landfill; an estimated direct economic toll of $75 billion, not including the consequential huge costs of increased security. There was also the twisted, ironic logic of hijacked planes becoming self-delivering bombs, with ordinary citizens travelling inside on involuntary suicide missions, which was hard to reflect upon. And there was the unfathomable purpose behind the terrorism, the fact that it came without a message, without a warning and without justification immediately afterwards.[10] 'Terrorism ultimately has no meaning, no objective, and cannot be measured by its "real" political and historical consequences. And it is, paradoxically, because it has no meaning that it constitutes an event in a world increasingly saturated with meaning and efficacy', Baudrillard observed.[11]

But although events, according to philosophers like Žižek and Baudrillard, overwhelm the human capacity to absorb them, we can discern them retrospectively as an idea, an image, a series of facts and explanations, mediated through the retelling. Human instincts kick in, wanting to know the causes of the event, the consequences and explanations. We need to find out the motivation for sudden acts of violence and the timescale of the separate incidents during the critical day. We also seek details about the individual people involved, comparing our experience with that of others, hoping for more information about the decisions taken by the victims on their last day in order to be able to feel the appropriate compassion for those who lost their lives. In other words, we frequently try to turn the traumatic event into a tragic plot. We fill in the sublime gap blasted by the Event with words, feelings and explanations. To coin a phrase from Paul Ricoeur, we attempt to respond to the 'aporias of time [and the sublime moment] by a poetics of narrative'.[12] If we do think about an event, it is most likely that what we are contemplating is the *reporting* of it or even the translation of it into some more familiar image or story in our imagination. Indeed, Žižek and Baudrillard claim that it is virtually impossible to experience an Event. Instead we experience *the experience of an event*, and thus we substitute the 'image' for the 'Real'.

The experience of September 11 was swiftly transformed into 9/11 and woven into a network of narratives and dramas. In fact, of course, it did not actually come out of the blue but out of a larger context of American involvement in the Middle East and beyond. It was a 'monstrous calling card from a world gone horribly wrong'.[13] To claim that the attacks on September 11, 2001, erupted out of nowhere is to perform a political act of erasure, to abrogate any sense of responsibility or context in relation to American's foreign policy over the decades. But that political and historical story was not interesting for people. Far more widely disseminated were the spreading rumours of plots and cover-ups. Mention 9/11 to anyone in America today and it will probably not be long before they bring up the issue of conspiracy theories: the strange, internal collapse of the Twin Towers; the later collapse of World Trade Center 7, which was not directly hit by a plane; the nationalities of the victims and those not in the towers that day; and – above all – the unlikelihood that just nineteen hijackers could cause such momentously destructive disaster. The explanation is that rather than a plot hatched between a few young men, masterminded from a cave in Afghanistan, this was a much larger plot organized by the American CIA or by Israel's Mossad. Rather, as the ancient Greeks ascribed disasters to the gods, who watched over men's affairs, the conspiracy theorists seek forces that are in overall control of events. Better to have explanations and plots in the world than accident, unpredictability and lack of control, even if those forces behind the plots are malevolent and insuperable. Conspiracy theories work therefore a little like tragic fate, with the lone conspiracy theorist similar to the soothsayer or priest divining the predestined fortune by deciphering the riddling oracle or reading the runes. The truth is to be found hidden beneath the surface. It is somehow comforting to the conspiracy theorist to find confirmed, through their reading of the event, their pre-existing distrust of politicians, intelligence agencies and the forces that allegedly protect us. The conspiracy theory fills in the void; it offers the first spiral in an ever-expanding series of circular narratives that characterize this event.

Along with what could be called a new 'theology' of entreaty and conspiracy on September 11 (for not by chance did witnesses gasp 'oh my God' as they watched the towers collapse), there was the filter of the media and fantasy. Almost one-third of the world's population is estimated to have watched the event on television. The attack happened in the city where four of the major American television networks – ABC, CBS, Fox and NBC – are headquartered, with CNN also broadcasting from the Time Warner Center there. It took place also in front of two of the nation's premier newspapers – *The New York Times* and *The Wall Street Journal* – and near the headquarters of international photo agency Magnum. The iconic Twin Towers, then, collapsed in the heart of the media capital of the world, watched live by approximately two billion viewers. And because the event was recorded on film, it was watched again and again on an endlessly repeated loop. Viewers found it challenging to get the measure of the scale. On the one hand, the towers were staggeringly huge. At 110 storeys high, the experience on the top of the South Tower from the outdoor viewing platform had been one of being disconnected from the ground, closer to the experience of looking out from a plane than from a building.[14] The towers had no recognizable face, no façade, their very architecture defied figurative apprehension. And as they collapsed, they seemed to dwarf any human scale of comprehension. But on the other hand, the repeated sensation of those watching the disaster on television was that they were watching a movie. Reduced to the television screen, the towers were toy-like in collapse, an unreal, special effect. As critic Alex Houen has noted, 'the scale of the attacks could, in reality, only be assimilated in mediated forms'.[15] They were 'im-mediated', *immediately* translated into spectacular form, or even 'pre-mediated', in the sense that collapsing, burning towers had been anticipated by Hollywood in films like *The Towering Inferno* or *Independence Day*.

However, as well as the theology of conspiracy theory and the 'immediating' spectacle of celluloid horror, there was another frame within which the event was absorbed and understood: the act of lamentation which tragedy both dramatizes and enacts. When the distraught Ophelia in Shakespeare's *Hamlet* mourns her father Polonius, who was killed accidentally by Hamlet, she draws on well-known tropes of grief and ritual to produce a 'speech of nothing / Yet the unshaped use of it doth move / The hearers to collection'.[16] 'He is dead and gone, lady, / He is dead and gone' is one of the common ballads that she sings.[17] And she hands out flowers traditionally thought to symbolize remembrance, love and 'thoughts', seeking in her half-delirious state to set her private bereavement within a larger cultural practice of mourning and commemoration. Tragic dramas lament loss by self-consciously drawing attention to the generic function of ritual mourning which they perform, thus setting the particular in a larger context. Of course, *Hamlet* explores the distinction between acceptable forms of mourning and unacceptable ones. Both Ophelia and Hamlet are deemed to be excessive and hysterical in their grief at various points of the play. How far lament can be managed properly at times of tragedy is an ongoing concern in tragic drama and in the aftermath of September 11.

As well as setting private grief within a longer cultural tradition, tragic dramas simultaneously do the reverse, reminding the audience of the value of the individual in the midst of a much larger disaster. Homer's *Iliad* made vivid the deaths of so many warriors on the plain of Troy by recounting the last moments of each man's life individually and illuminating them with a striking image drawn from the natural world. These became tragic vignettes within the larger epic.[18] Greek tragedy drew on this Homeric model in the messenger speeches that recounted the individual deaths with

detailed attention and in the songs of the chorus. Plays like Euripides'
Trojan Women raise the question of who is to be lamented: only
a select few aristocratic figures or a whole city full of abandoned
women, each with her own sorrows and fears?

'Names, singly and together, ... offer a hope of bridging the
spaces between the particular and the cosmic, between each single
case and the vast, morally ungraspable size of their aggregation',
the historian Thomas Laqueur has declared in his cultural history
of death.[19] Commemorative monuments list the names of the dead:
more than 57,000 on the Vietnam Memorial and nearly 3,000 on
the 9/11 memorial wall. Their power lies both in the totality and
uniformity of the whole and in the specificity of each individual
name. The names of the dead on monuments also stand in place
of the body. As the shortest form of epitaph or eulogy, they take
on the task of registering the loss, of deliberately offering a visible,
if metaphorical, presence in the place of absence. They demand a
'remarkable feat of imagination' on the part of the living.[20] In this
sense the work of tragedy, lament and the epitaph overlap. These
related activities for commemorating the dead, which coalesce
around place, word, the absent body and the grief of the living,
strive to mediate between the individual and the generic, between
the transient life and the permanent record, between insignificance
and significance.

Tragic portraits

One of the chief acts of public mourning for the victims of the
September 11 attacks was to read the brief biographies of the dead
that appeared in the newspaper. Published each day from mid-
September until 31 December in the *New York Times* and soon
well known collectively as the 'Portraits of Grief', these short 200-
word profiles, accompanied with a photograph, became a daily
opportunity to remember and lament those who had so suddenly
and cruelly disappeared. According to the novelist Paul Auster, 'one
felt, looking at those pages every day, that real lives were jumping
out at you. We weren't mourning an anonymous mass of people, we
were mourning thousands of individuals. And the more we knew
about them, the more we could wrestle with our own grief.'[21]

The 'Portraits' tried to give shape to the September massacre by transforming ordinary lives into significant narratives:

˙ Pictures of Jose Cardona show him dancing on a conga line with his wife and friends ... He cried when the couple found out that she was expecting their first child and the baby would be a son ... Mr Cardona, 35, had been working for Wall Street companies for 14 years, most recently as a clerk at Carr Futures. The baby is due in January.[22]

Or

Laura Rockefeller was an aspiring actress, singer, and director who paid the rent on her one-room apartment on West 85th Street with freelance work for Risk Waters, a London-based company that produces seminars for financial managers. On Sept 11, she was stage-managing one at Windows on the World .... Her animal-loving friends were the first to figure out that she might be among the missing at the World Trade Center ... If she was even 15 minutes late to walk J.T. [her dog], something was surely wrong ... J.T. continues to resist the finality, running to the door ... ears perked, each time a car approaches.[23]

Each profile mingled small anecdotes with poignantly detailed absences, the baby without a father or the dog waiting for an owner who would never come home. The noted gaps in the story became the source of their power.

As I read the profiles myself each day online, in order to give substance to the compassion I yearned to feel, it seemed as if the text with its quirky personal details conjured up eighteen hundred, recognizable but heterogeneous individuals in place of a set of statistics. One critic, Nancy Miller, has compared the 'Portraits' to quick sketches, to the writing of anecdotes in a notebook. The brevity of the writing paradoxically and poignantly evokes the copiousness of grief. 'In measuring disaster, the smaller the marker, the bigger the loss, seems to be the rule of incommensurability', she writes.[24] Words are not adequate to represent the depth and breadth of a human life, and so they break off short, replaced by a photograph, a 'snapshot' of a life. This is all true but it seemed to me that what the team of journalists who interviewed the victims' families in order to compile these 'Portraits' were doing was not just turning the pages of a family photo album but was also shining a light on each unique person in a way which is similar to the self-conscious illumination of the value of each individual life undertaken by the ancient Greek tragic dramatists. They were setting grief in a wider generic tradition.

Euripides' *Trojan Women*, in which the women of the defeated city of Troy wait to be shipped off to slavery, following the death of all the men in the war, is one prime example. Composed in 415 BC, the year after the Athenians had sacked the island of Melos during the Peloponnesian War, killed all the men and sent the women to be slaves, the play subtly alluded to difficult events and thus shaped very recent history into a long tradition of tragic narrative. One by one, the main protagonists – daughters of the queen Hecuba – demand mournful attention: Polyxena, whose sacrifice offstage at Achilles' tomb is described by Andromache so that it can be appropriately lamented; Cassandra, driven spectacularly mad by the gods and her misfortune; Andromache, who even tries to outcompete Polyxena for misery. Astanax, her baby son, is thrown from the city's battlements by the vengeful Greeks and his broken body brought in for mourning. Hecuba remains onstage throughout, directing the lament and asking the chorus and the gods to look at her. She claims to find a comfort in the sorrowful telling of her story: 'I wish to sing my swan-song over the blessings of my life. In this way I shall enhance the pathos of my sufferings.'[25] But the ordinary women also demand attention in their lyrical choral songs and retell the story of where they were the night that Troy fell, a narrative which is both vividly specific and common to all.[26] Reminding us that every life is grievable in similar ways, the chorus sing to Andromache, as she bemoans her miseries, 'Your tragedy is the same as ours. As you lament your own fate, you teach me where I stand in my woes.'[27] In this play, the drawing of lots to allocate the women to their new owners becomes the focus for a tragic form of individuation, since as the messenger explains 'each woman was assigned to a different man. You were not all allocated together' (243). The chorus collectively sing of their desire to know what misery awaits them individually: 'Oh, oh! / Which Argive, which Phthian / or islander will lead my unhappy self / away from Troy to his land?'.[28] Specific destinies are listed and the isolation becomes almost as much a source of pain as the abjection: 'To whom have I been allocated as a wretched slave?' (185). However, the chorus's question to Hecuba, 'You know your fate, my queen. But which of the Achaeans or Greeks is master of my fortunes?' (292–3), is never answered. Euripides' tragedy thus both proposes and simultaneously throws into question the extent to which all lives are equally lamentable.

Like tragedies such as the *Trojan Women*, the 'Portraits' were an attempt to restore individual faces and lives in the place of a disaster's statistics. They drew attention to the fact that they had to *seek out* the information, they had to carve out a life from scanty information. 'We began dialing the phone numbers on the flyers. What we wanted were stories, anecdotes, tiny but telling details that seemed to reveal something true and essential about how each person lived', one editor, Janny Scott, explained.[29] What became clear was that the form and nature of the 'Portraits', the characteristics that they all held in common, became as much part of their significance as the quirky, individual details. They were, as the editor pointed out, 'utterly democratic'. No matter whether they were high or low status, the sort of person who was usually given an obituary in the *New York Times* or not, they were all caught in the same event, allocated the same number of words in their 'Portraits' and accorded the same tribute of grief. The generic quality of the biographical sketches made them grievable, within the tragic tradition, allowing both communal and communicable lament and also individual recognition.

The self-conscious act of illuminating the ordinary thus became the half-hidden subtext behind the portrait. This was simultaneously highlighted by Anne Nelson's play *The Guys*, which was written and staged in TriBeCa, Lower Manhattan, around the same time in late 2001 that the 'Portraits' were appearing in the newspaper. Based on Anne Nelson's experience of helping a firefighter compose tributes to eight of his men for their upcoming funerals, the simple play – more of a meta-tragedy than a tragedy – consists of a writer (Joan) and firefighter (Nick) discussing what little he knew of each man and then developing and reading out the finished eulogy. Part of the firefighter's grief is focused on the fact that he cannot recall the men very well, that he cannot find anything meaningful to say that might illuminate their lives. But Joan manages to create accounts of value out of the very scanty details she is offered and, in the process, discovers a sense of connection with the New York community and a useful purpose; her words are 'her tools',

Nick tells her. He is able to mourn his fellow men, both through the task of talking about them and as a result of having those emotions channelled through the writer's eloquence. She has created a 'memorial of words' for him. The encounter between the two protagonists, and more widely between the actors and the audience, created a new, unexpected form of community, brought together by the disaster and the need to lament, to recollect, to ask the question, 'How can we share the suffering of those whose suffering is personal and visceral?'.[30] As Nelson commented, 'A play couldn't cure anyone. But it could bring people together in a dedicated space and allow them to experience emotion together.' She compared the experiment to Greek tragedy.[31]

The public mourning of the dead after 9/11, then, participated in a similar tragic need to record a life before it was forgotten as the ancient Greeks demonstrated. It focused upon the illuminating, therapeutic possibilities of the 'memorial of words'. As Hecuba declares in the *Trojan Women*: 'If god had not turned the world upside down, we would vanish into obscurity. We would never have given men to come the inspiration to sing of us in their song' (1242–5). Greek tragedy is focused on the benefit of such 'song', of tragic performance transforming 'obscurity' and loss into permanent memory and worth.[32]

But there was a second anxiety underlying the 'Portraits'. The dread of not recalling the victims or having anything significant to say about them was accompanied by the horror of having no bodies to mourn. At the same time that the 'Portraits' were being published in the newspaper, a major excavation was being undertaken on the ground in Lower Manhattan to retrieve traces of the bodies. For eight and a half months, workmen dug down into the ruins of the World Trade Center and sifted the debris, looking for the remains of the 2,606 dead. They prised apart the concrete and the metal. They laid out the piles of grey ash for firefighters to sift through. And they carted off rubble and dust to the medical examiner's office and to the landfill site at Fresh Kills, Staten Island, for further sifting and DNA analysis. According to one firefighter, 'You look for anything that resembles human. Anybody, anything. Could be clothes, could be bone, a shoe.'[33] Progress was measured statistically: 1.6 million tons of rubble removed from the site, 105,000 truckloads of material and the remains of about 1,200 more individuals still to be identified forensically. But the answer that was emerging during those months was that most of the victims had been utterly vaporized by the intense fire; there were no body parts to find.

The macabre process of trying to distinguish significant body parts from insignificant dust testified to a desperate need to honour the dead in the face of its obliteration which tragedies bear witness to over and over again. *Hamlet*, for example, ponders what is significant about human life through an obsession with decomposition. The whole world of Denmark is 'out of joint', as Prince Hamlet memorably observes, and in that atmosphere, even the basic human anatomy cannot hold steady or be offered up in its reliable form for contemplation, despite Hamlet's melodramatic 'What a piece of work is a man! How noble in reason, how infinite in faculty, in form and moving how express and admirable' (2.2.293–5). For the body as a symbolic whole itself disintegrates, under Hamlet's relentless questioning, beginning with his opening wish that 'this too too solid flesh would melt, / Thaw, and resolve itself into a dew' (1.2.129–30), through his bitter observation that the 'paragon of animals' is but a 'quintessence of dust' (2.2.297–8), right to the scene by Ophelia's grave when he reflects upon the skull of Yorick.[34] The body is reduced to its minute constituents in an environment which appears to be without order or meaning, a 'foul and pestilent congregation of vapours' (2.2.293), no longer safely monitored, 'roofed' or contained.

The other reason for Hamlet's sense that the body can no longer be relied upon to retain its shape and consoling anatomy in the face of tragic events is the prospect of its afterlife, whether in spiritual purgatory or physical decomposition. The grave is not a final resting place. Not only might the soul 'dream' and travel relentlessly through the 'undiscovered country' of death but the material body will disintegrate and be reconstituted in an endless cycle of repetition, a 'fine revolution'. Hamlet reveals the absurdity of death which allows 'a king' to 'go a progress through the guts of a beggar', since 'a man may fish with the worm that hath eat of a king, and eat of the fish that hath fed of that worm'.[35] In this radical migration nothing rests long enough to allow for the serious concentration of grief or lament: 'Why may not imagination trace the noble dust of Alexander till he find it stopping a bung-hole?' (5.1.187–9). The climax of Hamlet's interrogation of death occurs in the scene at Ophelia's grave. Egged on by the gravedigger, Hamlet considers the impermanence

of the body ('How long will a man lie I' the earth ere he rot?')
and the frangible material constituents of any person like the old
court jester Yorick ('Here hung those lips that I have kissed I
know not how oft').[36]

The two acts of mourning following the attacks on September 11 –
the obituaries of the dead and the forensic search for human
remains – follow tragic tropes: the 'Portraits of Grief' like
Euripides' *Trojan Women*, picking out individuals for lament amid
a whole city laid waste; the trucks' journey to Fresh Kills after
forensic examination recalling Hamlet's half-agonized, half-jocular
questions beside Ophelia's grave. The tragic intervention is also
located precisely in the disparity between the two, between the
narrative response of the 'Portraits' and the material response of
the excavation: the human bumping up against the non-human;
narrative reaching its limits against the intractability of the material;
the symbolic confronting the literal; question met by answer – or
maybe no answer but just further questions.

In March 2002, with only the basement of the South Tower
remaining to investigate, one firefighter expressed the desperation
felt by the workmen as the debris ran out, summing up admirably
the archaeological significance of the ground, the meaning it
discloses and the emotion located in the absences:

> It's not over, but it's definitely winding down. You've got a great
> number of people that you want to find, and you've got a certain
> amount of dirt that's left. And there's a gap. That gap is going to
> be a sorrowful one. But we can't make more dirt.[37]

The 'sorrowful' 'gap' to which this firefighter drew attention is
metaphorically the gap to which tragedy regularly attends. This
is the gap between our expectations and the intractable world,
between our desire for significance and order and the perception
of the world as without meaning or purpose. It's a gap which both
literally and metaphorically hollows out the ending of Euripides'
Bacchae. In that play, Agave has unwittingly torn apart the body
of her son Pentheus along with the other women driven mad by
Dionysiac frenzy. She enters the stage, still raving and clutching
what she believes is the head of a lion. Only after her father has
slowly brought her round from her mad delusion can she recognize
it for what it is, the head of her son. Devastated by this knowledge,

Agave focuses on solid facts, the recovery of her son's body. But this produces further physical and emotional challenges:

> **AGAVE** And the dear body of my son, father – where is it?
> **CADMUS** I found it with difficulty, and have brought it here.
> **AGAVE** Are all his limbs joined decently [*kalos*] together?
> **CADMUS** [missing line in text].

Cadmus's response to Agave's hope for 'decency', for order and wholeness, is hard to fathom, hard to articulate. Pentheus is literally scattered in bloody pieces across the hills of Cithaeron. The fragmentation of his body testifies to the wider disorder of the city of Thebes, to Dionysus's excessive punishment and the questionable justice of the gods. It challenges the notion of *kalos*, of beauty, goodness and decency to which Agave appeals. Nothing coheres any longer, nothing can be relied upon or makes rational sense. The aporia of Cadmus's response is matched by the physical lacuna in the text. His words are literally lost here. The silence, lost to history and the wastage of time, seems appropriate.

Of course, Cadmus would not have been lost for words when the *Bacchae* was originally staged back in 405 BC. Scholars have pondered what would once have filled that 'gap' and have tried to recreate the text, based on their knowledge of performance conventions and traditional ritual. One view is that although Cadmus would have answered his daughter's query in the negative, she would have put the pieces of Pentheus together in order that father and daughter could mourn over the dead. An ancient commentator noted that Agave 'taking each of his limbs in her hands, laments over each one of them', presumably referring to a lament which occurred at this missing point in the drama.[38] This restoration of text and body was re-enacted in the 2015 production of the play at London's Almeida Theatre, directed by James Macdonald in a way that attempted to stick closely to the ancient performance conditions. Cadmus and Agave crouched quietly over Pentheus' remains, carefully placing pieces back into a human shape and lamenting the whole, including the head.[39] In this case, ritual lament took the place of a solid body of text. Communal mourning (father and daughter coming together over the son's scattered remains) restored beliefs that had been shattered by the violent tearing apart or *sparagmos* of Pentheus. 'Restoring' the body of Pentheus, however imperfectly, allowed him to be lamented. It made him more recognizably human and grievable.

The power of tragedy lies in the disparity between the material remains of the body and the community's attempts to make them seem significant. It lies in the gap between excavating and lamenting. So I disagree with the interpretation of the 'Portraits of Grief' by one critic, David Simpson, who has claimed that the obituaries were generic, 'oddly flattened out', a 'very simple picture of features common to all'.[40] Their common quality was, he argued, designed to convey a notion of American wholesomeness, marshalled to instill a sense of national pride which ultimately led to vengeance and war. The 'Portraits' seem 'regimented, even militarised, made to march to the beat of a single drum', he wrote.[41] But the significance of the 'Portraits' was not only in their attention to quirky detail, a commitment to individualize the catastrophe and restore human faces to the statistics. It was also in the self-conscious effort of narrative itself, of interposing all these stories in the yawning absence of bodies. The 'Portraits' should be read in that context of the depressing search for fragments which could be distinguished from the dust. They were like the messenger speeches of Greek tragedy. The violence has happened offstage; a messenger enters to report in vivid detail what has happened. The chorus demand to hear more, wanting to learn all the facts so that they can lament properly. And afterwards, sometimes the body is brought out for additional mourning – the small body of the boy Astyanax in the *Trojan Women*, Pentheus in *Bacchae*, Haemon in *Antigone* – but sometimes it is not. The body may be too dismembered, too unsightly or too scattered in many pieces to be displayed for the expression of grief. And, thus, the dramas reflect upon the disjunction between words and objects, narrative tributes and human remains, significance and insignificance. Tragic lament gathers these disjunctions in its collective purpose.

The sense of an ending?

Ancient lament followed an established ritual. The mourners would sing, shed tears, raise their arms and lay their hands on the dead body. They would loosen their hair and pluck at their cheeks and clothes.[42] By the time of classical tragedy the lament was known as a *kommos*, the word literally meaning a 'beating' since the women would beat their breasts rhythmically to register their grief. But, earlier, a distinction was made between two types of lament: the organized, polished *threnos* of professional mourners ('a proper song') and the unorganized, raw *goos* of the kinswomen, who 'merely wailed'.[43] It is because of this origin in two groups of people mourning that lamentation developed as an antiphonal form, the professional mourners leading the song and the relatives responding. A repetitive cry of lament would be sung, the sorrow batted back and forth between the mourners, with different individuals taking it upon themselves to lead the grieving. This antiphony becomes developed into the *kommos* of the tragic Greek chorus, which structures its traditional call and response into 'verses' known as 'strophe' and 'antistrophe', so called because they indicate the movement of the dancing chorus across the stage, progressing in one direction for the strophe and then turning to go back again for the antistrophe.[44] Movement, rhythm and song combine to organize and give structure to the grief.

At the end of Aeschylus's *Seven against Thebes*, after the city has survived attack but the king and his enemy brother have killed each other in a single blow, the chorus divides in two, singing the dirge to each other in endless, reiterative phrases:

> **A.** Cry sorrow! **B.** Cry sorrow!
> **A.** My heart is mad with lamenting.
> **B.** My heart within me is groaning.
> **A.** Oh, oh! You shall have all our tears!
> **B.** You too, your wretchedness complete![45]

The original ending of Aeschylus's play is lost, so we can only surmise how far the collective mourning at the conclusion produced what might be described now as satisfying closure. Certainly, if the model of the *Iliad* is taken, it seems as if the ritual cry and song of lament brought a feeling of relief. In that poem, Achilles and Priam break down weeping together at the end of the epic, each weeping for his own source of sorrow:

> And the two remembered, the one weeping without cessation for man-slaughtering Hector as he lay curled before Achilles' feet,

and Achilles wept for his own father, and then again for
Patroclus; and the sound of their lament was raised throughout
the hall.[46]

But Achilles stops weeping with Priam when he 'had taken his
fill of lamentation / and the yearning had gone from his breast
and very limbs' (24.513–14). And in Troy, after Hector has been
cremated and the bones carefully gathered in a golden box and
buried, the citizens hold a 'glorious feast' in Priam's palace. In both
cases, the ritual of lament offers relief and the appropriate sense
of an ending. It's likely that a similar collective mourning, repeated
antiphonally, brought the city's grief to some form of resolution
in *Seven Against Thebes*. Mourning, notes Margaret Alexiou,
involves 'the balancing of cries', a 'kind of refrain' that brings
people together and forms a natural stopping point for grief.[47]

But according to classical scholar Nicole Loraux, the repetition of
mourning does not necessarily amount to a rhythmic pattern tending
towards closure. Instead it can just become endless reiteration,
stuck fast in a spiraling loop of sorrow. Ingeniously playing with
words, Loraux points to the pun on the word '*aiai*', the Greek word
usually translated 'alas' but really amounting to an untranslatable
cry or howl. '*Aiai*' sounds like the word for 'forever' in Greek: '*aei*'.
Howling a lamentation can last forever, with no natural, rhythmic
closure. Here is Loraux on lamentation in tragedy at her typically
most lyrical and complex:

> Thus, for the spectators the bewitched memory of the intractable
> *aei*, 'always', unallied with wisdom, will surely be stronger than
> any moral lesson – all the more so as the curious impulse which
> regularly brings the tragic genre back to the multiform evocation
> of the despairing *aei* of mourning is coupled with the perceptible
> and even sensual sonorous pleasure that the ear is invited to
> enjoy when tragedy intensifies *aei* into *aiai*.[48]

So Alexiou's ritualistic pattern or Loraux's shapeless but endlessly
seductive sound of grief? Lamentation pulls one in, with the
complicated traditions of expressive mourning, but it is not
necessarily the case that repetition can be worked through to
produce catharsis.

The lament for nearly 3,000 dead at 9/11, repetitive and ritualistic as it was when it appeared in the *New York Times*, could not offer the catharsis described at the end of the *Iliad*. The scale of the attacks, the lack of bodies to mourn, the disjunction between grief and objects: all combined to create a sense of unrepresentability, of disproportion and disruption, of work left undone, as I have described. All that could be offered were reiterations of the experience and reflections on the task of mourning and its limitations which tested the boundaries between the traumatic and the tragic. The dance-theatre piece by Pig Iron Theatre, entitled *Love Unpunished*, is one typical example of this intervention of collective grief.[49] Featuring simply a spiraling staircase, down (and occasionally up) which the cast repeatedly walk, dawdle or scamper, the 65-minute performance is supposedly an evocation of the evacuation of the North Tower of the World Trade Center. There are business men in suits, construction workers in hard hats, a couple of women (one of them speaking Japanese on her cell phone) sipping lattes. It begins slowly, with those descending unconcerned, chatting, checking their laptops. But then it builds in speed and intensity, until firefighters start appearing climbing the stairs in the other direction, and then coffee cups are scattered, people run down the stairs, the background alarm sound grows much louder. The lights go out, only for them to come back on again a moment later and for the whole process to be repeated, the rhythm returning to the idle, slow descending of stairs. Repetition becomes hypnotic but ultimately troubling in the piece. Since the same figures appear descending the stairs again and again, with echoing gestures and reiterated words, one is left uncertain whether this is a portrayal of the same characters descending several storeys down or whether this is the repeated loop of a traumatic memory. As later in the dance piece some characters stumble and fall at the side of the staircase, maybe free-falling down the side of the tower, the whole performance comes to evoke the unsteady, traumatized, fragmentary quality of shattered memory and collective loss. 'The piece tries to let you sit with really simple repetitions about simple details and unlock a kind of compassion', the director, Dan Rothenberg, has commented.[50]

Traumatic repetition is the hallmark of Don DeLillo's '9/11 novel' too, with the uncanny recurrences of the towers and the famous image of the man falling head first from them puncturing DeLillo's haunted prose. *Falling Man* does not really describe the disaster as such, or not at least until the very end of the novel, but it follows the weeks and months after September 11, with its characters held fast by their traumatized flashbacks in an emotional limbo.[51] The 'falling man' is recalled in the parodic and mysterious stunts that a performance artist pulls off at various points in the novel, dangling upside down from buildings or above the train tracks. But he is there too in the insistence of the word 'falling' repeatedly throughout the text, the 'downdraft of memory', the 'drifting smoke' of a cigarette, the 'timeless drift of the long spiral down' experienced during lovemaking.[52] And the towers keep making their ghostly presence felt. As one character Lianne looks at a painting hanging in her mother's apartment, her mother's lover, Martin, observes, 'I keep seeing the towers in this still life.' The painting simply depicts bottles and other indefinable domestic objects, yet Lianne agrees with him. 'She saw what he saw. She saw the towers.'[53]

Are we all similarly haunted by 9/11, that unresolved, lamentable trauma in our collective psyche? When I saw Jasper Johns's recent work, entitled 'Farley Breaks Down', which is based on Larry Burrows's photograph of an exhausted Vietnam veteran, the first thing I noticed was the grey silhouette of the towers at the back before I could make out any other shape.[54] Did Jasper Johns intend this or is it just that I am preoccupied by 9/11 and its symbol, the missing World Trade Center, rather like Lianne in DeLillo's novel? Or is Johns inviting that act of projection with his shadowy and indistinct image? Is he suggesting a parallel between Vietnam and 9/11, two open wounds in America's recent history? Ostensibly a painterly invocation of the Burrows' photo, repeated in many different versions, still the two open French doors from the original photograph become for me, in Johns's rendition, the ghostly twin towers looming over the scene. It is a fascinating palimpsest of defeat, unresolved trauma and the layered perceptions of public history, as Vietnam and 9/11 are made to read – or misread – each other.

The twin towers produce a series of uncanny repetitions. Of course, they echo each other, doubling so iconically. And then they replicate themselves in our imaginations, appearing as shadowy repetitions in the oneiric qualities of art, in novels, theatre, paintings. Their image is repeated again and again but is unresolved in the public imagination. Indeed the repetition is an indication of the lack of resolution, the lack of a conclusion. Our lament for them, for New York and for whatever it is that

9/11 represents, is without closure, stuck fast in the melancholic state of trauma. All that can be done is to metaphorically wail the lament, the *aei/aiai* of tragedy.

Creating the memorial

The memorial site in Downtown New York, where the Twin Towers once stood, has been hotly contested since it was first discussed in the months after the attacks. The area, known as Ground Zero, was simultaneously a graveyard and prime real estate, a vortex of grief and mourning and a catalyst for determination and rebirth. Daniel Libeskind's original winning master plan for the site, selected in 2003, transformed the area into a heavily symbolic topography of loss. The buildings were designed to let the sun shine without shadow down into the plaza just once a year, precisely on September 11 between the hours of 8.46 am, when the first airplane hit, and 10.28 am, when the second tower collapsed. They were thus intended to offer their own commemoration annually 'in perpetual tribute to altruism and courage', as Libeskind explained in his winning proposal. Meanwhile, the centre of the plaza was to be dominated by a vast chasm into which the public could descend to the slurry wall, since it 'withstood the unimaginable trauma of the destruction and stand[s] as eloquent as the Constitution itself asserting the durability of Democracy and the value of individual life'. The footprints of the towers were to be left, sunken down to the bedrock 70 feet below the ground, as places of reflection, while the eye was to be swept up to a twisting tower, symbolically 1,776 feet tall, the date of the declaration of American Independence, and the tallest building in the world, echoing the asymmetrical thrusting arm of the Statue of Liberty. But Larry Silverstein, leaseholder of the World Trade Center, has filled Libeskind's symbolic voids and rhetoric with commercial priorities in the years since until all that is really left of the original plan are the footprints of the towers and the slurry wall.[55]

While the site is almost completed now, it continues to oscillate between grief and determination, between waste and resolve, reflecting the persistent sense of trauma at the heart of the nation. Walking past the vast transport station building, known as the

Oculus, which rises like a white phoenix from the metaphorical ashes of the ground, you arrive at the memorial plaza, which is dominated by two huge fountains, created in the footprints of the original Twin Towers. Water plunges down into the abyss, with a roar closer to a natural waterfall or a giant industrial weir than an ornamental fountain. Around the rim, the names of the victims are carved in the metal wall, marking the boundary between the public and the sounding waters of grief, with letters deep enough to insert a tributary flower in memory of an individual. The poignant poetics of what is missing – 'allowing absence to speak for itself' – lay at the heart of why the design of Michael Arad and Peter Walker for the fountains was chosen, according to the Memorial Jury's statement in January 2004.[56] Over the plaza and the two fountains looms the new World Trade Center, otherwise known as the Freedom Tower. This is supposedly the victorious future as opposed to the defeated and doubtful past.

Beneath the plaza, however, the 9/11 Memorial Museum excavates the extent of public grief and trauma still further. Visitors are taken down a ramp, past the remains of the slurry wall which was built to hold back the waters of the Hudson River from the World Trade Center foundations and a buckled section of the steel façade of the North Tower and past disappearing projections of posters of the missing, which were displayed around the city in the subsequent days and weeks of the attack. 'As hope for survivors faded, the missing posters themselves became memorials', reads the caption, the flickering nature of the projection reflecting the tragic ephemerality of mortality captured by the Greek poet Pindar ('Creatures of a day! What is man? What is he not? A shadow's dream').[57] The descent passes a crumbling flight of stone stairs, the 'Survivors' Stairs', which took people from the plaza to the Vesey Street sidewalk as the North Tower was burning above them. At the foot are the material traces of the towers themselves. The steel columns which formed the skeleton of the buildings were cut down to their foundations during the clear-up and recovery process and these box-like stubs remain, marking out the contours of the ghostly, absent towers. Within these skeletal square boundaries are the twin functions of memorial and museum, a rotating projection of each victim in the memorial South Tower which draws on and extends the 'Portraits of Grief' and a museum of recovered artefacts, archived audio recordings, video footage and detailed information in the North Tower. In between the two towers, the recovered remains of the dead are buried, behind a sky-blue mosaic wall.[58]

Just as the retrieval of the dead at Ground Zero drew attention to the 'gap' between the missing relatives still to be found and the amount of debris still to sift, so the emotional power of the memorial museum lies in the gulf between what can be seen and what can never be recovered. Inevitably this absence is chiefly apparent in the attention to the objects recovered from the debris. There is a Yankees baseball game ticket, a bus pass, a Metrocard, a room key from a hotel, shoes, keys: the detritus of ordinary lives interrupted. Each object now takes on the status of a relic, standing in for the life and in most cases also the body that was never recovered. The objects are prosaic but for the fact that they take on the onus of substitution and survival. Thus, the memorial museum resorts to a familiar form of mournful reflection and lament, one which draws attention to the common human experience of a life lived and lost. But the most disturbing object in the museum, resonant of the particular nature of this tragedy, is the 'Composite' displayed towards the end. Only about 1 or 2 metres in height, this is the fused and compacted remains of five storeys of the building, originally about 19 metres in height. So intense was the heat that all material melted and condensed to this, like a dense black hole or collapsed star, making – as the museum caption tactfully puts it in understated terms – the 'preservation of human remains impossible'. Dense, material, shapeless and hard to contemplate, the solid composite evokes the spectacular disproportions of scale between the human and inhuman in this tragedy. As the caption puts it:

> As material evidence of the devastation and condition of the towers' collapse, the composites represent a unique historical record of these events. As objects connected to the unfathomable circumstances in which thousands died on 9/11, they also represent the unknowable.

What is 'unknowable' traditionally lies at the clotted core of trauma. It is, according to Freud, what cannot be understood, assimilated and absorbed into the healthy memory. It returns, again and again, only to be 'repeated' rather than properly 'remembered'.[59] And those repeated flashbacks become the locus for further confusion and pain, necessitating additional spirals of non-recognition or understanding and only further circulating narratives that fail to address the initial wound. The tour around the 9/11 Memorial Museum winds round and round the two tower footprints like the spiraling patterns of traumatic grief. The story of that day is told and retold, through objects, voice recordings, news footage, from different perspectives and in different media. And each narrative thread coils into the next, like the next strophe or antistrophe of a chorus of lament. There are, admittedly, some shortcut exits, some emergency doors, but to stay the ambulatory course is to find oneself disorientated and immersed in a claustrophobic, circulating and repeated experience of storytelling and retelling. Alice Greenwald, director of the museum, has herself said that 'this is a museum without ending'.[60] The sense of endlessness is palpable in the museum experience itself.

When does an event begin and end?

Trauma is traditionally resolved into tragedy, as I described earlier. The wounding, unapprehendable event is made intelligible or manageable through the patterning of tragic narrative, which shapes experience into a 'plot' with a beginning, a middle and an end. A similar transformation takes place in epic. Tragedies are assimilated into a larger epic narrative, so that tragic episodes become shaping nodes in the bigger historical journey towards the goal or the quest's end. Virgil's *Aeneid*, for example, tells the story of Aeneas's journey as a refugee from the burning city of Troy around the Mediterranean to the sanctuary of Italy, where he establishes a colony, conquers the local population and begins the race of people that will go on to become the ancient Romans. But punctuating this epic narrative are the tragic tales and vignettes of those whose lives were sacrificed along the way. Aeneas abandons his lover Dido, queen of Carthage, and she commits suicide in despair in Book 4; he encounters her ghost in the Underworld in Book 6, but she turns away in silence. Shadows and echoes of the traumatic violence experienced in the destruction of Troy reoccur as reiterated events and uncanny flashbacks throughout the epic and especially in the various battles and victories in Italy. Tragedy keeps coming back, unresolved, dragging Aeneas and the reader back to the unfinished past.

On the wall of the repository in the 9/11 Memorial Museum where the remains of the victims are laid to rest, a line from Virgil's *Aeneid* is displayed. Formed from letters fashioned out of World Trade Center steel that was recovered from the rubble, the line reads: 'No Day Shall Erase You from the Memory of Time'. The words serve as an epitaph upon a communal grave. The symbolism of repurposing the metal, so that it becomes burnished and renewed as stirring sentiments, testifies to the desire to express resilience and defiance in the face of destruction. Memory here both pays respects to the victims' lives and also, through the molten metal, indicates a mode of renewal and transformation. The material aesthetic object that the letters have become is so different from the 'Composite'; this is shaped and crafted, a thing of beauty. But as the Homer translator Caroline Alexander has pointed out, the line from Virgil omits the context.[61] It is a quotation from one of those tragic episodes in the epic which pulls the reader back to the unresolved, traumatic and violent vengefulness of the past. The two men 'remembered' have slaughtered a defenceless, sleeping military camp on a raid and then themselves been killed. In the Nisus and Euryalus episode in Book 9, from where the quotation is taken, we hear an echo of the traumatic attack on the unsuspecting city of Troy which Aeneas himself suffered. This is a tragic vignette of repeated, unresolved trauma, the Trojans unconsciously visiting upon others the brutal destruction they themselves experienced. The day may not erase them from the memory of time, but they have erased their own memories, replacing them with forms of forgetting and flashback, circling around episodes of trauma and tragedy.

If it is impossible to distinguish an event from the response to an event, as Raymond Williams said, then when can we say an event has finished? What is an event? When does it start or stop? How is it experienced? Where is the sense of it as a tragedy located? How does it get co-opted by a set of desires or fears that we might not fully acknowledge? 9/11 continues to be repeated, remembered and worked through. Its story is told and retold like the winding tour of the museum. On the ground, the reconstruction work is still going on while forensic efforts to identify remains continue. The repercussions are played out both psychologically as private and national trauma, and politically in the War on Terror and its knock-on results. The events of 9/11 are mediated, thought about and rethought, commemorated as anniversaries, co-opted by political rhetoric, and transformed into a cycle of recollection and forgetting and retelling.

At the end of *The Guys*, the playwright Anne Nelson records in an 'Afterword' the response of the firefighters to her play and to the work of recovery at Ground Zero after 9/11. She observes:

> Periodically, I hear people comment that 'it's time to move on', that 'the firefighters need to understand that'. All I can think of is what the fire captain told me late in the fall: 'For us, every day in the firehouse is September 12'. And it will be, for some time to come.[62]

It is September 12 not only for the firefighters but arguably for the rest of the nation and indeed for the wider world. There is no sign of 'moving on' or 'closure' or indeed of 'understanding'. The lament, the grief and the anger persist and the circling spirals of recognition and non-recognition.

The rest of my book considers this unfinished and continuing event. While we will travel from downtown Manhattan to the wars in Afghanistan and Iraq, from revolutions and conflicts across the Middle East to the refugee crisis in the Mediterranean, from the rise of political division and racist populism across Europe and the United States ultimately to the planetary climate crisis, each chapter follows the next inexorably as if 9/11 had never ended but is traumatically and tragically repeated in each of these spheres. The rest of this book, in other words, could justifiably be entitled September 12.

3

The Dogs of War

On 11 September 2004, waking up to a hot, late-summer Saturday morning in New York City, I caught the subway down to Chambers Street for the annual commemoration of the 9/11 terrorist atrocity. The hallowed site of Ground Zero, where once the two great towers of the World Trade Center had soared, had by this date been completely cleared of the rubble of the past. The diggers had reached bedrock, the hard, grey granite on which Manhattan was founded. But in 2004, the massive new construction which now dominates downtown had not yet begun. Instead, Ground Zero was a huge pit, ringed by a high-wire mesh fence on which pilgrims and tourists had attached flowers, tributes and messages over the years.

When I arrived at the site that September morning, it was already thronging with people peering through the wire squares of the fence at the city dignitaries, the firefighters and the families of the victims gathered beneath the stars-and stripes in the pit below us. Mayor Bloomberg spoke over the loudspeaker. A minute's silence was observed by the whole arena to mark the moment the first plane hit the North Tower at 8.46 am. Governor George Pataki quoted President Eisenhower: 'There's no tragedy in life like the death of a child.' Rudolf Giuliani, the former mayor, read out a letter from Abraham Lincoln, comforting a mother whose sons had been killed in the civil war. Another minute of silence to mark the moment the second plane hit the other tower at 9.03 am. A lone trumpet struck up the Last Post. And then the voices of bereaved parents and grandparents began to read out the names of the dead in alphabetical order, the sound echoing against the empty shells of buildings behind us and the rock below – Gordon A. Aamoth, Jr. Edelmiro Abad. Marie Rose Abad.

Later that evening, I made my way down to the Hudson River for the alternative 9/11 ceremony. Gathering at a pier on the west side of the city, and looking across at the beam of light shooting into the sky where the World Trade Center once loomed, the informal group lit paper lanterns, in the traditional Japanese *toro nagashi* fashion, and set them on the water to float away down the river in the sunset and out to the open water, past the Statue of Liberty, past Staten Island. Different family members of those who had died in the September 11 attacks made speeches and offered prayers. 'I want to remember all those who died on 9/11', said the brother of one woman who had died three years earlier. 'But I also want to remember all those who have died since in the name of 9/11.' This was 2004. The Taliban had been toppled and much of Afghanistan flattened. Saddam Hussein had been captured. Civil war was beginning, with hundreds of Iraqi civilians and police being killed by Sunni-led bombings. The first battle of Fallujah had erupted a few months earlier. And American abuse of Iraqi prisoners in Abu Ghraib had recently been exposed by the publication of a few photographs.

These two ceremonies to remember the dead were both versions of tragic ritual. Like tragic performances there were some principal 'officiants' reading the names, making the speeches, throwing the paper lanterns out into the Hudson – and of course there were the 'heroes' whom we were remembering and lamenting – but the rituals were participatory, designed to draw the mourners and the city together.[1] The whole crowd held the minute's silence with the city mayor or joined together in reflective memory by the water's edge. And like a tragic performance, what was said was intended to represent what could not be said. The words were offered in place of the actual bodies of those commemorated on this day, 'managing loss by narrating it', as Rowan Williams has described the activity of tragic performance, and 'uncover[ing] not so much the unknown as the *fact* of our not-knowing'.[2] Yet in other respects, these two ceremonies were in marked contrast. The first focused entirely on the American lives lost in New York City three years earlier. It was marked by grief and respect for those who had died and by a collective resolve to continue to fight for the perceived American values of freedom and democracy. The crowd turned inward to the empty bedrock at our midst. The second ceremony looked outward and was prepared to acknowledge that the events on September

11, 2001, had not ended neatly on that date. A parallel was being drawn between 'us' in New York and 'them' in Afghanistan or Iraq, those 'who had died in the name of 9/11'. As the lanterns floated out in the Hudson, traditional boundaries were being questioned.

These two responses to the catastrophe three years earlier strikingly mirrored the stark choice facing the American people that Rowan Williams had articulated so presciently in the aftermath of the attack. He himself had been there on the morning of September 11, 2001, amid the destruction and confusion of downtown Manhattan. As American Airlines Flight 11 was crashing into the North Tower, the clergy of Trinity Church in Wall Street were sitting down just a few blocks away with invited guests to record a discussion about religious practice and belief. They were 'interrupted', said Rowan Williams, the future Archbishop of Canterbury and head of the worldwide Anglican Communion, by terrorists driven by their own version of religious belief. Williams joined everyone else in the area stumbling out of the building in a thick dust of burning ash. There were shouts, sirens, the 'indescribable long roar of the second tower collapsing'. What he remembered particularly, however, was his lack of feeling that morning and the apparent silence of the streets as he perceived them in his state of shock. In the middle of terror and pain, there was just a sense of emptiness, he recalled. He was numbed, or even – as he put it – living 'in the presence of the void'.

Reflecting on the event a few weeks later, Rowan Williams attempted to do justice to this void, to write about its challenges, its potential and its temptations. There were, he said, two courses of action for the American people and indeed everyone around the world who were shocked and still grieving. One option was to use the initial passionate and understandable anger about the injury done to us and turn it into a violent response, continually fuelling the rage with recollections of the attack and 'cling[ing] harder and harder to the rock of our threatened identity'.[3] In effect, this would mean seeking revenge, acting quickly for the sake of being seen to do something and bombing the enemy in return. The other option was to pause and reflect, to think about our own vulnerability and that of others, to learn a radical and risky compassion. 'The trauma ... is not just a nightmarish insult to *us* but a door into the suffering of countless other innocents', wrote Williams.[4] His pamphlet professed to offer 'hope that risk and reconciliation are a new and living way to avoid the relentless spiral downward to more and worse aggression'.

Writing in the Dust appeared in January 2002 but it is extraordinarily clear-sighted about the times we live in now. For everything that Williams foresaw and warned against in his pamphlet has, sadly, happened. The world did not opt for the second choice, the invitation to reflect and to pass through the 'door' into the suffering of others. Instead, the void was filled with anger, with violence and with military force. On 7 October 2001, less than a month after the attacks, the United States launched Operation Enduring Freedom together with the United Kingdom, bombing Taliban forces and al-Qaeda training camps in Afghanistan. They captured Kabul on 13 November. By this time most of Taliban, as well as bin Laden, had escaped over the border to Pakistan, but the US attention was already being distracted towards its other focus for military action. Just over a year later, President Bush and his White House team had ratcheted up the punitive demand for justice so intensely that they were able to launch a military invasion of Iraq under the false claim that it was connected to the 9/11 attacks. On 9 April 2003, Baghdad fell and Saddam Hussein was toppled, with Bush declaring on 1 May that the mission was accomplished. An insurgency against coalition forces was already beginning, however; it reached a peak in 2006, to be followed by sectarian violence, the so-called US 'surge' of 2007, the rise of ISIS and the chaotic ungovernability of the country. Meanwhile in Afghanistan, a Taliban insurgency began to grow from 2004 with more and more Western troops being committed to the campaign from 2007. By 2018, the US military were still involved in Afghanistan and Iraq, with both countries torn apart by continuing conflict. Casualty figures are almost impossible to collate, but according to a combination of various estimates, it may be that around 120,000 lives have been lost in the conflict in Afghanistan while well over *half a million* people have died in Iraq since 2003 as a direct or indirect consequence of the invasion.[5] These figures dwarf the number of deaths (2,996) on 9/11.

The tragedy of the post-9/11 world is located in the choice identified by Rowan Williams. He set out the two options and foresaw the consequences of each one clearly. We had the opportunity to learn from the past and from careful reflection on the global situation and to choose an alternative to military air strikes. Other voices spoke out with similar warnings too. Martha Nussbaum argued that the shock of 9/11 could usher in a new era of mutual understanding, noting that 'compassion and terror now inform the fabric of our lives'.[6] And Judith Butler also questioned 'whether the experiences of vulnerability and loss have to lead straightaway to military violence and retribution' and 'what, politically, might be made of grief beside a cry for war?'.[7] But the alternative use of grief was the choice not taken; instead we opted for the other course of action, with disastrous results.

The wars on Afghanistan and later Iraq, 'in the name of 9/11', were waged supposedly for the causes of justice and freedom. 'On September 11, enemies of freedom committed an act of war against our country', declared President George W. Bush to a joint session of Congress, just nine days after the attack. 'I will never forget the wound to our country and those who inflicted it. ... Our grief has turned to anger and anger to resolution. Whether we bring our enemies to justice or bring justice to our enemies, justice will be done.' Bush's eliding of trauma, grief, anger and justice, in the short space of nine days, is telling here.[8] When the demand for justice is fuelled so swiftly by anger and when collective trauma is apparently to be healed by violent reparations, it becomes hard to distinguish between justice and vengeance. The wars in Afghanistan and Iraq and Bush's wider 'War on Terror' were punitive campaigns which carry all the hallmarks of revenge, from the invocation of necessity to the neglect of 'means' for the sake of a dubious 'end'. And revenge tragedy is one of the oldest and bloodiest and morally murkiest in the Western canon.

The war of choice

Tragic narratives of revenge usually begin with a choice. To avenge or not to avenge? To seek to impose rightful punishment or to keep quiet and turn the other cheek? But revenge tragedies mostly operate as if in fact there is no choice, as if everything compels the protagonist to one course of action. At the beginning of the Trojan War, Agamemnon, leader of the Greek army, is presented with a terrible decision. The goddess Artemis is angry with him and is preventing the wind from blowing and thus the ships from sailing over to Troy. She can only be appeased by the sacrifice of Agamemnon's daughter, Iphigenia. When Agamemnon hears this injunction from the prophet, he realizes immediately the starkness of his choice. Either he can refuse the goddess's demand and thus he will betray the army or he must kill his daughter and thus store up the seeds of violent hatred in the hearts of his family. In Aeschylus's *Oresteia*, as recollected by the chorus, he weighs up the options:

> The senior lord spoke, declaring
> 'Fate will be heavy if I do not obey, heavy as well
> if I hew my child, my house's own darling,
> polluting her father's hands
> with slaughter streaming from a maiden
> at the altar: what is there without evil here?
> How can I desert the fleet
> and fail the alliance?
> Why, this sacrifice to stop the wind,
> a maiden's blood,
> is their most passionate desire;
> but Right (θέμις: *themis*) forbids it. So may all be well!'[9]

In Robert Icke's recent adaptation of the play, Agamemnon's choice is put even more starkly, in terms that draw on the classic ethical dilemma commonly cited in philosophy: 'What you're being told is that the road is about to split, that an action is coming which you either perform – or you don't. Make that judgement', says the prophet Calchas.[10]

Yet the choice is not portrayed as a neutral one. Fate has already tipped the scales. Agamemnon seems compelled to choose the course for war. He must opt for the male, public demand for vengeance rather than the female, private alternative of refusing the rush to the military campaign. In Aeschylus's famous words, he 'dons the yoke of necessity' (ἀνάγκας ἔδυ λέπαδνον: *anankas edu lepadnon*; *Agamemnon*, 217) and from then on is committed to the war effort, filled with daring and the capacity for violation. In Euripides' version of this scene, Agamemnon is influenced by the intense pressure of a scarcely controllable army, a huge crowd of men desperate to go to war and baying for blood. 'We are slaves to the common people', he complains, and those common people are driven by a 'mad desire' (or '*aphrodite*' in the original Greek) to sail to 'the land of the barbarians and put an end to the rape of Greek wives'.[11] His efforts to change his mind and overturn the demand for Iphigenia to be brought for sacrifice are thwarted by Menelaus, Odysseus and the other Greek generals. You can't overturn the will of the people, they tell him. The policy is irrevocably set for human sacrifice and the countdown to war. In Robert Icke's adaptation, a momentum builds behind Agamemnon's killing of his daughter based partly upon the rational argument that the sacrifice of one individual will save countless others, since Iphigenia's death will ensure that the foreign war will finally come to an end. There are also additional motives for Agamemnon, whose characterization in Icke's version owes much to the figure of Tony Blair. He's also driven by pressures arising from public criticism of him as a leader, as well as his own religious sense that some 'things are just *right*', and fears of the threat of blackmail if he tries to back out of the commitment.[12] But in Aeschylus's version the compulsion comes from the complex Greek understanding of fate and divine determination. Agamemnon is driven by Necessity (ἀναγκη), an impersonal, fateful force. Yet he also *voluntarily* slips his head into the yoke, and thus steels his will to go through with the murder of his daughter. The compulsion and the apparent lack of choice are self-willed and not unnegotiable. 'For mankind is emboldened by wretched delusion, counsellor of ill, primal source of woe', comment the chorus.[13]

According to President Obama, the military invasion of Iraq was a 'war of choice', whereas the bombardment of Afghanistan was not. After September 11, he declared in a speech in Chicago in 2002, it was right to 'hunt down and root out those who would slaughter innocents in the name of intolerance' (implicitly referring to the war in Afghanistan) but the war in Iraq was a 'dumb' and a 'rash war', a 'war based not on reason but on passion, not on principle but on politics'.[14] Later, looking back as a newly elected president over the whole decade and defending his decision to increase American military involvement in Afghanistan, he again drew a distinction between the two conflicts. 'We must never forget. This is not a war of choice. This is a war of necessity', he told army veterans. 'Those who attacked America on 9/11 are plotting to do so again. If left unchecked, the Taliban insurgency will mean an even larger safe haven from which Al Qaeda would plot to kill more Americans.'[15]

But the 'necessity' of Afghanistan was closer to Agamemnon's 'yoke of necessity' into which he voluntarily slipped his head. According to foreign policy expert Richard Haase, a distinction should be drawn between wars of necessity and wars of choice. He defines them thus: 'Wars of necessity involve the most important national interests, the absence of promising alternatives to the use of force, and the certain and considerable price to be paid if the status quo is to stand.'[16] By contrast, wars of choice have viable alternative options and thus 'increase the pressure on the government of the day to demonstrate that the overall or net results of employing force will be positive, that is, that the benefits outweigh the costs'.[17] While the rhetoric of the US campaign in Afghanistan was one of 'no viable alternative', in fact the Taliban tried diplomacy in the weeks after September 11, offering to extradite bin Laden, but their offer was rejected. Indeed, details later emerged of a covert, deep relationship between the United States and the Taliban, dating back to the mid-1990s, chiefly in relation to a possible oil and gas pipeline which would run from the landlocked central Asian republics through Afghanistan and ultimately out to Pakistan.[18] By the summer of 2001 discussions about the pipeline had stalled, following a breakdown of trust on both sides and the suspicion that America was supporting the anti-Taliban opposition.[19] There were allegations that the Americans, anxious to put in place a more stable and US-friendly government to aid their oil interests, were exploring military options for regime change ('either you accept our offer of a carpet of gold or we bury you under a carpet of bombs') and indeed, according to one account, anticipation of their planned assault on Afghanistan that summer may even have triggered al-Qaeda's attacks on 9/11.[20]

Behind the 'necessity' of the war of revenge in Afghanistan, therefore, lurked many causes and motivations, rather like the ones that lay behind the Trojan War. In that mythical case, the *casus belli* was supposedly to avenge Menelaus for the abduction of Helen, but, as archaeologists have recently confirmed, there were also geopolitical motivations behind the conflict. Trade and access to the Dardanelles, the rival empires of the Hittites and the Mycenaeans, geopolitical tensions in the region: these were the underlying reasons behind the war. Homer translates these dimly remembered historical details into his epic verse, converting mercenary prose into the heroic poetry of individual glory. Setting out the reasons why he has gone to war, Achilles declares that he is not interested in taking vengeance on the Trojans since they have never 'driven off my cattle, or my horses / nor even in Phthia, where the rich earth breeds warriors, / have they destroyed my harvest' (I: 154–6) and it was not his wife that they stole. As far as he is concerned, the war is not a necessary, unavoidable decision. Instead, it is a voluntary choice which he has made initially out of loyalty to Agamemnon and later to win glory for himself, a goal which he thinks has now proved illusory:

> it seems there is no thanks
> for doing battle against enemy men without respite, forever;
> the fate is the same if a man hangs back, and if he battles greatly,
> in equal honour are both coward and warrior;
> and they die alike, both the man who has done nothing and he
> who has accomplished many things.[21]

The voluntary nature of the choice means that it can also be interrogated and challenged. Achilles transforms the whole conflict, through his existential questioning, into a vision of futility in a radical way. The retribution visited on Afghanistan was one of choice, not one of necessity – but for most people around the world, it was impossible, after the 9/11 attacks, to imagine an alternative.[22] Carpet bombing Afghanistan to the point where, as Donald Rumsfeld quipped, the military were running out of targets seemed to be an inevitable necessity. And the number of Achilles-type dissenters was limited to a few independent minds dismissed as 'Liberals'.

Meanwhile, even as the bombs were dropping on Afghanistan in October 2001 and later as the Northern Alliance, along with American air support and special forces ground troops, were taking Kabul, the campaign to widen the 'War on Terror' to include Iraq was beginning. Indeed, according to Richard A. Clarke, the Bush administration viewed Afghanistan as simply a 'detour along the road to Iraq'.[23] In Bush's State of the Union speech in January 2002, he indicated that 'what we have found in Afghanistan confirms that, far from ending there, our war against terror is only beginning'. Terrorists, he said, were now 'spread throughout the world like ticking time bombs, set to go off without warning'.[24] It was in this speech that he named Iraq, along with Iran and North Korea and 'their terrorist allies', as part of an 'axis of evil'. Key spokesmen in President Bush's administration started to claim or insinuate connections between Saddam Hussein and Osama bin Laden. Dick Cheney, for example, declared in a television interview in late 2001 that it was 'pretty well confirmed' that one of the chief 9/11 hijackers had met with a senior intelligence officer from Iraq.[25] Iraqi operatives were alleged to be funding al-Qaeda, while the hijacked planes and the supposed weapons of mass destruction that Saddam Hussein was stockpiling were frequently mentioned in the same breath. George Bush's speech at the United Nations General Assembly in September 2002 singled out Iraq as the world's most dangerous state in its supposed continuing support for international terrorism.[26] The international community was urged to 'meet [its] responsibilities' and 'overcome this danger' by pressing Iraq to disclose and destroy its [non-existent] weapons of mass destruction and to 'end all [non-existent] support for terrorism'. For Iraq had necessitated the war against it by its own action, Bush assured the assembly. In a classic trope from revenge tragedy, the protagonist had apparently set in motion the inevitable mechanism of the retribution about to be reaped upon itself. 'By breaking every pledge, by his deceptions and by his cruelties, Saddam Hussein has made the case against himself', Bush stated.

When Hamlet is first informed by the ghost of his father about how his father was 'dispatched, cut off even in the blossoms of my sin' and he is enjoined to 'revenge his foul and most unnatural murder', he becomes passionately committed to the plan.[27] The ghost stirs him up to so much anger and disgust at his uncle ('that incestuous, that adulterate beast / With witchcraft of his wit, with treacherous gifts') that he is prepared to 'wipe away' all other thoughts, 'saws of books', distractions and compunctions and focus exclusively on the task of vengeance.[28] Memory is an essential, obsessive aspect of the revenge plot and Hamlet duly sponges everything else from his mind except the ghost's injunction to 'remember me'. His companions are sworn into an alliance of secrecy. But as time passes, he appears to doubt the ghost and to consider the need to double-check the necessity of revenge. He engages in some performative madness, for reasons that remain opaque, and he seizes on the opportunity some wandering players present to stage a play that will test the reactions of his uncle. The tragedy explores the tension between the freedom of individual choice – could Hamlet act differently? – and the compulsion of generic expectation. This is a revenge tragedy with origins in a now-lost early sixteenth-century play known as the *Ur-Hamlet* and in Thomas Kyd's *Spanish Tragedy*, and it is dramatically inevitable, given this generic history and its conventional assumptions, that the prince will ultimately avenge his father and kill Claudius. It is this tension – between the traditional expectations of revenge tragedy and Shakespeare's strange version – which lies behind Hamlet's famous cry: 'The time is out of joint. O cursed spite / That ever I was born to set it right!'.[29]

In the countdown to the invasion of Iraq, the principal actors gave out the illusion that there were other options, that the narrative could go down other routes. The UN passed one more resolution in November 2002, declaring that Saddam Hussein was in breach of previous resolutions and sending inspectors once more into Iraq looking for weapons of mass destruction. In September 2002 Tony Blair claimed that Saddam's 'WMD programme is active, detailed and growing' and presented an intelligence dossier (now known as the 'dodgy dossier') in which it was stated that Saddam had 'existing and active military plans for the use of chemical and biological weapons, which could be activated within 45 minutes'.[30] Colin Powell produced supposed visual evidence of Saddam's weapons programme in a presentation to the UN Security Council in February 2003 and argued that there were terrorist links between Iraq and al-Qaeda, with Iraqi cells visiting Osama bin Laden in Afghanistan. On the eve of the launch of the attack, the British parliament held a vote on whether or not to go to war. The focus, especially of Tony Blair, was to give the impression of presenting a coherent case for war on which politicians could form a judgement and actively take a decision.

In all this careful preparation, then, Blair and Colin Powell gave the impression of there still being a place for reasoned argument and choice, of other narratives being possible. They acted as if they needed to *persuade* people to make the right decision, as if things could go differently. But, in fact, it is now clear that the decision had already been made to wage war on Iraq. When Tony Blair and George Bush met at Bush's ranch in Crawford, Texas, in April 2002, and subsequently in a letter sent to Bush in July, it is now known that Blair pledged his support for the military operation 'whatever' the circumstances, long before the UN resolution was drafted or the weapons inspectors had gone back into the country and found nothing.[31] It was to strengthen the US case for the war that Tony Blair's administration 'sexed up' the intelligence dossier in September 2002, greatly exaggerating the inconclusive intelligence reports about Saddam's missile programme and thus misleading parliament and the wider public. Any dissent in the rush to war was either ignored or crushed. The massive protest march around the world on 15 February 2003, for example, in which 2 million people participated in London alone, made no impact upon the political decisions. The US and UK coalition decided not to go for a second UN resolution, even though members of the security council had only agreed to the first one the previous autumn on the understanding that it did not make 'automatic' the recourse to war if it was not obeyed. Urged on by the military who warned that the weather conditions for an effective military strike were running out, the massive aerial bombardment and land invasion, known as 'shock and awe', began on 20 March 2003. The overwhelming sense was that there was no choice but to inflict massive punishment on the man who had survived the military campaign of Bush I (George W.'s father) humiliatingly twelve years earlier. The time for debate and delay was over. Like the final act of *Hamlet*, the revenge plot was now moving swiftly and inexorably.

Symmetry of revenge

Traditionally in revenge tragedy, the avenger feels that he or she occupies the moral high ground. In the absence of a higher objective justice – whether that be a court of law or the governing establishment – the protagonist decides that he or she must take matters into his or her own hands. The avenger becomes judge, jury and executioner. Indeed, trial by jury does not even exist as a concept at the beginning of Aeschylus's *Oresteia*. Clytemnestra has been nurturing anger for ten years at her daughter's murder by her husband, Agamemnon, without any access to public justice, while the Trojan War has rumbled on. So, after she has killed him on his return home, in three blows accompanied with a prayer like another sacrifice to echo that of her daughter, she is defiant in her declaration that her retaliation was rightful. Justice (or δίκη: *dike* in the original Greek) guided her hand that struck the blow; it was to Justice, along with Ruin (Ἄτης) and Fury (Ἐρινύς), that she sacrificed Agamemnon.[32]

But Clytemnestra's deed, murdering her husband, immediately provokes a reprisal. Just as there was no law court to try Agamemnon's sacrifice, so there is no court of law for Clytemnestra. The chorus sing that 'there is a law that bloodshed / dripping to the ground demands another's blood', as if earth and blood organically bring about justice, but in fact that process requires individual agents to implement it.[33] It falls to Agamemnon's son, Orestes, to avenge the deed, and it is at this point – the second play of the trilogy – that the ambiguity of δικη really becomes apparent. As Orestes says, in killing his mother to avenge his father, 'War will meet war, and justice meet justice!' (Ἄρης Ἄρει ξυμβαλει, Δίκᾳ Δίκα).[34] His sense of justice will clash with his mother's sense. Two sets of values are in ethical collision with one another: Is it more just to condemn child murder or the killing of a husband? Orestes' sister, Electra, appears not to have grasped the complexity of the issue when she responds simply with the plea to the gods to sanction their prayers justly (κραίνετ᾽ ἐνδίκως). But Orestes is slightly more clear-sighted that revenge culture interrogates what is justice anyway. Certainly, he claims after the deed that he acted with justice, as Clytemnestra did. He displays the dead body of his mother and her lover, just as she displayed the bodies of Agamemnon and his enslaved war booty Cassandra. And he produces the net that trapped his father to remind viewers of the 'impious work' of his mother and to act as a witness ('μάρτυς') that he killed his mother with just cause. But even as he claims justice for himself, the symmetrical nature of these acts of display, deliberately recalling Clytemnestra's gestures in the previous play, calls into question the unique superiority of his moral and legal position and melds moral certainty into relativism. As John Kerrigan noted about revenge tragedy, 'the symmetry of revenge is inseparable from a dramatic irony which complicates the moral situation of the revenger'.[35]

The Iraq invasion, code-named Operation Iraqi Freedom, began with a strong sense of moral purpose and an unfortunately phrased crusading vision. Within three weeks, the coalition forces were entering Baghdad and scenes of joyful citizens pulling down the statue of Saddam Hussein were beamed around the world. The contrast between the sides appeared to be stark. On the one side was a dictator who tortured and oppressed his people. On the other side was a massive military coalition bringing freedom and hope. 'We have fought for the cause of liberty and for the peace of the world', announced President Bush without any sense of irony when he gave a speech in front of a banner with the words 'Mission Accomplished' behind him on 1 May. The principles appeared to be clear. And in line with the retributive war of revenge for 9/11, which was how Bush and others portrayed the 'Battle of Iraq', the symmetry appeared to be carefully planned and ordered, in a way that made Iraq and the United States sharply distinct.[36] Bush declared that 'in these 19 months [since 9/11] that changed the world, our actions have been focused, and deliberate, and proportionate to the offence'.

But already by the end of May 2003, the BBC were reporting doubts about the 'dodgy dossier' and its claim that Saddam could launch weapons of mass destruction with only 45 minutes warning. The original intelligence reports, on which the dossier was based, had not been as categorical in their claims but the reports had been 'sexed up' to make the case for war stronger. In July, David Kelly, the British scientist responsible for leaking the facts about the insubstantial evidence for WMD, apparently took his own life, under the pressure that the Blair government was piling upon him. It was a private tragedy and a national scandal, the first indication that the moral argument for the conflict was murky and the product of coercion. If Saddam's 'offence' was non-compliance with the UN resolution to disarm, but the nature of the armament was being exaggerated, how could any action be 'proportionate'? And how could the coalition governments of Bush and Blair be trusted?

The *cause* of the war was compromised and morally open to attack. And as 2003 moved into 2004, the *conduct* of the conflict undermined the clear distinction between ally and enemy still further. 'Bullying's the fucking job. That's what you have a fucking army for', says one character in Gregory Burke's award-winning tragicomic play *Black Watch*.[37] Dramatizing the controversial deployment of the Scottish regiment from October 2004 in the so-called 'Triangle of Death' south of Baghdad to replace US troops transferred north to Fallujah, Burke's play mixed cynical humour and male banter with lyrical balletic movement, raw emotion and angry questions about the purpose of the whole conflict.[38] Underneath the hilarious comedy lies a seething violence. One soldier boasts about blowing away a donkey and cart. Another, suffering from PTSD, threatens to break the arm of a writer who has come to interview them. It's all partly a product of the massive disparity in firepower between the

occupying army and the local insurgents which provokes a mixture
of terror and hubris. Here are two of the Scottish soldiers as they
watch a huge aerial bombardment rain down on a town on the
horizon:

> **Cammy** This is nay fucking fighting. This is just plain
> old-fashioned bullying like.
> **Rossco** It's good fun, though.
> **Cammy** D'you think?
> **Rossco** Aye.
> *Beat.*
> It's good to be the bully.

Meanwhile, up in Fallujah and other towns in Iraq, reports of the
killing and abuse of civilians by the occupying US army began to
circulate. Fallujah in 2003 and 2004, Haditha in 2005, Al-Ishaqi in
2006: these were some of the infamous place names and dates of
'massacres' in a catalogue of mistreatment and killing of civilians
by the occupying army.

Haditha, for example, which was the subject of an initial cover-up,
subsequent investigation and court case, has been preserved in the
memory by film-maker Nick Broomfield, whose tragic film *Battle
for Haditha* blends fact and fiction, using professional actors, former
Marines and Iraqi refugees to portray semi-fictionalized characters.[39]
After an IED kills a Marine and injures two others, their fellow
Marines led by Corporal Ramirez (representing the original Frank
Wuterich) execute five Iraqi civilians, who had stopped in their car
by the roadside, in cold blood. They then 'clear' four nearby houses
supposedly in the search for the insurgents, shooting nearly all the
inhabitants (unarmed family members of all ages) without stopping
to investigate them. In the space of a few hours, twenty-four Iraqi
civilians have been brutally killed.[40] The film is a study of revenge,
a portrayal of soldiers hardened and haunted by war who watch
DVDs of previous IED attacks on their fellow men at the film's
beginning and say 'if they're going to do this stuff to us, we should
go and kill more of them' and who shoot old Iraqi grannies at close
range while yelling 'you fucking killed my buddy'. Meanwhile, the
Jihadi fighters, who detonated the IED, film the massacre from a
nearby minaret for use in further recruitment. 'The world will see
today how the Americans behave', the Sheik masterminding them

says. 'Look at your children. Look at your families. We shall get our revenge on the Americans. Enough orphans. We want our revenge.' All sides are driven by passions and pressures larger than any one individual's will, with some of the Marines suffering from PTSD and a culture that clearly values American lives more than Iraqi ones and with the local Jihadi fighters manipulated by al-Qaeda leaders.[41] Indeed, *Battle for Haditha* discloses structural vengeance beneath the murky fog of war, blaming less the individual soldiers and more the Iraq War as a 'giant butt hole' (as one Marine puts it).

The coalition brutality, which far exceeded the ferocity of the opposition in places like Haditha, gave rise to the impression of American lawlessness and hypocrisy, particularly when there was no accountability afterwards.[42] Meanwhile revelations were emerging about the American abuse of prisoners. Abu Ghraib had been the prison used by Saddam Hussein for his regime's practice of extensive torture and executions. Consequently, the revelation that the US military were also carrying out physical, sexual and psychological torture in that same prison was lent an extra irony, which forced the uncomfortable parallels between enemies and allies still further. The war was being waged partly on the pretext of liberating Iraq from its torturing, cruel dictator, but now it appeared that the Americans were mirroring those same practices in the very same building. Initially there were only unsubstantiated reports. But then, amazingly, pictures emerged, snapped as trophies by the soldiers and guards themselves. Just as a revenge hero exults over the spectacle of his tortured victim (think Vindice in a 'throng of happy apprehensions' in *The Revenger's Tragedy* over the sight of the Duke kissing the poisoned skull of a woman he killed years before), so these soldiers were happy to pose for the camera beside a pyramid of naked, degraded Iraqi prisoners.[43]

The Pentagon strove to suppress reports of the atrocities or to pass them off as the regrettable responses of a few stressed individuals. Lynndie England, the private soldier who appeared in several of the pictures posing beside naked prisoners and dragging one on the floor by a dog leash, became the most prominent scapegoat, vilified for her brutality and ignorance which were said to be the consequence of her childhood in a trailer park, abused by her own father, as well as her learning difficulties. But then the series of documents sent between members of the Bush administration and their legal advisers, ultimately to be known as the 'Torture Papers', were brought to light by the investigative work of *The Washington Post, Newsweek* and the American Civil Liberties Union, and subsequently released and acknowledged by the government. These showed that the administration had sought and found legal justification for 'enhanced interrogation techniques' amounting to torture and had authorized this policy at the highest level. This was a systematic effort 'to argue away the rules against torture' and to 'misuse' the skills of a lawyer 'in the cause of evil'.[44] The rights and reciprocity of the Geneva Convention were rescinded from the 'unlawful combatants' in America's charge, and thus, as the months went by and the legal loopholes and 'strained analysis' were increasingly exploited, the government slid more and more into a 'moral morass'.[45] Donald Rumsfeld actually admitted in an interview at the time that 'we have to work sort of the dark side', and that, in effect, the US interrogators were joining the terrorists in their darkness since 'that's the world these folks operate in'.[46] The legal wrangling legitimized interrogation methods such as the use of stress positions, isolation, sensory deprivation, sleep deprivation, forced nudity, forced grooming and the exploitation of phobias. Waterboarding, for example, seems to have become commonplace.[47] But working the 'dark side' had harmful consequences on the Americans as well as their victims. As Colin Powell put it in a memo on 26 January 2002, following the campaign in Afghanistan but before the invasion of Iraq, to announce that the Geneva Convention does not apply in the War on Terror would 'undermine the protections of the law of war for [US] troops' and carry 'a high cost in terms of negative international reaction'.[48] International law was being systematically undermined which ultimately had long-term implications for how Americans would be perceived and treated around the world. According to legal journalist Anthony Lewis, 'torture does terrible damage not only to the victim but to the torturer'.[49]

In addition to establishing a legal 'flexibility' (Colin Powell's word) regarding the use of torture, the Bush administration and their legal advisers also dealt with the legality of the indefinite detention of prisoners at the US base at Guantanamo.[50] The memoranda collected in *The Torture Papers* reveal that Guantanamo fell into a 'legal black hole'. According to the Bush White House's careful legal parsing, it was not covered by the Geneva Convention because the normal 'laws of armed conflict' did not apply in the case of al-Qaeda and the Taliban: they were not enemy combatants since Afghanistan was 'not a functioning state' and the Taliban merely a 'militia', al-Qaeda was a 'non-State actor'[51] and the United States was at war anyway with 'terrorism',[52] not with Afghanistan per se or, later, Iraq.[53] But the camp was not covered by the US courts either, since it was an offshore base and the prisoners were 'unlawful combatants' or 'aliens', not civilians. There was no 'habeas corpus' here, no state with jurisdiction over a prisoner's rights, no proper tribunal to which one could even bring one's appeal to be considered a rightful subject and therefore eligible for fair trial. The camp slipped outside the law, even while it was covered supposedly by US jurisdiction, and so remained beyond the scrutiny of international lawyers and journalists. The scandalous product of America's dark casuistry, Guantanamo was thus the paradigmatic example of Giorgio Agamben's paradoxical 'state of exception', which lies both outside and inside the law and which tests the boundaries and assumptions of what we think of as hard-won democratic principles and human rights.[54] Since 2001, the legal 'indeterminacy' of Guantanamo has spread across the wider reach of America's 'War on Terror', making it a 'laboratory for the perfection of CIA psychological torture' and facilitating the establishment of other secret interrogation centres and sites for 'rendition'.[55]

Law and lawlessness operate in tandem in a vengeful so-called state of exception.[56] The initial suspension of law leads to a perverted re-imposition of the law which itself is destructive of all principles of justice and order. 'In the very act by which state sovereignty suspends the law, or contorts the law to its own uses, it extends its own domain, its own necessity, and develops the means by which the justification of its own power takes place', Judith Butler has observed.[57] This invidious co-dependency of law and lawlessness is a central feature of revenge tragedy. The attempt to restore justice and what John Kerrigan calls 'equilibrium' compels the avenger to resort to means as murky, cruel and violent as the original perpetrator. This results ironically in even more disorder, violent turbulence and shocking *coups de theatre*. Hieronimo in Thomas Kyd's play *The Spanish Tragedy* (1587) concocts an elaborate plot, to be enacted within a play (taking method acting to violent extremes), in order to descend to the brutal level of his enemies. Here poetic or dramatic justice becomes conflated with – or corrupted by – the private justice of the vigilante. His audience watch the theatrical role-playing and suddenly discover that it is not 'fabulously counterfeit' but that art and life are horribly mingled and their sons (actors in the play) will not 'revive to please tomorrow's audience':

VICEROY
Why hast thou murdered my Balthazar?
CASTILE
Why hast thou butchered both my children thus?
HIERONIMO
O, good words!
As dear to me was my Horatio
As yours, or yours, or yours, my lord, to you.
My guiltless son was by Lorenzo slain,
And by Lorenzo and that Balthazar
Am I at last revenged thoroughly.[58]

A couple of decades on, revenge tragedy was at the height of its vogue and Vindice's brother admires his 'constant vengeance / The quaintness of thy malice' in *The Revenger's Tragedy*. As Vindice himself observes, he must replicate the iniquity of his foes for 'who would not lie when men are hanged for truth?'.[59] So elaborate and excessive is the spectacle of Vindice's vengeance that he becomes synonymous with the vice he initially set out to oppose. ''Tis time to die when we are ourselves our foes' is his famous conclusion (5.3.118). Even more ethically ambiguous, the duke Ferdinand and his brother the Cardinal in Webster's *The Duchess of Malfi* (1614) appear to uphold morals but are really the prey of many passions – lust, jealousy, cruelty – which they hide in duplicity and hypocrisy, charging the duchess, their sister, with lechery and subjecting her to psychological torture. After her eventual death, at the hands of the henchman Bosola but on the orders of Ferdinand and the Cardinal, Bosola hits back in criticism at them:

You have a pair of hearts are hollow graves,
Rotten, and rotting others; and your vengeance,
Like two chained bullets, still goes arm in arm. (4.2.309–11)

The supposed centres of authority and morality (church and government) turn out to be the chief architects of corruption, persecution and manipulation. Rotten and rotting others indeed.

And then, of course, there is *Hamlet* (1601), with its vision of corruption permeating both the kingdom ('something is rotten in the state of Denmark') and individuals ('how long will a man lie in the earth ere he rot?').[60] While Hamlet is tasked by the ghost of his father to avenge his assassination and kill Claudius, his reparative plot results in many more dead bodies by the end than after the initial murder. He is absorbed and tainted by the archetypal revenge plot he finds himself in, implicitly accusing himself of being a 'Bloody, bawdy villain! / Remorseless, treacherous, lecherous, kindless villain!' for failing to kill Claudius and only 'unpack[ing his] heart with words'.[61] Earlier, after hearing the ghost's tale, he has noted down in his 'tables' that 'one may smile, and smile, and be a villain' (1.5.109). It is indicative here of the rottenness of both the state of Denmark and Hamlet's own mind that one cannot tell with certainty whether his various outbursts about 'villainy' refer to Claudius or to himself. Definitions and distinctions of value have begun to 'melt' within the paradoxical symmetries and moral disorder of revenge, until the world is no more than a 'foul and pestilent congregation of vapours' (2.2.293), an amoral, dismal 'revolution' (5.1.83) of dirt, dust and decay in which lives can be won or lost on a wager, signifying nothing.

In the remarkable *Guantanamo Diary*, Mohamedou Ould Slahi recorded in great detail his treatment in the US base at Guantanamo. Taken in for police questioning in his native Mauritania in November 2001, he was rendered initially to Jordan, where he was subjected to physical and psychological terrors and interrogated for eight months, and then transferred to the American Bagram air base in Afghanistan, where he continued to be badly treated. He was subsequently transported – shackled, blindfolded and with no food or water for more than 30 hours – to Guantanamo where he was to be detained without trial for the next fourteen years. For part of that time, he was subjected to the 'special interrogation plan' for which Donald Rumsfeld and the Bush administration had prepared the legal justification: months of sleep deprivation, hours of standing in stress position, psych ops involving sexual and religious degradation, suffocation and waterboarding with sea water. His legal claim to be tried in American courts under habeas corpus was granted in 2010 and then rescinded on appeal, where it stalled for six more years. The hand-written diary, sent out confidentially to his lawyers initially in 2005 as part of the preparation of his case, became a case in itself, the subject of legal wrangling. Repressed or 'protected' for seven years, it was finally released for publication in heavily redacted form. Nevertheless, even censored, the book, first published while Slahi was still in Guantanamo in 2015, allowed his side of the story to be known. It was 'my way of fighting the U.S. government's narrative'.[62] What emerges in Slahi's writing is a strange reversal of expectations. The moral Americans, supposedly upholding freedom and the rule of law, become mired in a malaise of their own making, while the suspected terrorists, detained for years without charge, much less a trial, appear patient, stoic and still apparently hopeful about American justice. Even after a couple of years in Guantanamo, Slahi just 'couldn't believe that a democratic government with more than two hundred years of experience in upholding the rule of law could really rig trials, with everyone on board'.[63] He does not set out to portray the American interrogators and guards badly but only to record their incompetence, fear and ignorance, as they themselves enact it before him. And in contrast, he comes to articulate an enlightened vision, on the side of the good, even quoting the American founding fathers against them:

> I trusted the American justice system too much, and shared that trust with the detainees from European countries. We all had an idea about how the democratic system works ... With every day going by, the optimists lost ground. The interrogation methods worsened considerably as time went by ... those responsible for GTMO broke all the principles upon which the US was built and compromised every great principle such as Ben Franklin's 'They that give up essential liberty to obtain a little temporary safety deserve neither liberty nor safety'.[64]

Slahi was himself granted liberty in October 2016, and returned to Mauritania, with no charges ever brought against him. He claims to feel only forgiveness for his captors and guards. John Kerrigan noted of traditional revenge tragedy that 'when B, injured by A, does to A what A did to him, he makes himself resemble the opponent he has blamed, while he transforms his enemy into the kind of victim he once was'.[65] At Guantanamo, the Americans achieved just this moral reversal, rendering themselves terrorists degraded by their own punitive regime and allowing the prisoners to become victims or even enlightened, brave victors. Even the text of *Guantanamo Diary* which has been re-published in a new edition, now with its redactions visible, makes apparent the vindictive silencing of the prisoner. The shaded, originally censored words become silent marks of the corruption of American justice.

Endless wars

When President Bush gave his State of the Union speech in early 2002, after what was considered to be the successful campaign in Afghanistan, he was careful not to draw a conclusion upon the revenge for 9/11. This was, to coin Churchill's phrase, not the end nor even the beginning of the end, but merely the end of the beginning:

> We'll be deliberate, yet time is not on our side. I will not wait on events, while dangers gather. I will not stand by, as peril draws closer and closer. The United States of America will not permit the world's most dangerous regimes to threaten us with the world's most destructive weapons. Our war on terror is well begun, but it is only begun. This campaign may not be finished on our watch – yet it must be and it will be waged on our watch. We can't stop short. If we stop now – leaving terror camps intact and terror states unchecked – our sense of security would be false and temporary. History has called America and our allies to action, and it is both our responsibility and our privilege to fight freedom's fight.[66]

Bush was, of course, preparing the ground for the war in Iraq. He needed to fuel the sense of fear and imminent threat, in order to justify widening the theatre of conflict. But in avoiding calling an end to the War on Terror, he was conforming to the traditional contradictory structure of revenge. For while revenge tragedies operate apparently teleologically, with the avenger in control and shaping events and destinies to their desired conclusion, in fact there is always a surfeit. Blood will have blood, in an endless cycle of retribution. The notion that order can be simply re-imposed – the fantasy of the revenge hero – turns out to be a delusion.[67]

At the end of the first play of Aeschylus's *Oresteia* trilogy, Clytemnestra's lover Aegisthus arrives on the scene. The chorus of old men are making things difficult for Clytemnestra, not accepting her justification of the murder of her husband and warning that there will be inevitable retribution for her deed: the one who acts must suffer (παθειν τὸν ἔρξαντα: *pathein ton erxanta*: 1564). Aegisthus threatens to kill them, hands on sword and with his loyal men close by. But Clytemnestra calls a halt. 'ἅλις' (*halis*) is the word she keeps using; '*enough*' of killing, this means. We have had enough misery. Now is the time to start ruling and setting the house on the right (*kalos*) path (1673). But Clytemnestra is deluding herself. There can be no '*halis*' or '*kalos*' in revenge tragedy, no boundary to the surfeit of killing. Instead the *Oresteia* dramatizes the endlessness of retributive justice as one play in the trilogy follows the next.

Once you start down the path of revenge, how do you know when there is 'enough' retribution, when the killing should end? What are the natural limits of vengeance? 'Revenge should have no bounds', observes Hamlet's uncle Claudius towards the end of the play; retributive tragedy naturally runs to surfeit and limitlessness.[68] The seventeen-year campaign in Afghanistan has ebbed and flowed in violence and governance, from the fall of Kabul in 2002, to a growing Taliban insurgency especially around 2007–9, to a surge in Western troop numbers, the crushing of opposition and the killing of Osama bin Laden in May 2011 and then the withdrawal of British and American troops in 2014, supposedly handing over responsibility to the Afghan government for their own security. With around 13,000 foreign troops remaining in support, the Afghan government, as I write this, only controls 30 per cent of the country with the Taliban either in control or actively engaged in the remaining 70 per cent. They are particularly strong, as they have always been, in the southern Helmand province, where more than 450 British troops died trying to keep them from power. After more than 10,000 civilian casualties in 2017 alone and with even the capital Kabul coming under frequent attack, the Afghan president called for a ceasefire at the end of February 2018 and invited the Taliban to engage in peace talks. History seems to have come full circle after seventeen years of conflict and the huge, incalculable loss of life and livelihood.

Afghanistan, it seems, has become synonymous with futility, the endlessness of the conflict there a product of the unrealistic desire to impose order and the corrupting malaise of retributive violence. Lives are sacrificed and battles waged to gain territory that is subsequently relinquished just a year or so later. *Restrepo*, the award-winning documentary film made by photographer Tim Hetherington, captures just this stalemate and pointlessness.[69] Hetherington was embedded with a US army platoon on their fifteen-month deployment in the Korengal Valley, eastern Afghanistan, for the period of 2007–8. Their mission was to clear the area of the insurgency and to gain the trust of the local population. Early into the deployment, two of the soldiers are killed, one of whom is named Juan Restrepo. The outpost which they strive to construct and sustain through the year is named after him. The film charts the year's progress – or lack of it – without comment, not directly declaring its futility. We merely witness the difficulty the soldiers experience communicating with the locals and the lack of mutual understanding, as well as the loss of an army sergeant's life under enemy fire. But the dedication of the men to the mission and the loyalty they show to each other is made even more ironically poignant with the film's statement in the coda: 'In April 2010, the United States Army withdrew from the Korengal Valley. Nearly 50 American soldiers died fighting there.' The valley reverted back to Taliban control. American lives – and an uncounted number of Afghan lives presumably – were lost for no purpose and no gain.

The effect is the reverse of the equation that Hamlet proposes when considering the invading army of Fortinbras. While the Danish court is trapped in the claustrophobic plot of intrigue, surveillance and suspicion which form the obsessions of the play, the country is being threatened by the encroaching army led by Fortinbras who is determined to avenge his father's defeat at the hands of Hamlet's father and to win back his land. 'We go to gain a little patch of ground / That hath in it no profit but the name', the army captain tells Hamlet.[70] Hamlet marvels that men will risk their lives in such numbers 'even for an eggshell'. In a tortuous bit of syntax, indicating the difficulty of thought, he appears to argue that it is more noble to fight for a trivial purpose and minimal gain than to avoid action even when the cause is great:

> Rightly to be great
> Is not to stir without great argument,
> But greatly to find quarrel in a straw
> When honour's at the stake. How stand I then,
> That have a father kill'd, a mother stain'd,

Excitements of my reason and my blood,
And let all sleep while, to my shame, I see
The imminent death of twenty thousand men
That, for a fantasy and trick of fame,
Go to their graves like beds, fight for a plot
Whereon the numbers cannot try the cause,
Which is not tomb enough and continent
To hide the slain?[71]

The implication of Hamlet's perverse equation is that the more trivial and 'straw'-like the cause, the more noble the action. Military action, when 'honour is at stake', ennobles and gives meaning to the meaningless plot of land gained or lost. But the converse is surely lurking behind this reasoning, indicated, as I said, by the tortuousness of the syntax, that the futility of the military exercise, which is evidenced by the waste of lives and money, out of proportion with tactical gain made, undermines any notion of nobility, honour or significance.

Iraq seemed to be following a more successful narrative arc than the one in Afghanistan. The mission was 'accomplished' in 2003, and after the insurgency from 2003 to 2008, the 'surge' of American troops in 2007 appeared to be putting the country back in order or making it *kalos*, as in Aeschylus. Troops were withdrawn in 2011, after an eight-year occupation. But then the country broke down into different militias – Shia, Sunni, the Mahdi army – possibly when the American money which had been used to bribe Sunni groups as part of the 'surge' campaign dried up and the situation descended into civil war, with old scores settled and a political and moral vacuum. It was in this anarchic context that Abu Bakr Al-Baghdadi and his organization which became known as ISIS emerged, with a series of atrocities in violent retaliation supposedly for the death of Osama bin Laden. Large regions of the country fell to ISIS in early 2014: Fallujah, Mosul, Tikrit – names etched on the popular consciousness because of the battles there a decade earlier. And the turmoil in neighbouring Syria exacerbated the violence with Islamic State fighters crossing the virtually non-existent border between the two countries. The huge refugee crisis which had begun with the American invasion of 2003 (2 million people fled abroad at that time and 1.7 million were internally displaced) became even worse. Iraqi refugees in Syria had to flee again once the civil war there took off.

So, the millions of lives devastated by the war were sacrificed for nothing. The revenge war – true to the ancient dramatic tradition – brought only turmoil and further killing and a failed state.

There is only one thing worse than losing a life or a limb in a war – and that is losing a life or a limb in a pointless war. According to Jonathan Shay, the psychiatrist and author who works with severely traumatized combat veterans, the worst wound a soldier can suffer is the psychological or what he terms 'moral' injury which arises from the sense of betrayal or abandonment. 'Veterans can usually recover from horror, fear, and grief once they return to civilian life, so long as "what's right" has not also been violated', he states.[72] 'What's right' – or θεμις (*themis*) in Greek – can be something relatively simple like the strategic orders of the commander or the fair treatment of his men. *Themis* can also come to represent a whole moral framework and a set of beliefs and assumptions. Risking one's life on the battlefield or taking revenge on one's enemies is *themis* if the cause is just and – crucially – the end purpose is achieved. But what if it all turns out to be for nothing? Victory, which might mean ridding Afghanistan of the Taliban, would make the notion of 'setting [the world] right', to coin Hamlet's phrase, acceptable. But defeat, which relinquishing hard-fought territory back to the Taliban might seem to constitute, would throw the whole moral order and psychic stability into question. As Shay notes, 'the unanchored dead', restless from this moral uncertainty, endlessly recur following the pointless war, troubling the veterans' dreams.

Almost immediately after Orestes has proclaimed the justice of the murder of his mother in the *Oresteia*, he qualifies what he describes as his 'victory' by calling it an 'unenviable pollution' (ἄζηλα ... μιάσματα: *azela miasmata*: 1017). Yet again, the vengeful blow is not the 'be all and the end all', but rather it triggers a continuing series of repercussions. Orestes feels his wits whirling away like a chariot and horses and then the Furies arrive to drive him mad, the monsters with the reach of swarming snakes and the nose of bloodhounds. They are set to pursue him across the earth to the end of time if necessary. 'When will things be finished?', the chorus wonder. When will the force of anger have burnt itself out? Only Orestes can see the Furies at the end of the second play of the *Oresteia* trilogy, rather as the ghost of Hamlet's father is seen by Hamlet alone and not by Gertrude (3.4.100–41). The ancient Greeks believed in the externalization of pollution and guilt; violently spilt blood would literally call up the hounding, punishing Furies. But Aeschylus's Furies become psychologized in modern adaptations of the play, a form of internal torment rather than external harassment. So Lavinia (the Electra character) at the end of Eugene O'Neill's version of the trilogy (*Mourning Becomes Electra*), set immediately after the turbulent period of the American Civil War, shuts herself up in the family mansion to abandon herself to her past history and inner agony: 'I've got to punish myself! ... I'll live alone with the dead, and keep their secrets, and let them hound me, until the curse is paid out.'[73] And in Robert Icke's *Oresteia*, Orestes is left alone on the stage at the end, not released by the 'innocent' verdict of the trial and doubting what is 'real' and what is not. The play appears to end as it began, with Orestes caught in a psychological impasse of his own making:

> But I still killed her.
> Where does it end?
> ,
> Perhaps I always *feel* guilty
> ,
> What do I do?
> What do I do?
> What do I do?
> What do I do?[74]

America is still replaying the loop of 9/11, caught again and again in the memory of that attack rather as the crowds held onto the metal fence at Ground Zero back in 2004. The notion that the trauma could be resolved by revenge and the imposition of 'order' and 'freedom' in Afghanistan and Iraq was flawed by the very logic of revenge itself, with the violations and replications and moral malaise it unleashed. That flaw was further ruptured by the failures of the campaigns and futility of the endeavour, an endless punitive war not on a specific enemy or a place but on the nebulous, hydra-like form of 'terror'. And futility brings further trauma, a circular and self-destructive stalemate of doubt and torment. In this context, we are presented with one further choice, to follow the alternative direction that Rowan Williams presented his readers with back in 2002. We can choose to acknowledge the empty benefits of revenge and the futility of the war, finding a form of healing only in the sense of recognizing and communicating these failures. Or we can choose to tell stories of honour and heroes and sacrifice, trying to restore a by-now scarecrow form of *themis* and deluding ourselves that we are winning the War on Terror.

At the moment, the tragedy is located in the fact that the world is choosing the second option. There is, however, always the possibility that we may eventually choose the first option and, in that case, dare to lose the illusory hope that vengeance offers.

4

Shooting Conflict

The production of *Antigone*, directed by Polly Findlay, at London's National Theatre in the summer of 2012 placed the play in an oblique relationship with the ongoing war in Afghanistan. As the play opened with the sound of a helicopter whirring overhead, the ensemble appeared to be anxiously masterminding a battle in an underground war room, checking screen monitors, collecting and delivering paper messages issuing from fax machines, criss-crossing the stage with ever-increasing urgency. Then briefly the actors all gathered around one desk and watched a closed-circuit television in a rare moment of stillness (Figure 1). On the day I saw the play, the *tableau vivant* produced a gasp of recognition from the audience. It was a visual echo of the well-known photograph by White House photographer Pete Souza of Barack Obama, Hillary Clinton and the national security team in the situation room watching the capture and killing of Osama bin Laden (Figure 2).

The reference to Osama bin Laden illuminated something new in Sophocles' play, and vice versa. The stage business, of course, was designed to indicate the war between Eteocles and Polyneices, the action immediately before the play opens. By suggesting a contemporary setting in the 'War on Terror', the director was nudging the audience towards seeing Polyneices and his allies as 'insurgents' or 'terrorists' and Eteocles – and, later, Creon – as 'our' leader, desperately trying to prosecute a complex, ambiguous war. So far, so not unusual. What was innovative was the issue of image-making itself which the tableau raised by its allusion to the situation room picture and the self-conscious connection between theatre and photography.

FIGURE 1 Antigone. *Directed by Polly Findlay. National Theatre, June 2012. © Johan Persson/ArenaPAL.*

FIGURE 2 *The White House Situation Room. May 2011. © Pete Souza/ Reuters.*

Greek tragedy, and *Antigone* in particular, is very concerned with what can be seen and what cannot. Two of the main concerns in *Antigone* are the questions of how one treats one's enemies and what is the proper way to dispose of the dead. Eteocles, the brother who died defending the state, is to be buried with full honours by the state; he is to be viewed and celebrated by everyone. His dead brother Polyneices, the traitor or terrorist, is to be left to rot outside the city; nobody can even witness him. When Antigone transgresses Creon's law and attempts to bury Polyneices, she is walled up alive beyond the city's gaze and purview of justice.

The Pete Souza photograph, conjured up in Findlay's production of *Antigone*, is interesting because it focuses on the witnesses of the action on the television, rather than on the CCTV footage to which they were supposedly attending. Indeed, there has subsequently been speculation on what exact moment of the special operation the national security team was watching when the photograph was taken. What was it that made Hillary Clinton raise her hand to her mouth?[1] Does it indicate that she could scarcely bear to look at the screen, that the hand covering her mouth could as easily have been covering her eyes? The central subject of the event – Osama bin Laden himself – is missing from the photograph; the television is turned away from the image's spectator. The occlusion of bin Laden continued with the decision to dispose of his body at sea. There was, therefore, no official photograph of the killing of Osama bin Laden. There was no verified image of his dead body. Through a fleeting reference to a hidden image, Polly Findlay's production of Antigone made strikingly visible the invisibility of one of the great 'enemies' of our time.

Photographs of the wars in Afghanistan and Iraq, taken by professional photojournalists, have been almost exclusively of Western soldiers. Unlike in previous conflicts, and most strikingly in contrast to Vietnam, press coverage of the wars has been strictly controlled. Western journalists must be 'embedded' with allied troops for their own security and they inevitably therefore shoot from the perspective of the American or British military. It is true that as professionals, aware of these constraints, they often think of ways of indicating, and thereby paradoxically eluding, the 'frame' of embeddedness.[2] Tim Hetherington's and Peter van Agtmael's award-winning photographs from Afghanistan, for example, taken when they were embedded with the US military, seek to critique subtly the partiality of their viewpoint from within. Hetherington's images, many of which show literally and punningly the American soldiers *in bed* asleep, combine a surprising intimacy in the war zone with a sense of the vulnerability and questionable purpose behind the Western campaign.[3] This is, as one commentator put it, 'the other side of Afghanistan'.[4] Meanwhile, Peter van Agtmael shot soldiers at work in Iraq and Afghanistan, either tenderly caring for their wounded comrades or indifferently standing by as enemy combatants are taken prisoner or their houses are violently searched, reflecting the contradictions of war.[5]

Despite these sophisticated ironies from professionals, however, it is fair to say that our visual sense of the perspective of our 'enemies' has been limited. We have seen very little of the enemy casualties and even less of how daily life has been devastated by the seventeen-year conflict. This lacuna in our visual understanding is matched by the lack of factual information about the numbers of the dead and injured in Iraq and Afghanistan, the detailed statistics on the consequences of war. There was no body count performed for the Iraqi and Afghan victims of the two wars – a decision announced by Donald Rumsfeld on CBS news in March 2002 with the words 'I don't do body counts' and echoed by his chief general in Afghanistan, General Tommy Franks, a few days later. The policy, by the US Defence Department, of not counting the enemy combatant and civilian casualties has been interpreted by many as indicative of a form of blindness to the human cost of US military intervention, a troubling indifference which has been complicated by the revelation from WikiLeaks that allegedly the Pentagon did in fact count the enemy dead, but deliberately withheld publication.

But the paradox is that the technology of war has made the enemy more visible to the military, and easier to target, than ever before. Drone pilots track the movements of their enemy, 12,000 miles away in Afghanistan or Pakistan, from their bunker outside Las Vegas. They conduct the conflict with the aid of predator drones and computer algorithms. This is a war of maximum visibility, a scopic conflict. In order to assist their hunt and to determine the identity, motivations and imminent plans of their prey, they must learn about his daily routine and habits and notice any changes or aberration. Drones thus lend war the illusion, at least, of intimacy. The surveillance is global but the technical knowledge of particular enemies, anywhere around the world, is local, precise and specific.

These paradoxical areas of visibility and invisibility in the prosecution of the War on Terror point to important questions about how we think of the people we are fighting, the so-called Other, and about how we think of ourselves. These polarities between 'us' and 'them' are intensified by the harsh caricature that spectacle can produce or by the ignorance that neglect encourages. But the division between allies and enemies can also be broken down by forms of intimacy and reciprocal understanding, which visual representation (in photographs or the theatre, for example) can facilitate. Questions about how we are to think of the Other or ourselves are encapsulated in the important task of recognition which lies at the heart of the business of tragedy as well as at the foundation of democratic society today. How do we view the ongoing conflict? Does the accumulation of visual data really lead to greater self-understanding and compassion for others? This hypervisual, never-ending military campaign gives rise to forms of collective recognition and misrecognition which are deeply tragic in nature and in their effects.

Recognition and acknowledgement

The act of recognition is central to current ethical and theological thinking, and it is similarly at the core of both tragic theory and the performance of tragic drama. Indeed, we might say that it is the act of recognition which brings together our experiences both in the theatre and in the world. Through these acts of recognition, we attempt to explain terrible decisions taken or suffering inflicted upon ourselves or others. We do this in narratives which seek to understand the knowability or unknowability of other selves. In this way we acknowledge our interdependence, bringing to our cognition something about our relationship to the world and the society in which we live. This act of attempted recognition might ultimately lead us to the Socratic paradoxical conclusion that 'we know that we know nothing', but even that is conventionally deemed to be valuable for the flourishing of a healthy civic community.

According to Aristotle, *anagnorisis* or 'recognition' is a crucial component of tragedy, along with reversal (*peripeteia*) and suffering (*pathos*). On the one hand, this term refers simply to 'discovery', usually through visual means. Aristotle elaborates upon his theory of recognition by pointing to the visual signs by Agamemnon's tomb in the *Oresteia* and their function as evidence that the exiled Orestes has returned.[6] The term also seems to mean 'identification', or in other words discerning and naming the familiar. By way of example, Aristotle cites the identifying scar by which the nurse recognizes Odysseus when she washes his feet as a model of *anagnorisis*.[7] There are, of course, other famous moments in Greek tragedy when characters fail to recognize other characters in this way. For instance, Electra is fooled by the disguised Orestes in Sophocles' play, so that she mourns her own brother's death while he looks on.

But beyond these literal visual acts of identification or misidentification in Aristotle's account of tragedy, there is also a more cognitive meaning to *anagnorisis*. The protagonist comes to understand something about his past action, which then recalibrates everything that he believes about himself, the world, the gods and the relationship that sustains them all. Oedipus believed he knew everything, had solved the Sphinx's riddle and was 'the best of men', but comes to recognize that he is 'accursed in my conception, and in my marriage, and in him I slew'.[8] Similarly, Creon, in *Antigone*, having spent the play trying to assert his sovereignty, realizes at the conclusion that he is a 'cipher, less than nothing'.[9] The chorus, witnessing and learning from what they see, come to a comparable recognition that no man should be considered blessed until he sees his last day, that – in other words – identity and fortune are fluid concepts definable only at the end of a life. And the audience, made self-conscious of the process of witnessing events by the chorus's continuous presence in the orchestra after their first entry, go through a similar cognitive process of understanding.[10] Aristotle declared that emotions were most likely to be stirred when things happen unexpectedly, making it clear that he believed *anagnorisis* happens for the audience as well as the protagonists on stage.[11] The theatre thus becomes a shared, ritualistic act of recognition at a particular moment in a particular space. 'The not-knowing of the characters becomes a disturbing reflection of our own not-knowing as observers', Rowan Williams has observed of the experience of watching tragic drama recently.[12] 'Speaking about and showing the risk of disaster and the cost of different sorts of loss, in a language that is not just individual but allows listening and the sharing of perception and emotion – this liturgical activity is a way of affirming our recognition of one another as participants in a continuing labour.'[13]

According to various philosophers and theologians like Rowan Williams, a sense of interdependence, based upon the act of recognition, should be foundational to the constitution of the citizen body. For some that recognition involves identifying and respecting what is termed the 'sovereign' independence of others, attending to their particularities, or understanding society as the 'reciprocal recognition among equals' and allotting power and rights accordingly.[14] For others, recognition involves acknowledging conversely the frailty of ourselves and others and our necessary dependence upon each other. Judith Butler develops the notion of what she calls our 'common human vulnerability', based upon a mutual recognition of 'what is precarious in another life or, rather, the precariousness of life itself'.[15] The process is not so much one of uncovering what is already known but of moving towards new states of mutual understanding through the self-conscious attention to the process itself. Consequently, some philosophers prefer terms such as 'acknowledgement' or 'witnessing', on the grounds that these words seem less categorizing and fixed in definition.[16]

But since the term 'recognition' actually carries this double sense of discovery of the unknown and identification of the already known, it can cover both the process of acknowledgement and the reinforcement of existing categories. Aristotle argued that tragedy provoked both pity and fear, which could be solidified into bonds of friendship or enemity. 'Recognition', he said, 'is a change from ignorance to knowledge, bringing characters into either a close bond, or enmity, with one another'.[17] While fear can be based upon a recognition of common human fallibility (a man 'like ourselves'), resulting therefore in a situation rather like Butler's recognition of our shared precariousness, it can also produce hostility, since friends or enemies are structurally closer than those who have no connection at all. Even if active fear and hostility are not intended or produced, certainly the act of recognition, granting sovereign agency to another, can actually reinforce and perpetuate structures of inequality, subordination and dominance, making the world 'intelligible' by 'stratifying it', as Patchen Markell has argued.[18]

These political possibilities and pitfalls of recognition are present in the viewing of photography as well. It is a commonplace nowadays to lament the plethora of visual images of misery around the world and our inability to respond to them with the appropriate degree of concern. Since the influential book on photography by Susan Sontag in the 1970s, we have been critical of the mediating effect of the camera and sceptical about the belief that a photograph will inevitably convey the truth and awaken compassion. According to this critical tradition, photography is exploitative, detached and voyeuristic; it 'cuts sympathy, distances the emotions'.[19] But in the last few years, there has been a backlash against this academic and popular orthodoxy and writers have been reaffirming in photography what Sontag called an 'ethics of seeing'.[20] Photographs confront their viewers with the need to focus upon the embodied repercussions of war and violent action, 'making suffering palpable so that people far removed cannot overlook or excuse it', as one writer has said about the work of photographer James Nachtwey.[21] To ignore shocking images of suffering is to be guilty of 'moral defectiveness'.[22] Without the empathy that looking at photographs gives us, 'the politics of human rights devolve into abstraction, romantic foolishness, and cruelty'.[23]

So, when we look at images of suffering, we are forced to think about the human consequences of what might seem a 'clinical strike' in war. But visual images also raise the issue of the limits of understanding and compassion. As Susie Linfield observes, 'in bringing us close, photographs also illuminate the unbridgeable chasm that separates ordinary life from extraordinary experiences of political trauma. In this sense, photographs teach us about our failure – our *necessary* failure – to comprehend the human'.[24] Recognition in photography can involve acknowledging, or indeed failing to acknowledge, the inability to understand the Other and, by extension, the human condition. In this sense, as Margaret Olin has argued, 'in the area of interpersonal relationships, photographs act rather than represent'.[25] They make us aware of what cannot be seen or understood as much as what can, if they are viewed and reflected upon deeply, and therefore affect our orientation to the world. If we consider photographs as shared or collective 'events', which participate in the larger political questions of sovereignty, citizenship and who has the power and security to look at whom, then viewing pictures can help to foster a 'civil imagination'.[26] But it is much easier to fall back into established ways of viewing and interpreting what one sees. Visual recognition can lead to stereotypes and caricatures of fear and hatred. While communities or what Ariella Azoulay calls a 'citizenry of photography' can form around images leading to political awakening and activism, they can also easily be formed around a picture in prejudice and hostility.[27] Recognition, in this sense, involves a degree of self-awareness, being attentive to the blind spots and distortions that are in the image before one and which also shape one's own viewing. This chimes with the philosopher Patchen Markell's caution about the difficulties in the act of recognition, located 'not in the failure to recognise the identity of the other, but in the failure to acknowledge one's own basic situation and circumstances'.[28] So it is a question of looking at the looking or even looking at the not looking. Making the viewer aware of the complicated pitfalls of viewing, and the problematic relationship between ethics and aesthetics, might therefore be considered one of the challenges of tragic representation.

(Not) looking at the enemy

It is relatively easy to shoot conflicts from the perspective of the allies, albeit at some risk to the photographer's life. There are the pictures of deployment, of injury, of homecoming. Nina Berman's *Purple Hearts*, a portrait series of injured veterans back from Iraq, is one of the most powerfully tender examples of this body of work.[29] But it is far more complicated, in terms of the politics of recognition, to shoot war from the perspective of the opposition. How do we view the enemy? Do we look at them in the same way or different? During the conflicts in Afghanistan and Iraq, the images of enemy soldiers or indeed leaders have been either objects of spectacle or, in some way, hidden from us. In either case, it seems to me, we have found ourselves looking at the looking or not looking at the not looking.

Take the fate of Saddam Hussein, captured in a 'spider hole' on 13 December 2003, seven months after the fall of Baghdad. Images of him were widely disseminated. First, footage was released of a disheveled, confused Saddam being subjected to medical examination, his hair checked for fleas and his mouth probed open ostensibly to look for a hidden cyanide capsule but implicitly to humiliate (Figure 3). We gazed at the brutal examination, the

FIGURE 3 *Looking into Saddam. Army footage of the inspection of the captured Iraqi leader.* © *AP.*

flashlight a scopic form of torture 'penetrating the head' and the yawning mouth a symbol of the fruitlessness of the coalition's search for Saddam's weapons of mass destruction.[30] So empty and permeable was our great enemy! Then there was a televised trial, which continued for a little over a year, from October 2005 until November 2006. 'This is all theatre. The real criminal is Bush', he declared at the first pretrial hearing in July 2004. And then finally, on 30 December 2006, the execution by hanging was officially filmed by the Iraqi state television news agency up until the moment of actual execution. An amateur video, shot on a mobile phone by one of the guards, actually showed the entire hanging, complete with the shouted taunts by the other prison officers. This was a spectacle designed to unite the viewer in hate and a sense of purpose at a time when Iraq was at the height of chaotic and violent insurgency.

Contrary to the treatment of Saddam Hussein, we heard very little about the last day of Osama bin Laden or the fate of his body. The best-selling account by 'Mark Owen', the Navy Seal who was in the team that killed bin Laden, describes his efforts to verify whether it was indeed bin Laden's corpse. The examination of the body seemed to involve some rough treatment, described with the violence associated with the age-old, traditional disrespectful treatment of an enemy's body: Owen 'pull[ed] his beard to the right and then the left', 'peeled back the eyelid, exposing his now lifeless brown eye', 'jammed [a cotton swab] in Bin Laden's mouth to get a saliva sample', 'slammed my syringe into the fleshy part of Bin Laden's thigh', and 'pulled [the body bag] off the truck [where] it flopped on the cement floor like a dead fish'.[31] In other respects, 'Mark Owen' engaged in familiar tactics when confronting the body of an enemy, dwelling on his effeminacy as evidenced by bin Laden's apparent use of hair dye.[32] But the prevailing theme in his account is the discrepancy between the popular image of bin Laden and the dead body he witnessed.[33] He actually took many photos of bin Laden as part of his verifying evidence that he had indeed killed 'the most wanted man in the world'. But a decision was taken by the White House not to release these photographs nor to give any details, visual or descriptive, of the disposal of the body at sea.

It was allegedly to avoid the complicated repercussions of the American treatment of Saddam that the decision was taken to allow Osama bin Laden's body to disappear, so that there would be no reprisals on American forces nor would a bin Laden grave be transformed into a martyr's shrine. In Saddam's case, the body was displayed for mockery; in Osama bin Laden's, it was arguably not given the respect of a public funeral. The hypervisibility and invisibility of the ultimate fate of America's two major enemies both had their pitfalls, in terms of managing the interpretations of their deaths.

There are other photos of the enemy from the wars in Afghanistan and Iraq which conflate the hypervisible and the invisible in a single picture. In other words, the body is on display but the face is hidden. In these examples, who is it who is not seeing? Jean-Marc Bouju's picture of an Iraqi man held captive at the US military holding camp in Iraq won the 2004 World Press Photo award. The picture, shot through a barbed wire security fence, shows the man's head covered in a black plastic hood while he cradles his young toddler son in his arms (see back cover). Bouju has explained that the boy witnessed his father being hooded and handcuffed and was terrified, and that a guard cut the plastic handcuffs to allow the man to comfort his son. The violent hooding and the tender paternal gesture pull against each other in this picture, so that the polarities between the supposedly liberating allies and fiercely hostile opposition are questioned. The camera, stuck between the wire mesh, bears witness to a scene that the official US Army 101st Airborne Division does not see. The implicit question of the photograph is whether the hood really shrouds the eyes of Western allies rather than that of the prisoner.

More complicated still are the images that were taken not by professional photographers but by soldiers and in ways that make them very hard to read. The set of scandalous images from Iraq, depicting the torture of prisoners in Abu Ghraib prison, shocked the world when they were published in 2004, as I discussed in the last chapter, and they played an important part in changing attitudes to the war.[34] The most notorious picture shows a man forced to stand dressed only in a blanket on a box with his arms spreadeagled in a mockery of the crucifixion, with electric wires indicating some threat of electrocution formed part of the torture. What sears itself into our memory is the fact that the figure is hooded. We do not see his face. In a similar way to the paradoxical effect of the Jean-Marc Bouju photo, we start to question, when viewing this picture, whose gaze is hidden. We see him not looking at us, and his not looking draws attention to our not looking, both literally and more cognitively. The hood therefore has the capacity to see into us. But wait. Who are the 'us' in this context? Unlike the sophisticated and questioning perspective of Bouju, these Abu Ghraib snaps were taken by the soldiers as part of the 'enhanced interrogation techniques' ordered by their commanders, by Guantanamo commander General Geoffrey Miller and ultimately by Donald Rumsfeld. Officially sanctioned to be creative, then, the ordinary soldiers were recording, and inviting each other to share in, their 'fun' without seeing the humiliation suffered by Iraqi prisoners. The pictures were circulated trophies for a mobile phone generation.[35] But when they were published in the *New Yorker*, they were viewed differently, the fun interpreted as cruelty and the perpetrators seen as more degenerate than their victims. In this case, the viewers distanced themselves from the soldiers. They recognized what the soldiers did not. But did we recognize the third layer of recognition, the ideology of Rumsfeld and others that relied upon such acts of evasion and deflection? The hood of the crucified prisoner serves a similar function to the redacted passages of Mohamedou Slahi's *Guantanamo Diary*, testifying visibly to a non-visibility, to the legal black holes in the system and the tragic gaps in mutual recognition and understanding.

Looking with *Antigone*

While Greek tragedy avoided onstage violence, it did place great emphasis upon looking at dead bodies after violence had occurred. The invitation to look was often accompanied with an appeal to the justice or injustice of the death, or the improbable simplification into friendship or enmity of the living's relationship with the dead. Thus, in Aeschylus's *Oresteia* Clytemnestra shows the bodies of Agamemnon and Cassandra, clarifying that they are 'enemies who had seemed to be friends' (*Agamemnon*, 1374–5), and in the next play in the trilogy Orestes shows the bodies of Clytemnestra and Aegisthus, displayed with the same net in which Clytemnestra trapped his father (*Libation Bearers*, 973–89). Similarly, at the end of *Antigone*, Creon brings out the body of his son Haemon for public mourning, highlighting his close identification with him despite their argument earlier in the play and his (Creon's) indirect responsibility for his son's self-inflicted death. 'Look at us, the killer, the killed / father and son, the same blood', he mourns, emphasizing their reconciliation.[36] By contrast, while Creon attends eventually to the proper burial of Polyneices, he does not bring his body out on stage or offer it the same public act of witnessing and mourning afforded to his son. As far as Creon is concerned, there is still a division between friends and enemies, indicated by that onstage or offstage recognition.

However, although Polyneices's body is never seen, we hear about it throughout the play, lying exposed to the sun, stinking so much that the guards must station themselves upwind of it, eaten by animals and vomited up over the city's altars by birds. The body polarizes opinion, for while Creon desires to make it 'an obscenity to behold' (αἰκισθέν τ᾽ἰδεῖν: *aikisthen t'idein*; 206), Antigone wishes to 'join in love, not hate' (οὔτοι συνέχθειν, ἀλλὰ συμφιλεῖν: *outoi sunechthein alla sumphilein*; 523), and the reactions of Ismene and the guard are different again. While Ismene thinks Antigone is out of her mind (ἄνους: *anous*), to disobey Creon by burying it, she is still 'rightly (ὀρθῶς: *orthos*; 99) dear to those who love [her]'. Ismene's 'ὀρθῶς' functions here to interrogate the very notion of orthodoxy, and indeed, as Simon Goldhill has pointed out recently, Ismene serves to complicate the notion of what is 'common' (κοινὸν: *koinon*; 1) and normal in the play.[37] Despite Creon's attempted simplifications, therefore, the unseen body of Polyneices radically challenges the easy conventions of loyalty and enmity which war apparently demands.

Greek tragedy wrestles with the perennial need to bring things to the light, with our natural desire to be witnessed and with the significance of withholding that act of witnessing. Antigone wants her act of burying Polyneices to be made public, to be 'proclaimed' to all.[38] Creon is determined that she should be buried alive away from the city, that her death should not be seen:

> I will take her down some wild, desolate path
> never trod by men, and wall her up alive
> in a rocky vault. and set out short rations,
> just the measure piety demands
> to keep the entire city free (ὑπεκφύγῃ: *hupekphuge*) of defilement.[39]

Creon's evasiveness is emphasized by the verb *phugein* here, a word which is repeated many times in the whole play, indicating the desire to escape recognition and responsibility.[40] When Antigone comes out to give her final speech as she is being led to her death, she asks the chorus to look at her, but it is possible (as I once saw in a production in New York, at the height of the Iraqi insurgency, to great effect) for the chorus specifically not to watch Antigone at this point, to avert their gaze, and just occasionally not to be able to prevent their eyes gliding onto her lone figure.[41]

Looking at the enemy, actually seeing his face, noticing the details of his person – his clothes, his customs, his feelings – can lead to contradictory effects. It can apparently elicit respect and compassion for the Other. Or it can result in a grotesque objectification, a humiliating transformation of the hostile combatant into a fantastical display of the subject's worst fears. Aeschylus's play *The Persians*, which dramatizes the defeat of

Xerxes, the king of Persia, and his army at the battle of Salamis, compelled the ancient Athenians to look at their very recent enemy. That the effect of such an act of looking in the theatre is ambivalent is testified to by the production history of the play. The ancient tragedy has been performed both as a morale-boosting way of grotesquely ridiculing the enemy and as a means of looking at the enemy and eliciting compassion. In 1983, for example, in the last years of the Cold War, the Berliner Ensemble in East Germany portrayed the protagonists – the Persian king and queen – as examples of Western decadence. This was effectively a transformation of the enemy into satirical spectacle.[42] But by contrast, the 1993 production by Peter Sellars, which toured the United States and Europe not long after the first Gulf War, aimed to compel its audience to think about the humanity of the enemy by casting the protagonists sympathetically as Iraqis. 'In America', commented Sellars, 'the war in Iraq was shown with no Iraqis at all – dead or alive [...] We're saying come and meet a few'.[43] Seeing the enemy from their point of view, according to Sellars, effectively awakens compassion and 'tests people's tolerance of different opinions and of difference in general'. Thus it is 'crucial to the functioning of democracy'.[44]

So looking at the enemy can lead to very different effects. Not looking at the enemy is also multivalent. It can be interpreted as a form of neglect, the Other registered as insignificant because it is displaced to the realm of the invisible. But on the other hand, not looking at the enemy evades the possibility of familiarizing him, of rendering him understandable through caricature or the projection of exotic spectacle. The photograph after all, according to Barthes, is an 'institutional activity' whose 'function is to integrate man, to reassure him'.[45] If one accepts Barthes's notion of the photograph's capacity to pacify and sublimate the traumatic, then one must consider the lack of an image of the enemy as a failed attempt at sublimation, as a continuing haunting presence of the traumatic. The impact of a figure remaining invisible, therefore, is ambivalent but should not be underestimated. 'There is real power in remaining unmarked', observed Peggy Phelan in her fascinating claim for the value of invisibility in photography and performance, 'and there are serious limitations to visual representation as a political goal'.[46] Being unmarked allows the subject to remain un-trapped by surveillance, not co-opted by hegemonic culture. Polyneices, the unseen enemy of Thebes, persists as a powerfully absent presence throughout Sophocles' play.

Drone vision

The philosopher Hannah Arendt, writing in the catastrophic aftermath of the Second World War, Hiroshima and the Holocaust, declared that technology shapes and determines our capacity for thought, the meaning of our politics and the 'fundamental experiences of our age'.[47] She noted that 'the modern age ... was born with the first atomic explosions' and that the potential for nuclear Armageddon, together with the genocides committed by totalitarian regimes in the twentieth century, altered the very parameters of thinking about power, agency, freedom and politics.[48] If we reflect upon the implications of Arendt's thesis for our contemporary predicament, then we are compelled to conclude that the technology of conflict is fundamentally different now from the Cold War nuclear age and that therefore the 'meaning of our politics' and our moral thinking must be altered.

In the past cameras were metaphorically compared to weapons, the shutter like the trigger of a gun. Sontag pointed out the sometimes violently aggressive aspects of the act of taking a photograph: 'We talk about "loading" and "aiming" a camera, about shooting a film', she wrote. 'Just as the camera is a sublimation of the gun, to photograph someone is a sublimated murder – a soft murder, appropriate to a sad, frightened time.'[49] Photojournalists and photo-editors are said to be interested in the 'bang-bang', partly because it is dramatic images of conflict that sell newspapers and win press prizes but partly also for the adventure of being on the front line.[50]

But now in the era of drone warfare, the distinctions between cameras and weapons have become far more blurred. Cameras do not only metaphorically shoot pictures but also literally shoot targets. Although unmanned aerial vehicles (UAVs) or drones have been used for surveillance since the Vietnam War it was in 2002 that armed drones (UACVs) were first used to fire missiles. During the Gulf War of 1990 we first witnessed, on the television news, the targeted missiles that the military view on a computer screen, but these became far more familiar to us during the second bombardment of Iraq in 2003.[51] So-called precision bombing and 'intelligent' conflict is conducted through the medium of a screen, with minimal or no risk to the person who fires the missile. And as such, following Arendt's lead, it necessitates a rethinking – or even a 'complete reversal' – of our relationship to war, to allies and enemies, and to the structuring polarities of pity and fear, recognition and misrecognition.

Drone warfare has become a key strategy in the War on Terror, developed under the Bush administration but hugely increased under the presidency of Barack Obama. Indeed, more drone pilots are trained now than fighter and bomber pilots. The emphasis is upon the use of machines in the actual battlefield while the human 'fighters' are safely out of harm's way in a bunker outside Las Vegas, looking at a computer screen. The drones are given deathly names, like Predator and Reaper, and the missiles are called Hellfire, but the killing is arguably conducted by committee. Every Tuesday the head of the CIA meets with the President in the White House to review the latest intelligence and surveillance reports and to draw up that week's 'kill list'.[52] The drone pilots are then commanded, within the next sixty days, to seek out their targets, zoom in and fire. One recent estimate is that more than 3,000 people have been 'assassinated' by drones. While the attacks are deemed to be more precise than traditional methods of warfare, there is still 'collateral damage'. An unknown number of innocent civilians have been killed by drones in Pakistan, Afghanistan and Yemen. One estimate is that 'for each person the US has targeted, an average of nine children have been killed'.[53] Meanwhile, 'autonomous drones' – unmanned aircraft programmed with algorithms to meet a number of potential challenges and to carry out strikes – are already undergoing military testing, although they have not been authorized for use yet. In that case, even the sight and insight will have been automated.

The effect of this rapidly developing technology of conflict is to make warfare unilateral. Vietnam was described as an asymmetrical war, because of the marked imbalance between the manpower and weaponry of the Americans on one side and that of the Vietcong on the other. But drone warfare is unilateral, completely one-sided, indeed without really any 'sides' at all. The targets go about their lives, not obviously in any clear conflict zone, until they are attacked while the drone pilots watch them in safety 12,000 miles away in

Nevada. The designated 'kill list' makes warfare more like a form of animal hunting, according to Grégoire Chamayou.[54] The pilots seek their targets globally, wherever they happen to be; there is no respect for boundaries or national sovereignty. The nebulous definition of 'Terror' means that there are no limits to drone warfare, either geographically or temporally. It results in a war 'of infinite violence, with no possible exit', according to Chamayou.[55] Geographer Derek Gregory has called it an 'everywhere war', in which the enemy's body is the battlefield wherever he happens to be.[56]

So what forms of recognition – both recognition of others and self-recognition – does this new type of warfare produce? On the one hand, the drone pilot using his aptly named 'predator' is deeply *intimate* with his victim, monitoring his every movement, surveilling him inside buildings in domestic settings. Like Shakespeare's Coriolanus with his military opponent Aufidius, the drone pilot knows the name of his antagonist, knows his individual history, becomes bound up in his fate. In Shakespeare's tragic drama, Coriolanus and Aufidius face each other in a series of battles until they become deadly rivals: 'the man of my soul's hate, Aufidius, / Piercing our Romans', says Coriolanus (1.6.10–11). They seek out each other in the field and showing more obsessive respect for each other than for their fellow men. Indeed, the strange intimacy of combat even becomes tinged with an erotic attraction drawing them together. When Coriolanus is expelled from Rome by his fellow citizens and arrives at his enemy's encampment, asking Aufidius either to use him in his campaign or to kill him, Aufidius greets him more than warmly:

> Let me twine
> Mine arms about that body, whereagainst
> My grained ash an hundred times hath broke
> And scarr'd the moon with splinters. Here I clip
> The anvil of my sword, and do contest
> As hotly and as nobly with thy love
> As ever in ambitious strength I did
> Contend against thy valour ….
> … that I see thee here,
> Thou noble thing, more dances my rapt heart
> Than when I first my wedded mistress saw
> Bestride my threshold.[57]

Military combat and sexual embrace become conflated in Aufidius's speech here, his enemy apparently closer to his nocturnal fantasies than his new bride. Individual one-on-one fighting produces these strange forms of intimacy. Sexual attraction or obsession is similarly latent in the rhetoric of drone warfare, brought on by the closeness of attention which the 'pilots' must devote to monitoring the movements of their antagonists. For example, they commonly use nicknames drawn from porn stars and striptease artists to designate their targets.

Yet on the other hand, the combatants do not really meet face to face, do not stare 'with piteous recognition in fixed eyes' like the enemies in the nightmare of Wilfred Owen's First World War poem 'Strange Meeting'.[58] Combatants now do not even share the same earth or airspace. They are hugely distanced from each other, cut off from reciprocal risk and respect. Viewing the enemy on a screen, or identifying 'heat signatures' or 'patterns of life' as an anomaly on an algorithm, is not the same as recognizing them on the battlefield.[59] The drone operates as a prosthetic extension of the pilot, functioning as if the pilot were *really* dropping into inaccessible locations in the desert, but in fact he and his body are 'indissociably tied to technology', intimately instrumentalized as a killing machine.[60] The contradictions of recognition and non-recognition are thus symbolized by this cyborg figure, half-man and half-machine. The technology gives the illusion of hypervisibility, power and insight but in fact stops up the passage of real compassion and understanding.

According to Kelly Oliver, there are some forms of witnessing which on the surface seem like proper acts of respectful acknowledgement of difference and diversity but in fact are really examples of what she terms 'false witnessing'. These involve 'closing off responses from others, otherness, or difference' and paying attention only to the self.[61] It seems to me that the obsessive attention paid to the psychological trauma suffered by drone pilots is a form of 'false witnessing'. While the pilot is the untouchable victor day after day, choosing which target he or she will erase, he or she deals with the burden of omnipotent power by inculcating an environment of victimhood, by taking on the burden of trauma and psychological damage. Tragic responsibility takes on the form not of concern for the enemy casualties of the drone bombings or the innocent civilians on the ground caught in the collateral damage but rather of care for the self.[62] The unilateral, dissociated nature of drone warfare is altering the understanding of guilt and responsibility, making it inward looking, self-contained and imprisoning. The rhetoric is one of trauma rather than tragedy.

The complications of drone warfare, the unilateral power of the pilots and their self-contained feelings of guilt and trauma animate George Brant's play *Grounded*. This play, which starred Anne Hathaway in its successful New York run, dramatizes, as a poetic monologue, the experience of a female pilot who conducts drone warfare in Afghanistan (not Iraq: as she says, 'different desert same war') from a bunker in the Nevada desert during the day and returns to her husband and child in Las Vegas each night.[63] The focus is upon the unreality of the situation, the fact that she can touch a button and kill somebody who is simultaneously 12 hours ahead and 1.2 seconds away. Unlike conventional warfare, she cannot be touched by her enemy. She is removed in all senses, sealed off, safe, in no way precarious:

> And them
> Look at them
> Poor saps
> You don't learn do you
> You can't hide from the eye in the sky my children
> We look down from above we see all and
> we have pronounced you guilty
> boom.
> Another grey inferno.[64]

Like the Olympian gods to whom they are explicitly compared, the drone pilots in their bunker ('the Chair Force') look down at the small mortals below and pass judgement upon them, deciding who to 'erase' and who to spare.

A recent cinematic treatment of drone warfare, *Eye in the Sky*, directed by Gavin Hood and starring Helen Mirren, focused at great length on the collective act of judgement about whether and when to release the missile by showing all the different links in the 'kill chain' of just one strike in Kenya, from a colonel coordinating the attack from her headquarters in North London, to drone pilots in Nevada and image-ID specialists in Hawaii, to local surveillance agents using micro flying robots on the ground in Nairobi and right up to the general watching the attack on a screen with the foreign minister and the attorney general in the Cabinet Office Briefing Room in Westminster.[65] The only risk in the operation is to the legality and the moral consequences of the action, but consequently the decision to strike is endlessly deferred, the politicians continually arguing that they need to 'refer up' before they can authorize the attack. While the drone pilots exhibit distress at the prospect of targeting the life of a young girl as collateral damage, in a faux and sentimental attempt to show moral compassion, the emphasis of the film is much more upon the clinical, mechanical nature of the warfare and the contrast between the cold, rational and lengthy decision-making in the offices and the gritty, dusty reality on the streets in Nairobi. Traditional tragic choice, on an individual basis, has been replaced by collective decision-making, diffused and abrogated by committee.

In contrast, *Grounded* is a one-woman play in which the character of the pilot becomes more and more isolated within her own limited agency, guilt and confusion. Despite the fact that there is absolutely no risk to her life, she is much more isolated and vulnerable than the pilots in *Eye in the Sky*. Indeed, although the warfare might be said to be 'unilateral', and, according to Elaine Scarry, successful military strategy 'is one in which the injuring occurs in only one direction', *Grounded* portrays a form of trauma for the impervious god.[66] The pilot's difficulty is that she gets to go home each night. In no previous war could a combatant serve 12-hour shifts, obliterating the enemy in the desert, and still go home at night to watch TV with the husband and take the child to day care the next morning. It is as if, she says, 'Odysseus came home every day'.[67] One desert (in Afghanistan) becomes confused with the other (in Nevada), one screen (the footage relayed back by the drone) interpolated by another (the entertainment TV screen at home). In a climactic penultimate scene, the pilot confuses the child she is about to target in the enemy desert with her own child whom she dropped off at school earlier that day and she pulls the drone away.

> The shrink asks me a question
> Like I'm the guilty
> I want to tell her
> You don't know guilty
> I know the guilty

I see the guilty every day
Don't speak to me of guilt
Don't speak to a god of guilt.[68]

'Guilt', a word intended to differentiate one group of people from the other 'innocent' group, has become confused by the end of the play and applied mutually: 'I see the guilty every day.' The pilot appears to be seeing the world in shades of grey, rather than black and white. But George Brant implies that this confusion on the pilot's part is an aspect of her mental breakdown, rather than a form of tragic wisdom. The surreal hallucinations under which she struggles at the play's end are more reminiscent of *Long Day's Journey into Night* or *A Streetcar Named Desire* than any cathartic recognition in the classical sense. Tragedy has become trauma, stuck fast without the clarity of recognition, in the modern age of drones.

Looking at the not looking

Greek tragedy and tragic photography confront suffering head-on, metaphorically with their eyes open. The war photographer Don McCullin 'serves as an eye we cannot shut', wrote John Berger, in the context of a discussion of how we confront shocking images. Photographs like the ones McCullin took in Vietnam 'are printed on the black curtain which is drawn across what we choose to forget or refuse to know'.[69] The camera, like the eyes of the mask of Greek tragedy, witnesses events 'because it is created with open eyes' and 'faces up to the muses', according to Tony Harrison.[70] On the other hand, both Greek tragedy and tragic photography can also register their lack of response, their moment of turning away, their drawing of the 'black curtain'.[71] Thus the chorus at the end of *Oedipus Tyrannus* twist and turn towards and away from the sight of the blinded and cursed Oedipus, a polluting and taboo figure:

Ah, most unhappy man!
But no! I cannot bear even to look at you,
Though there is much that I would ask and see and hear.
But I shudder at the very sight of you.[72]

And thus the Pete Souza photograph of the situation room catches the moment when Clinton puts her hand over her mouth, a hand which could have easily also been placed over her eyes.

While drone vision closes off its insight with its false witnessing, even while it achieves global surveillance and astonishing military intelligence, some visual recording of the War on Terror does go some way to giving us the kind of tragic recognition afforded by traditional drama and other mediations. These interventions are ones in which we become aware of the limits of what we can see and understand and the easy categorization into which we all frequently relapse.

The Pete Souza photograph of the situation room, which was given deeper resonance and significance by its invocation during the *Antigone* performance, did, later, have its uncanny double. I want to compare the Pete Souza photo with the other image of viewing and not viewing the enemy which emerged in 2011, to think about the role of revelation, (non)recognition and fear shaping our visual grasp of the decade-long War on Terror. When the Navy Seals stormed the bin Laden compound in Pakistan, they found a stash of home videos. Among these was film footage of Osama bin Laden, sitting on an old carpet in a dingy room, wrapped in a blanket and watching a television. In lieu of the photograph of the dead bin Laden, the Pentagon decided to release this video in May 2011, with the soundtrack censored so that we *see* but do not hear the scene. The inverted echo of the Pete Souza image is striking. Unlike the full view of Obama in the situation room, we see Osama from behind, and therefore only his back and side profile, not his face. But we see the television screen that he is watching; at various points it projects images of both Osama and President Obama against a backdrop of the events of 9/11 and the subsequent wars in Afghanistan and Iraq (Figure 4).

These two images, the situation room photo and the compound home movie, testify to a double failure or refusal to see, covered by an obsession with viewing (Figures 2 and 4). In the first, the ambivalent possibilities of depicting the spectators of a hidden picture aim to cultivate the notion of the enemy as opaque, mysterious, fearful but also insignificant. The spectating group are formed, and conformed, by what they see and recognize and fear or hate; our attention is carefully composed to be about them, not about what they are watching, although, as I have argued,

FIGURE 4 *Osama bin Laden watches Barack Obama on television,
Abbottabad, Pakistan.* ©AP.

the occluded television leaves open the space for speculation, for
pity and fear and uncertainty. In the second, haphazardly shot
image, the spectator, bin Laden, is also formed by what he sees,
the narcissism of watching oneself on television not lost on the
video's many commentators. The film was released, presumably, to
make him an object of ridicule; to what depths has our fearful
enemy been reduced! But the gap between the visible television
image and the shadowy, unseen viewer actually demands what the
Pentagon never envisaged, a sense of the pathetic, of pathos, or,
dare we say, of pity? All we see is bin Laden's hand clutching the
television remote control, flicking from one channel to the next,
although all seem to offer the same visual library. Choice but no
choice, a decision over a stock of images already archived, a hand
which seeks, through the touch of a button, a visual recognition of
polarized enmity: such is the tragic spectral image which haunts the
iconic Pete Souza representation of the war.

One image, it seems to me, calls up the other, invoking the
hidden blind spots that are paradoxically foundational for the
politically useful forces of fear and doubt and certainty. In viewing

these two images we are forced to face questions that are central to tragedy, about our sense of ourselves as a society, what we choose to recognize and what we do not, and, in an era of mass media and multiple images, the self-conscious and ambiguous function of bearing witness today.

5

The Year of Revolutions

The uprisings that swept across the world in 2011 – from Tunisia, Egypt, Bahrain, Libya, Yemen and Syria, to the European capitals of Greece and Spain, and on to the 'Occupied' city centres across the United States and beyond – filled their participants and supporters with something close to the bliss of paradise.[1] 'There is ecstasy present in the moment', gushed New York-based academic Hamid Dabashi in late 2011, 'not just in the revolutionary uprisings themselves but also in attempts to fathom and narrate them, imagine, embrace and define them'.[2] 'Look at the streets of Egypt tonight', wrote Ahdaf Soueif from the midst of the protests in Cairo, at 6 pm on Friday 11 February 2011. 'This is what hope looks like.' Reflecting later on those 'eighteen golden days' of revolution, she wrote that they 'brought out the best in us and showed us not just what we could do but how we could be'.[3] And over in the States, at the Occupy Wall Street which was directly inspired by the Arab Spring revolutions, Nathan Schneider was reaching for the language of religious revelation. 'For nearly two months in the fall of 2011, a square block of granite and honey locust trees in New York's Financial District, right between Wall Street and the World Trade Center, became a canvas for the image of another world', he recalled later. 'In the rupture of the ordinary that characterised those early days, everything felt in some sense religious, charged with a secret extremity and transcendence.'[4] Comparisons were made with other revolutionary moments in history: France in 1789, Europe in 1848, the beginning of the end of communism in 1989.

But the comparisons were made with these other dates in history not only because of their similar experiences of hope but also because of their comparable feelings of disappointment in the months after the initial euphoria. Across the Middle East, the Arab Spring turned into an Arab Winter. Egypt's revolution resulted in the election of Mohamed Morsi and the Muslim Brotherhood the following year, only for that administration to be overturned by a coup in July 2013 and the country to revert to harsh military rule.[5] The overthrow of Gaddafi in Libya has led to the country becoming a haven for terrorists and people traffickers. Bahrain's uprising was crushed by Saudi troops in March 2011. Yemen succeeded in ousting its hated ruler, President Saleh, in November 2011, but the subsequent civil war between tribal factions has provoked Saudi Arabia to intervene, resulting in numerous fatalities, destruction and famine. Meanwhile, the uprising in Syria descended into civil war, pulling in sectarian armies from the surrounding region and creating the chaotic political vacuum that allowed the death-cult Islamic State to take root in the region. Only Tunisia of the original revolutionary states seems, at this time of writing at least, to have transitioned to a functioning democracy and even that has been embattled by terrorist resistance. Revolution has led to violence across the region. Hope has turned to despair.

On a different scale in terms of physical death and destruction, but nevertheless still devastating for revolutionary aspiration, the Occupy movement of 2011 also ended in apparent failure. The encampment in New York was evicted on 15 November 2011, just around two months after it began. The Occupy camp outside St Paul's Cathedral in London was evicted on 28 February 2012, the last high-profile camp to go of the global protest movement, which at one point had spread to over 900 cities worldwide. Whether or not any of the demands of the Occupy movement were met, and indeed what those demands were, is very much a matter for debate.

Revolutions might seem to defy the traditional assumptions about tragedy. They replace passive fatalism with collective action and transformation. They substitute optimism and progress for misery and resignation. The 2011 revolutions across the totalitarian regimes of the Middle East and in the heartland of what was felt to be the exploitative capitalism of the West made people believe that change was possible. The world did not have to be governed in the way it had been for decades.

Yet, on the other hand, it is hard to envisage revolution without tragedy. Indeed, it is scarcely possible to find an example of a revolution in history or literature that has not resulted in failure. This is because the goal which is so frequently sought in a revolution – 'Liberty! Freedom! Tyranny is dead!' as the conspirators shout after the assassination in *Julius Caesar* – can so easily degenerate into anarchy and from there into violence.[6] The very process of liberation from rule and oppression, exhilarating as it is, can bring about its opposite. 'The world is topsy-turvy', one revolutionary declares in Georg Buchner's 1835 political tragedy about the French Revolution, *Danton's Death*. 'Virtue turns murderer, criminals die like saints.'[7] Revolution is tragic also because of the nature of human frailty and the corruption of power. Idealistic leaders, once they have achieved the overthrow of the existing government, then have to contend with the responsibility of rule, with the inevitable compromises that they have to make and with the temptations for private gain and aggrandizement. 'Shall one of us / That struck the foremost man of all this world … now / Contaminate our fingers with base bribes?', the noble Brutus complains to Cassius as the revolution fractures in the second half of *Julius Caesar*.[8] And revolution can be considered tragic, also, because we see, time and again, that the historical forces of reaction are stronger than the forces of hope and change. For as Raymond Williams pointed out, revolution exposes not only the necessary disorder and brutality of the revolutionaries but also – most importantly – the underlying disorder and brutality of the system which provoked the rupture.[9] Revolutions produce backlashes as they are counteracted by a conservative establishment eager to continue or restore that brutal system.

The question of whether or not revolution is considered to be tragic is partly determined by how much emphasis we place upon the collective good and how much upon the fortunes of individuals. According to the harsh radical Saint-Just in Buchner's *Danton's Death*, 'Nature obeys her laws calmly and inexorably' and 'if a man comes into conflict with them he is destroyed'.[10] Revolutions, from this perspective, would be no more tragic than an 'insignificant, almost imperceptible change in physical nature' since, as Buchner himself wrote in a letter, the individual is just 'foam on a wave'.[11] Buchner's Saint-Just was articulating views very similar to those of the philosopher Hegel, whose lectures on tragic drama were delivered some fifteen years before the play's composition. Hegel believed that historical change inevitably produces casualties but progresses towards ultimate justice. Watching tragedy impresses us with the 'absolute rationality' of what happens to its victims; 'only then can our hearts be morally at peace: shattered by the fate of heroes but reconciled fundamentally', he stated.[12] But despite Hegel or Saint-Just, we don't tend to repress 'mere sympathy and tragic pity' for individuals in the name of the greater good. Instead, the tragedy of revolutions is located in the violent plight of individuals sacrificed at what Hegel calls the 'slaughter-bench' of history.[13] As evidence of this, Buchner's *Danton's Death* focuses on the contradictory efforts of one man, Danton, to defy or surrender to death. Even Brecht's revolutionary plays, which attempted to school its audience away from bourgeois pity, still cannot help evoking sympathy for his suffering characters: the self-sacrificial gesture of Kattrin in *Mother Courage* or the last stand at the barricades of the Cabet family in his play about the brief proto-Communist occupation of Paris in 1871, *The Days of the Commune*.[14] So rather than thinking about the Arab Spring in the abstract or geopolitically, we might focus instead on the decision of twenty-six-year-old Mohamed Bouazizi, vegetable vendor and sole income earner for a family of eight, to set himself alight on 17 December 2010 in Sidi Bouzid, 300 kilometres south of Tunis, after he had been fined a day's wages for not having a licence and had his vegetable cart confiscated. Tunisia's revolution ultimately succeeded but Bouazizi was one of its individual tragedies.

The revolutions of 2011 raise the question of the purpose or futility of action. Can individual action make a difference or are there deep-seated forces at work, steering the direction history takes or ensuring that the status quo ultimately remains? The revolutions compel us to think about the meaning of freedom, about whether it is unambiguously desirable or whether it can be tragic, unleashing anarchic or populist danger as much as liberal possibility. But they also point us to think about the relation between tragedy, history and notions of justice, questions which run through tragedies like *Julius Caesar* or *Danton's Death*. Traditionally, dramatic tragedies explore the process of living *through* an experience as well as getting the measure of the whole. To what extent can we do that with the 2011 uprisings? At what point can one say that a revolution has been successful and is over? Or, indeed, that it has failed? Revolutions catalyse often imperceptible changes in the public imagination which might slowly lead to progress later, just as one revolution influences another in the collective thinking or revolutions in past history or literature inspire the present. What is the tragic, revolutionary imagination by which we can understand 2011?

Revolution and the course of history

'The arc of the moral universe is long but it bends towards justice', Martin Luther King Jr. famously declared during the civil rights struggle in the 1960s. But across the Arab world since 2011, the moral universe has felt less like an arc and more like a boomerang. In the first year, it soared out in cosmopolitan promise. First Tunisia, then Egypt, then Libya and Yemen, like beacons igniting courage and optimism across the region. The revolutions, according to Hamid Dabashi in late 2011, were creating 'a new geography of liberation' which moved beyond old 'colonial' or 'postcolonial' structures of domination' and were 'leading to a reconfigured geopolitics of hope'.[15] Yemeni Nobel Peace Prize laureate Tawakkol Karman also emphasized the tolerant, positive influence of globalization in her prize acceptance speech in Oslo in December 2011, connecting what was being achieved in Yemen with the uprisings across the Arab region and with wider pro-democracy movements worldwide.[16] Even by the end of 2012, Middle East expert Marc Lynch continued to be optimistic, deeming Libya 'a guarded success story against all the odds', Yemen 'for all its many woes ... doing better than anticipated' and Egypt 'emerg[ing] from its long months of polarisation and chaos with a shaky but real transition to civilian rule'.[17]

Meanwhile in the United States, in the summer of 2011, young people were taking inspiration from what was being achieved across the Middle East. An advertisement in the online magazine *Adbusters*, canvassing willingness to protest against austerity in the wake of the financial crisis, asked its readers: 'Are you ready for a Tahrir moment?'[18] The following month a meeting was held in downtown Manhattan at which people who had participated in the protests in Egypt, Spain and Greece spoke about their experience and passed on lessons to their American counterparts. The fantasy was born of a crowd of people occupying a central square in a city until the governing power – the 'corporate oligarchy' in the case of Manhattan – was toppled. The protesters began camping out in Zuccotti Park, near Wall Street, in mid-September and within a month they had inspired similar occupations in cities across the globe. International revolution seemed to be possible, as one Occupier wrote enthusiastically:

> The world becomes a very different place when members of the 99% stand up. The revolts in Egypt, elsewhere in the Middle East, and in Europe belie the story that popular uprisings are futile. The people occupying Zuccotti Park in lower Manhattan and in cities across the country have showed that Americans, too, can take a stand.[19]

But then first there was the brutal crackdown on the protest in Bahrain in March 2011, greatly assisted by a Saudi-led military intervention. And then, maybe emboldened by the Bahraini response to the uprising and cautioned by Gaddafi's fate in Libya, Syrian president Assad refused to step down and proceeded to bomb his own citizens. In Egypt, meanwhile, the democratic aspirations of the Tahrir Square protest morphed into the election success, a year later, of the Muslim Brotherhood, which formed an administration that became so unpopular that the coup against Morsi in July 2013 and the establishment of the hard-line military ruler, President Al-Sisi, attracted widespread support. Yemen, like Syria, has also descended into bitter civil war, after the initial euphoria over President Saleh stepping down in November 2011. The elected Sunni president Hadi continues, as I write, to fight the Shia rebels, who ousted him in 2014. In this case, the suffering is exacerbated by the external intervention of Saudi Arabia, which has bombed rebel strongholds with apparent indiscriminate concern for the civilian population. Revolution across the Middle East and North Africa has been transformed into a sectarian war between Shia and Sunni, a conflict by proxy between Iran and Saudi Arabia for control over the whole region.[20] As Marc Lynch observed in his most recent book on the Middle East, the 'entire regional order appears to be in freefall'.[21]

The reversal in the trajectory of the Arab Spring revolutions challenges our confidence in progress and the teleology of history. Is radical change to the status quo actually possible? Can individuals make a difference or is there an underlying structure ensuring that the established order ultimately persists?[22] According to Cassius in Shakespeare's *Julius Caesar*, we often use the notion of determining forces as a substitute for taking responsibility ourselves:

> The fault, dear Brutus, is not in our stars
> But in ourselves, that we are underlings.[23]

But Cassius puts forward this argument about individual agency when he is trying to persuade Brutus to join his conspiracy to assassinate Caesar; can we trust Cassius? Certainly Shakespeare's play, which is about a failed revolution, seems to turn on the mistakes of individuals. Julius Caesar ignores the warnings of the Soothsayer ('beware the Ides of March') and the fearful dreams of his wife and goes to the Senate where he is assassinated. Brutus resists Cassius's inclination to kill Mark Antony as well as Caesar ('Let's be sacrificers but not butchers') and later allows Antony to speak at Caesar's funeral despite Cassius's warnings against this. And at the battle of Philippi, Cassius misreads the fortunes of his captain and the troops, believes they have been defeated rather than victorious and consequently commits suicide, thus ensuring that he and Brutus will lose. The truth comes too late:

> O hateful Error, Melancholy's child,
> Why dost thou show to the apt thoughts of men
> The things that are not?[24]

If events had turned out slightly differently, if certain accidents and 'errors' had not happened, according to this interpretation, Brutus's and Cassius's revolution – returning Rome to its former liberty and nobility – would have been successful and long-lasting.

Yet there are many indications in the play that the causes of failure lie much deeper than individual fault and that there is an underlying structure – on a political, supernatural and even aesthetic level – which determines events. Shakespeare maps the story set in the pagan Roman republic onto the later Christian ideas of the political and religious violation incurred in killing a king. Supernatural portents are noticed even before Caesar is assassinated; after his death, at the battle of Philippi, his ghost appears. The implication is that the crime of king killing must be punished; the moral order is restored with the death of Brutus and the reversal of his revolution. 'Caesar now be still', gasps Brutus as he breathes his last (5.5.50).

The supernatural revenge is complete. Beyond this, the underlying order, of both state and individual, upon which characters depend for their decision-making, is revealed to be tumultuous and precarious. Rome turns out to be an illusory idea, based upon a nostalgic myth about its past. Brutus believes that he has been petitioned by the Roman people to rise up against the tyrant Caesar, urged by anonymous letters thrown in through his window. 'O Rome, I make thee promise, / If the redress will follow, thou receivest / Thy full petition at the hand of Brutus', he vows (2.1.56–8). But these letters have all been penned by Cassius, who needs Brutus to give legitimacy and the appearance of nobility to the assassination plot. Rome seems to be a place where a man has to live up to the noble example of his ancestors, thus continuing the distinction indicated by the specific family name. And yet men can seem precariously interchangeable; Cassius's lines, 'Caesar does bear me hard, but he loves Brutus. / If I were Brutus now, and he were Cassius, / He should not humour me', lurch with their torturous syntax into a confusion between subjects which mirrors the turbulent politics of late Republic Rome.[25] And the divisions of state are replicated in the divisions within individual characters, the extraordinary number of doubts and second thoughts and contradictions in this play. Cassius speaks of Brutus's 'honourable mettle' that can be 'wrought' and manipulated, but Brutus more memorably compares his inner self to a kingdom which is undergoing revolution:

> Between the acting of a dreadful thing
> And the first motion, all the interim is
> Like a phantasma or a hideous dream:
> The genius and the mortal instruments
> Are then in council, and the state of man,
> Like to a little kingdom, suffers then
> The nature of an insurrection.[26]

And finally there is the Roman populace, anarchic and capricious, discounted as ill-educated and manipulated to serve different political ends. They are driven 'hence' at the beginning of the play by the tribune of the plebs, but they return, whipped up by Mark Antony's clever and emotional rhetoric at Caesar's funeral. In a matter of a few minutes, they change from being convinced by Brutus of the justice of his insurrection – 'This Caesar was a tyrant', 'We are blest that Rome is rid of him' – to blood-curdling rage at Caesar's killers, moved by Antony's words to 'rise up and mutiny'. That this fickle crowd is a force to be reckoned with is confirmed by the desperate fate of Cinna the poet, who is torn apart by the people just because he bears the same name as one of the conspirators. No revolution can be successful without this crowd, and Brutus and Cassius have underestimated (or overestimated?) them while Antony has judged them just right, creating their metaphorical hunger in the first part of his speech and then carefully feeding them what they want to hear.

The crowds in Tahrir Square were not quite the same as the Roman populace, but they did appear to change their views radically on democracy, revolution, the army and strong government between January 2011, when they toppled Mubarek, and July 2013, when they welcomed back General Al-Sisi, his hard-line military colleague. Historians have suggested that the army cynically let the Muslim Brotherhood and Mohamed Morsi win the election in 2012 and 'sacrificed Shafiq [the military candidate] on the altar of democracy', thereby gaining the 'legitimacy and popularity to come back'.[27] They made Morsi's year-long presidency extremely difficult, impeding his efforts at reform for which his inexperience in government had ill-equipped him and thus provoking him into more autocratic measures and the country into further turbulence. As a result, when the coup was mounted against Morsi in 2013, the people were relieved. When a new constitution was passed in January 2014, making protest more difficult than it had been under Mubarek, they continued to be supportive. A protest rally at the end of January 2014, to mark the third anniversary of the revolution, coincided with the explosion of several bombs around Cairo. Within hours Al-Sisi had blamed the Muslim Brotherhood and linked those protesting in Tahrir Square with the Brotherhood, with those responsible for the bombs and with terrorists everywhere. Forty-nine people were killed, 247 injured and over 1,000 people were arrested. 'Within two hours of the first bombing, a crowd had gathered to cheer Sisi, shouting "The people want the execution of the Brothers", thus imitating and twisting the call of three years before', one historian noted.[28] In that shout, 'the people want the execution of the Brothers', one can hear echoes of Shakespeare's Romans' cry of 'We'll burn the house of Brutus' and 'fire the traitors' houses'.[29]

In the last few years, Egyptian writers have been producing terrifying dystopian fiction which testifies to their political

disillusion, the product of the failure of their revolution. Mohammad
Rabie's disturbingly violent novel *Otared*, set in Cairo in 2025,
although also looping back to January 2011 and historically to
1063, operates under the premise that everything is ultimately
controlled by underlying dark forces and that nothing therefore
can really change. Narrated by a police sniper called Otared, now
working for the resistance, the book imagines Egypt occupied by
an invader force, with its inhabitants struggling to eke out a bleak,
feral existence. The narrator is commissioned to undertake an
undercover mission as an *agent provocateur*, to target civilians with
the aim of creating such misery that they will readily rise up against
their perceived oppressors: 'In recent years, the people had been
led, sheep-like, into uprisings, revolutions, and demonstrations. We
ourselves prompted them to revolt against a previous revolution
that others had led them into.'[30] Referring implicitly here to the
coup against Morsi in 2013, Rabie evokes a world in which the
dark forces of a corrupt police force control the hopes and fears of
the populace, learning the lessons of the original protest in January
2011, engineering uprisings and driving the people to accept any
form of government so long as there is security. 'We now know when
to shoot them down and when to let them rise up', Otared is told by
a general. 'People called what happened a "revolution" and, in their
minds, that's how it stayed for years. Thank God they woke up in the
end and changed the term to "troubles."'[31] Rabie cynically ironizes
the notion of revolution here, since such rapturous change is only
a temporary delusion in what is a permanent state of corruption,
turbulence and violence. The novel concludes its nightmarish,
hallucinatory journey with an infernal vision of eternity:

> Then I saw that I had been a policeman in the world, and I saw
> that I had been a policeman in many different lives in many hells,
> and a million million images passed before me in which I saw
> everything: how I had tormented people and been tormented by
> them. And I saw that hell was eternal and unbroken, changeless
> and undying; and that in the end, all other things would pass
> away and nothing besides remain. And I knew that I was in hell
> forevermore, and that I belonged here.[32]

Otared's circular structure is infernal, beginning and ending with
shocking acts of killing. Fellow Egyptian writer Basma Abdel Aziz

has also captured brilliantly the futility and disappointment of the Arab Spring in her recently published work of fiction, *The Queue*, but with more Kafkaesque absurdist frustration. The novel portrays an unnamed, dystopian state in which two popular uprisings, known as the 'First Storm' and then the 'Disgraceful Events', have been crushed with the establishment of 'the Gate', which quickly 'controlled absolutely everything, and made all procedures, paperwork, authorizations, and permits – even those for eating and drinking subject to its control'.[33] Everyone must queue at the Gate for permits for all types of activity, including medical treatment, but the Gate never opens and the line gets longer and longer, a metaphor for the injustice and futility of life under the new regime. Like the surreal, nightmarish visions of Kafka in *The Trial* or 'Before the Law', the queue becomes a daily, weekly, monthly experience in itself, causing those in line to forget their past or their purpose.

> The queue was like a magnet. It drew people toward it, then held them captive as individuals and in their little groups, and it stripped them of everything, even the sense that their previous lives had been stolen from them.

Rather than the optimistic sense of living through an extraordinary historic moment and orientating towards a teleological future, as witnessed in the imaginative writing of the first year of the Arab Spring, works like Abdel Aziz's *The Queue* or Mohammad Rabie's *Otared* portray a dark, dystopian future which seems stuck fast in unchanging misery.[34] Their imaginary worlds have distorted time, and given way to injustice, oppression and bureaucratic unaccountability. The consequence is staggering violence, made all the more horrifying because it is inexplicable and without clear origins. Indeed, much of *Otared* is almost unreadable because of the extreme nature of the grotesque violence described. But particularly in the case of *The Queue*, the stasis of injustice and random brutality creates a form of absurdity close to that found in Beckett. Neither of these novels could really be termed tragedies because there is no space for any alternative vision, no point of contrast from which the characters have fallen. Instead, like Beckett, these novels are tragicomedies or grotesques that violate generic boundaries along with other forms of violation: political, moral, epistemological, ontological – and temporal.

What is the timeline of revolution? If the Arab uprisings raise questions about the notion of progress, could revolution rather be circular, revolving back to an earlier state of being? Certainly, the tragic revolution of *Julius Caesar* can be deemed a ring composition, beginning and ending with festivity. 'Hence! Home you idle creatures, get you home! / Is this a holiday?', the tribune chides the people at the start. Octavius closes with 'So call the field to rest, and let's away, / To part the glories of this happy day', the alliteration of 'h' (hence, home and holiday) at the start of the play subtly echoed in that 'happy' of the final line. Is history itself actually circular, rather than linear and progressive as we have been led to believe? 'History, with all her volumes vast, / Hath but *one* page', reflected Lord Byron towards the end of his melancholy epic poem *Childe Harold*, composed after the failure of the French Revolution:

> 'Tis but the same rehearsal of the past,
> First Freedom, and then Glory – when that fails,
> Wealth, vice, corruption, – barbarism at last.[35]

Each civilization or society is condemned to repeat the same pattern. And by extension, each revolution makes the same mistakes or is co-opted by the same conservative forces as the previous ones and falls into 'barbarism', leaving the people to seek their 'home' again in the comfort of the status quo.

According to the philosopher Walter Benjamin, history is not a Hegelian teleological progress towards utopia nor a neat coherent circle but a melancholy pile-up of wrack and ruin which is repeated endlessly. We do not have the vision to see this but the so-called Angel of History can do so. Here is Benjamin:

> A Klee painting named Angelus Novus shows an angel looking as though he is about to move away from something he is fixedly contemplating. His eyes are staring, his mouth is open, his wings are spread. This is how one pictures the angel of history. His face is turned toward the past. Where we perceive a chain of events, he sees one single catastrophe which keeps piling wreckage upon wreckage and hurls it in front of his feet. The angel would like to stay, awaken the dead, and make whole what has been smashed. But a storm is blowing from Paradise; it has got caught in his

wings with such violence that the angel can no longer close them. The storm irresistibly propels him into the future to which his back is turned, while the pile of debris before him grows skyward. This storm is what we call progress.[36]

The angel would like to 'awaken the dead' presumably to reverse wrong decisions that have been taken and to allow the lessons of history to be learned. But instead time keeps 'blowing' on, rushing humanity to make the same mistakes, to repeat similar catastrophes. Benjamin, who owned the painting 'Angelus Novus' by Klee, viewed history as disjointed, elegiac and non-linear, palpable to the historian at traumatic moments like clotted blood.

But for Slavoj Žižek, these piles of 'wreckage upon wreckage' are not confirmations of the melancholy ruins of history but, rather, paradoxical portents of better things to come or what he calls 'signs from the future'. Revolution will only happen when people truly suffer under oppression, when the situation becomes really intolerable, when there is an 'all-pervasive sense of blockage'. Is the counter-revolution which has followed the Arab Spring therefore necessary in order to provoke the far greater, deeper and long-lasting revolution to come? As Percy Bysshe Shelley wrote at the end of his revolutionary poetic drama *Prometheus Unbound*, freedom can only be brought about through wisely contemplating its threats and constraints:

> To suffer woes which Hope thinks infinite;
> To forgive wrongs darker than death or night;
> To defy Power, which seems omnipotent;
> To love, and bear; to hope till Hope creates
> From its own wreck the thing it contemplates.[37]

To do all these things, concludes Shelley, is to stand a chance of achieving a successful revolution. Writing in the wake of the French Revolution, the Terror and the re-imposition of the ancient regime in 1815, he was acutely aware of the brutalizing effect of oppression and the length of time it might take to recover from tyranny.[38] He was also wary of complacency, urging his readers to understand the fragility of hope and the precariousness of any appearance of freedom and justice. Revolution had to be paradoxically both apocalyptic and incremental, 'wreckage upon wreckage'. Karl Marx also pointed to an incremental state of progress in which the revolutionary vision was shaped by existing material conditions, influenced by the legacy of oppression and injustice. 'Men make their own history, but not just as they please', he wrote. 'They do not choose the circumstances for themselves, but have to work upon circumstances as they find them, have to fashion material handed down by the past.'[39] Freedom should be understood as recognizable and realizable within constraints. But Žižek's 'signs from the future' are to be thought of not as teleological but rapturous, disturbingly illegible, a 'jump into the unknown'. For him the brief, failed uprisings of 2011 were 'radical emancipatory outbursts' that can only be interpreted as 'limited, distorted (sometimes even perverted) fragments of a utopian future that lies dormant in the present as its hidden potential'.[40]

In thinking about these questions of history, tragedy and revolution, of course, one comes up against a crucial problem: When does an event come to an end? When does an event, indeed, become history, capable of interpretation? Hamid Dabashi's book or Marc Lynch's, published in 2012 in the first flush of revolutionary enthusiasm, gains an additional tragic poignancy now when read in the knowledge of subsequent events. But will the bleak resignation of Basma Abdel Aziz come across as equally short-sighted in the decades to come? Traditional tragedies produce a clear narrative pattern, with a beginning, middle and an end, as Aristotle stipulated. Unlike lived experience, they shape history into a linear arc so that it may become intelligible. And yet they often exceed that pattern, defying expectation and challenging the spectator to actively think about the arbitrary imposition of just these very narrative boundaries. 'Is this the promised end?', asks Kent at the close of *King Lear*, as the aged king staggers in with the dead Cordelia in his arms. 'Or image of that horror?', is the reply. The end is continually deferred, just as the desire for it grows.[41] And, to go back to *Julius Caesar*, the revolution of Brutus and Cassius ebbs and flows with a series of false starts and stops. This is not a conventionally coherent play but a drama of divided catastrophe in keeping with the messiness of history. The eponymous character dies at the beginning of Act 3; Cassius in the middle of Act 5 (5.3.45–6); Brutus two scenes later (5.5.51–2). And even while Antony and Octavius announce the return to order in the final lines, we know that civil war and the divisions of *Antony and Cleopatra* loom in the future.

Traditional tragic dramas thus impose endings of a sort and yet simultaneously make us acutely aware of the arbitrary nature of that sense of closure. We get an overview of the whole yet simultaneously feel the effects upon individuals as they occur. And in this sense, my task of writing *within* an event, uncertain whether the revolutionary event is over or still continuing, is similar. When do current affairs morph into history? How do we measure the success of a revolution and when do we measure it? Hannah Arendt acknowledged that 'all stories begun and enacted by men unfold their true meaning only when they have come to their end, so that it may indeed appear as though only the spectator, and not the agent, can hope to understand what actually happened in any given chain of deeds and events'.[42] But, just as she argued so forcefully that we should not be mere spectators but also active citizens, so I try to actively and attentively read the revolutions as both history and narrative, as an ongoing process and an archetypal tragic plot. Bridging these divisions involves thinking of the long connection between performance, politics and activism. It means both acting and spectating.

Protest as theatre, theatre as protest

One of the many criticisms that the 2011 uprisings incurred, particularly Occupy Wall Street, was that they did not know what they wanted. There was no simple demand, no clear-cut vision of an alternative future. They had no leaders. Typical of the critics was commentator Anne Applebaum who pointed out that the protesters in Zuccotti Park, New York, or outside St Paul's in London, by directly occupying central spaces rather than lobbying their senators or members of parliament, were – ironically – rejecting the conventional democratic, constitutional processes for which the crowds in Tahrir Square were calling.[43] There was nothing, she said, to unify them all; rather they seemed to be in direct contradiction with another.[44] Certainly many of the protesters were motivated by what was perceived to be the unjust response to the 2008 financial crisis, the bailout of the banks and the policy of austerity for everyone else, while others were concerned about the crisis of climate change. Gender, race and class were other motivating issues, as well as a general protest against inequality and frustration at not being heard. There was criticism of the way that corporations and big business had taken over elected government, with the insight that 'no true democracy is attainable when the process is determined by economic power'.[45] This was not one big movement organized along class lines, like resistance movements in the past, but rather a disparate collection of various political and social identities. Many of the protesters came from what has been termed *the precariat*, those whose lives are 'dominated by insecurity, uncertainty, debt and humiliation' and who 'knew what they were against but not yet quite what was wanted instead'.[46]

The loose coalition of people in Occupy was matched by a lack of leadership. Those in the movement spoke about the advantage of decentralization. Hydra-like, they were more challenging to pin down, more difficult to crush. By contrast, we might think of various tragic dramas of revolution, from *Julius Caesar*, to Buchner's *Danton's Death* to Ibsen's *Emperor and Galilean*, in which the individual flaws of the leaders of rebellion result in the failure of their original revolutionary aims.[47] Charismatic leaders stir the masses but then get enamoured of their charisma itself; rebellions which depend upon a few individuals falter when those individuals prove fallible. Instead, decisions in the Occupy camps were made by committee, and the connection between one camp and the next was loose and undefined. Contrary to the demands both from some of the protesters and from reporters and critics wanting to characterize the uprising, there was no slogan. Or if there were slogans, they were rather ones that drew attention to the process, rather than to the end goal: 'We are the 99%' or 'This is what democracy looks like.'

And it was the attention to the process that particularly marked the performative quality of the 2011 occupations. The uprisings in Zuccotti Park and elsewhere were improvised as they went along and became, as editor and activist Sarah van Gelder said, 'not just places to talk about a new society ... [but] twenty-four-hour-a-day experiments in egalitarian living'.[48] There were discussions about the organization of food, on recycling, on governance itself. Activists have written about the exploration of ways of reaching agreements, the 'direct, consensus-based democracy' in which decisions were reached by agreement and compromise, not by voting.[49] There were debates, too, on different forms of activism, the 'diversity of tactics' used, the interpretation of that vague phrase and the decentralized control over the very task of its interpretation. The 'human microphone', in which a speaker's words were repeated by those listeners sitting close to him or her in order to communicate them more widely to others further away, was initially necessitated by the lack of amplification equipment and New York's regulations prohibiting the use of conventional megaphones. But it became a source of reflection and protest in itself, particularly in its inclusive and ritualistic form. People had to listen carefully to the words of others, repeat them and effectively thus assent to them, and performatively give the impression of consensus. In other words, aspiration was collectively enacted in the ritual liturgy of the human mic. These aspects of daily living and self-organization became both microcosms of how society at large could organize itself, 'fragments of a utopian future' and performative ends in themselves.

As Lara Shalson has recently explored, there is a long-standing connection between theatre and protest.[50] Theatre has been used as a form to stage protest: think of *Antigone* rewritten by Anouilh during the Nazi occupation of France or adapted by Athol Fugard to protest apartheid in South Africa. And acts of protest and revolution in dramatic plays have self-referentially compared themselves to theatre. The conspirators in *Julius Caesar* memorably compare their assassination of Caesar to an anticipated future re-enactment. Cassius reflects:

> How many ages hence
> Shall this our lofty scene be acted over,
> In states unborn and accents yet unknown!

And Brutus chimes in:

> How many times shall Caesar bleed in sport,
> That now on Pompey's basis lies along,
> No worthier than the dust![51]

These remarks are made as the conspirators are ritually bathing their arms in Caesar's blood, staging a dramatic tableau of their violent act of 'sacrifice'. The comparison with an imagined future performance of the scene is made partly to elevate the action, to make it seem significant rather than 'no worthier than the dust'. But this comparison is made more complicated by the fact that Cassius and Brutus are indeed actors and this is a 'lofty scene' staged many centuries later in an 'accent yet unknown' in ancient Rome. The self-conscious lines thus acquire the opposite effect to the one Brutus and Cassius apparently intend. Rather than adding to the significance of the action, the theatrical metaphor encloses the activity within a claustrophobic, self-referential bubble. The revolution is no more than a performative game, staged for its own sake, narcissistic and self-regarding.

Sometimes, of course, protests draw on the work of theatre groups and performance artists rightly to attract attention. The Rev Billy and the Church of Stop Shopping – a parodic gospel service with Billy preaching against commercialism and multinational corporations – performed riotously at Occupy Wall Street. The uprising was carnivalesque in the fullest, Bakhtinian, subversive sense: playful, anarchic and rupturous at the same time. With the continual drumming and the collective exuberance, this was revolution as festival.[52] But it was also performative in the sense that Judith Butler and others use the term, namely that language and other forms of signification and representation actually make something happen. To name something is to bring it into being; to make some gesture is to enact something. So, in this sense, the uprisings or sit-downs in cities across the world should be thought of as revolutionary gestures in themselves. Appearing in city squares, collecting together and making themselves visible, the Occupiers were both symbolically and literally performing acts of resistance. Language became performatively scrutinized and destabilized, through its ironic use in a new context. The term 'Occupy', for example, became no longer the word for a colonial usurpation of land or (when in the form of 'occupation') about 'one's place in the machinery of capitalism' but an act of subverting such notions and forging new meanings.[53] Performing gestures, like chanting 'we are the 99%' or 'I am Trayvon' (in the context of Black Lives Matter), drew upon 'the affective and instructive power of embodying the speech and actions of others' as an important act of witness.[54] But beyond these words or performative acts, simply assembling in a public space is itself a powerful form of protest, independent of any specific demands.[55] To march is to enact, in literal and symbolic terms, the right to free movement; to hold a sit-in or to occupy a central square is conversely to assert the right not to be moved on, not to be discounted.

Determining how far a *performance* of resistance translates into an effective *politics* of resistance continues to challenge activists and critics alike. Do protest marches make any difference? Did the few months of occupation in New York and London and elsewhere really change anything? In traditional tragic dramas of rebellion, the symbolic gesture is often matched by real political or social rupture, even while its value is also interrogated. In Brecht's play *Mother Courage*, for example, Courage's cynical struggle for survival through an endless war is contrasted with the action of her daughter, Kattrin, at the end of the play. Aware that soldiers are about to attack a sleeping village at night and kill innocent children and other civilians, Kattrin climbs up onto the roof of a building and bangs a drum loudly to sound the alarm. She continues until she is shot by the soldiers but by then the village is awake and able to defend themselves. On the one hand, the significance of Kattrin's gesture is largely symbolic. Her determination to go on drumming until she is killed publicly stages an act of self-sacrifice for the principle of altruism and love, which cuts against the principle of self-interest which her Mother has advocated and demonstrated throughout the play. Another set of values is performed before us. Yet on the other hand, we hear the sounds of the village waking up, the town cannon firing. The drumming has an immediate effect and makes a visible, practical difference as well as a performative one. Having said this, however, Kattrin dies, and the Mother and the war continue. 'Wherever life has not died out / It staggers to its feet again', she sings.[56] The play asks how long-lasting Kattrin's awakening really was and how effective.

Similarly, the symbolic or literal significance of Antigone's 'burial' of her brother has attracted much critical debate. Antigone is supposedly motivated by the religious need to bury the dead. She needs literally to scatter earth over the corpse to prevent it being eaten by dogs and polluting the land. This physical necessity is of such importance that she has to bury the body a second time when she finds it has been cleared of the first scattering of earth she heaped over it. Yet on the other hand, it seems as if Antigone places more emphasis upon the symbolic gesture of burying the body than on its physical interment, since she shows no concern about the continuing fate of the corpse after her arrest. She focuses more upon her act of defiance, wanting her act 'shouted from the rooftops' and drawing attention to her acknowledgement of the deed in her debate with the ruler Creon.[57] The play explores symbolic action as a form of resistance, as an act of asserting sovereignty or – according to Bonnie Honig's recent radical interpretation – collective sisterhood and self-sacrificial love.[58] As with Kattrin, Antigone's gesture appears to end in failure. And yet ultimately, the act of resistance results in the toppling of Creon. Polyneices is buried and Creon becomes 'nothing', subject to the decisions of the chorus of citizens.

By contrast, the 'street theatre' of the Occupy movement concluded in the dismantling of the camps. The glimpse of an alternative world was over in a matter of months. What was performed was on the one hand the 'lifting of the veil' or some form of apocalyptic vision but on the other hand a representation of narcissistic futility. For Slavoj Žižek, this was a necessary rupture of the hegemonic ideology, a 'gesture [which] opens up the space for a new content'.[59] The protesters had an important right not to know what they wanted. They had the right not to convey a meaning beyond their occupation of the square. Their empty gesture of protest was somehow more liberating than a concrete set of demands, full of insight concerning the impasse of conventional politics. And the fact that nobody listened or changed anything simply indicated the enormity of what was demanded. 'Disappointment is part of any apocalypse', Nathan Schneider reflected. 'The fact that the most radical aspirations of Occupy Wall Street remain unrealized is also a symptom of success.'[60] But subsequent events place that lack of realization in a new context. Not only did the Occupy camps get evicted and the Arab Spring uprisings lose their momentum, but politics generally moved to the right, to harsher dictatorships and to greater division and inequality. One might say that the loss of solid political content in the Occupy carnivals and the freedom to interpret their message how one liked opened up a vacuum in which hard-right populism seized control, threatening democratic institutions and hard-won civil rights.

Rupture and populism

After Brutus and Cassius and the other conspirators have assassinated Caesar, they are for a period unsure how to reassure the people about their motivations and intentions or, in effect, how to spin the story. By contrast Antony, the master of guile and popular manipulation, grasps how to seize the moment and turn the revolution around to his perspective. His soliloquy, addressed to Caesar's dead body after the assassination, includes a startling image of the populace whipped up to demand the words he gives them:

> Over thy wounds now I do prophesy –
> Which like dumb mouths do ope their ruby lips
> To beg the voice and utterance of my tongue –
> A curse shall light upon the limbs of men …
> And Caesar's spirit, ranging for revenge,
> With Ate by his side come hot from hell,
> Shall in these confines, with a monarch's voice,
> Cry 'havoc!' and let slip the dogs of war,
> That this foul deed shall smell above the earth
> With carrion men, groaning for burial.[61]

Caesar's wounds are metaphorically compared to the ordinary people ('dumb mouths'), to whom Antony gives voice. And once called into being by Antony's address, they become like a savage, hunting pack of dogs, let loose in the 'confines' of both Rome and the theatre, the political stage (in both senses) and the bear-baiting pit on which the Globe was built, driven anarchically and paradoxically by a 'monarch's voice'. It's a strange, reciprocal partnership between the people and the strongman, but one that is a hallmark of populism. The consequences of Antony letting 'slip the dogs of war' is the lynching of the poet Cinna, killed because he shares the same name as one of the assassins. 'Pluck but his name out of his heart and turn him going' is the cry (3.3.33–4). In the violent lawlessness created by the assassination and the failure of Brutus and Cassius to take responsibility for the post-revolution government, the mob can be led to believe anything and to act on it ruthlessly.

While the 2011 revolutions might be characterized as uprisings broadly on the Left, their failure from 2012 onwards has ushered in an alternative revolution on the Right. We can see this phenomenon in the growing popularity of Marine Le Pen's National Front party in France, the Freedom Party in Austria and the AfD (Alternative für Deutschland) in Germany. It has emboldened Hungary's prime minister Viktor Orban, first elected in 2010, to instigate more extreme policies, publicly to question the notion of 'liberal democracy' and to describe his country as an 'illiberal state', a 'work-based society'.[62] Recep Tayyip Erdogan in Turkey, first elected president in 2014 and prior to that prime minister since 2003, has been strengthened by his (popular) defeat of an attempted coup in 2016 to push through changes to the constitution, shoring up his authoritarian rule, and to repress any voices of opposition ruthlessly. Meanwhile, Narendra Modi's election as India's prime minister in 2014 has ushered in a fearsome, extreme Hindu nationalist regime, which has resulted in the lynching and intimidation of non-Hindu minorities, urged on and legitimized by government legislation. All these political parties and nationalist leaders, who acknowledge common political ground between them as they congratulate each other on their election victories, follow similar campaigning strategies and address themselves to similar concerns and constituencies. They point to a failure of the metropolitan-based, political establishment, position themselves as the spokesmen of the 'people', appeal to a nationalist sense of pride and whip up fears about immigrants. The refugee crisis (which I'll discuss in the next chapter), which was caused first by the wars in Afghanistan and Iraq but then intensified by the civil war in Syria, has fuelled anxiety in Europe and America and been exploited by the revolutionary extreme Right to justify their intolerant views and divisive policies. Populism, the appeal to the ordinary people and disparagement of 'privileged elites', is sweeping across the developed and developing world, driving frightened and neglected electorates into the arms of demagogues and authoritarian 'strongmen'. The 'dogs of war' are barking in this new revolution.

But nowhere is the revolution felt more sharply, with repercussions for the rest of the world, than in the United States, following the election of Donald Trump to the presidency in November 2016. Appealing to some of the same constituency as those who had been drawn to the Occupy camps five years earlier, or those in whose name or cause the Occupiers had gathered, Trump promised to end inequality and overturn the whole established system. His anatomization of the disparities felt by many in the country, especially since the 2008 financial crash, appeared to have some common ground with the grievances of 2011.[63] He talked about bringing back employment in simple slogans that people would remember. 'Washington flourished but the people did not share in its wealth ... The forgotten men and women of our country will be forgotten no longer.'[64]

But remembering the 'forgotten men and women of our country' meant denigrating everyone else. It meant stoking feelings of hatred and dread, pumping up fear and suspicion. The rallying cry of 'Drain the swamp' was accompanied with scorn for 'Liberal elites', which included academic, political and media leaders, and any professional experts. Trump continued after his inauguration with further attacks on almost all groups apart from his core base of supporters, including government intelligence agencies, foreign allies and international organizations and alliances like the UN and NATO, the judiciary, scientists and the National Football League. He neglected and insulted African Americans, Muslims at home and abroad, women's advocacy groups. He cut funding for the environmental protection agency, for the arts, for birth control. The alt-right seized upon his election victory as a validation of their white supremacist, Nazi-sympathizing belief and Trump did nothing to condemn them or check their rising power. This was a revolution against the notion of civil society, against the established checks and balances of democracy, against the liberal, humanist values of tolerance, compassion and peaceful bipartisanship. It was a revolution, too, against truth. Dismissing any opposition or different accounts of events as 'fake news', Trump spins lies and contradictions, pitting his 'alternative facts' against hard evidence and the commonly agreed consensus. In the post-truth environment that he has helped to create, people can be led to believe anything and treat any alternative account as false. Justice, accountability and democracy itself become undermined in the turmoil of mendacity and emotional manipulation, focused around the egotism and sensitivity of one 'strongman'. The White House lurches from crisis to crisis on a continuous war-footing against its own American citizens; the establishment has been ruptured and continues to fight over the questions of authority, power and the law themselves.

In the summer of 2017, the Public Theatre of New York put on a production of *Julius Caesar* in Central Park. The depiction of a 'petulant, blondish Caesar in a blue suit and red tie, complete with gold bathtub and a pouty Slavic wife' was immediately recognized as a dramatization of Donald Trump.[65] The audience were going to watch their president being assassinated night after night, all summer. Predictably the right-wing media outlets and various Trump supporters were quick to criticize the production, with Fox News reporting that the play 'appears to depict President Trump being brutally stabbed by women and minorities'.[66] After the president's son chipped into the discussion, questioning the public funding of the theatre production, a couple of key sponsors pulled their financial support, thus of course paradoxically adding to the show's international publicity. Certainly, the production appealed to a broad constituency who felt powerless and fearful under the onslaught of Trump's attack on what they perceived were the safeguards of American democracy, law and institutions. Perhaps there was some vicarious pleasure to be gained in watching the violent overthrow of what the actor Gregg Henry, who played Caesar, described as a man 'drunk with ego, drunk with power, drunk with ambition and the belief that he and he alone should rule the world'. In dark times, people need some crumbs of hope, whether that is through the humorous release of satire or the subtle resonance of Shakespearean theatre.

But the production was more complex than that. After all, as we have discussed earlier, *Julius Caesar* is a play about a failed revolution and the conspirators are themselves defeated by a counter-revolution. The play's director, Oskar Eustis, wrote about the complicated political message of the play: '*Julius Caesar* can be read as a warning parable to those who try to fight democracy by undemocratic means. To fight the tyrant does not mean imitating him.' Indeed, another recent production of the play, directed by Nicholas Hytner at London's new Bridge Theatre, and more implicitly rather than explicitly about Trump, highlighted the complications of Brutus's and Cassius's insurrection and the flaws in their actions. They were too cerebral, impractical; too middle class. 'Political revolution is too serious a business to be left to a self-regarding elite out of touch with the popular will' was the appreciative comment of reviewer Michael Billington.[67]

Freedom, it seems, has a dark and dangerous side to it. It can lead to uncertainty, anarchy, excess and violence. It exposes the lack of security in utopia, the corruption of the self in self-rule. Its challenges and risks were well known to Shakespeare and to many post-French Revolution tragic playwrights (Byron, Shelley, Buchner).[68] Once a revolution has overturned the established constraints, then either the revolutionary forces themselves become tyrannical – the hubris of *arche*, as Vassilis Lambropoulos has put it – or the political vacuum is so terrifying that the people retreat to the reassuring safety and protection of the strongman.[69] Either scenario is inherently tragic, in the sense of hope containing within itself the seeds of its own destruction. As the Arab Spring has turned into an ever more turbulent Arab Winter and the Occupy movement has been overtaken by a divisive and fear-mongering populist usurpation of power in the White House, we bear witness to the corruption and perversion of revolution and the flight from 'hope' and 'change'. Our dangerous dreams have turned into nightmares. Only through keeping watch may we curve that arc back to hope.

6

Claiming Asylum

The picture shook the world. A three-year-old child, dressed in blue shorts, red t-shirt and black trainers, lying face down on a stony beach. Around his head, the Mediterranean surf eddying in and out. His hands, resting open but slightly curled, as if ready to grasp the hand of an adult. His face, slightly turned as if about to look out at the shore or appeal to a parent for reassurance. Alan Kurdi, for a few months the world's most famous toddler, drowned on the night of 2 September 2015 while trying to move with his family to a new life in Europe and ultimately Canada, away from the war in Syria and the harsh conditions of a refugee camp in Turkey.

Kurdi's family of four had been attempting to evade the Turkish coastguards and make the 30-minute crossing to the Greek island of Kos, having been unsuccessful in their application for visas to Canada a couple of months earlier. They had paid people traffickers a large sum to smuggle them, with twelve others, on a small rubber dinghy designed to carry a maximum of eight. Alan Kurdi's father found himself in charge of steering the boat, in the dark, after midnight. Within five minutes of launching, the boat capsized. Alan, his older brother and his mother drowned and their bodies were washed back to shore by the waves; his father, after struggling to save his family, survived. Nine of the other twelve refugees in the boat also died, their names unrecorded.

Alan Kurdi's death, at the end of the summer of 2015, was not an isolated or unusual occurrence. There were a staggering total of 3,771 migrant and refugee deaths in the Mediterranean that year, with 805 of them occurring in the eastern Mediterranean, in the narrow strait between Turkey and the Greek islands of Lesvos,

Kos, Chios and Samos. Overall, well over a million refugees arrived in Europe by sea in 2015, five times as many as there had been the previous year, mostly on overcrowded, unseaworthy vessels. Numbers peaked in the summer: 78,464 in July; 130,849 in August; 163,597 in September; 221,454 in October.[1] Nearly half the refugees came from Syria; the others originated from war-torn Afghanistan, Iraq, Somalia, Sudan, Eritrea. The sudden surge in numbers was primarily caused by the desperate situation in Syria: the civil war that the Arab Spring uprising had degenerated into and the rise of the violent extremist army known as ISIS, which the political vacuum in post-war Iraq had facilitated. By the summer of 2015, ISIS was at the height of its power, taking Palmyra, Al-Hasakah and Qaryatayn, and President Assad had increased military conscription. There were three million displaced Syrians living in neighbouring Lebanon, Jordan and Turkey. Unable to work according to their refugee status, they were dependent on handouts and food was scarce. Fleeing war, deprivation and persecution, and the political and economic hardship which was the consequence (indirect or direct) of Western military intervention in neighbouring Iraq a decade earlier, the refugees were drawn to a Europe which in 2015 seemed easier to access and more welcoming than ever. Macedonia had opened its border with Greece, allowing refugees to trek through the Balkans to the wealthier northern nations of Europe. The rules relating to the Dublin Agreement, namely that migrants must claim asylum in their first port of entry – and therefore in the poorest fringes of the continent – had been relaxed. And then in August, the German Chancellor Angela Merkel announced that Germany would take in and welcome refugees. 'If Europe fails on the question of refugees, then it won't be the Europe we wished for', she said. 'If we now have to start apologising for showing a friendly face in response to emergency situations, then that's not my country.'[2]

Of course, the so-called refugee crisis in 2015 was nothing new or unique to Europe. There had been many waves of forced migration before. The Tutsis and then the Hutus had streamed out of Rwanda in the mid-1990s. The Kosovan Albanians fled the southern parts of Serbia, now known as Kosovo, in the late 1990s, prompting an international military response. And, overshadowing the whole century was the persecution and migration of the Jews from Central Europe in the 1930s and 1940s.

In recent years, huge numbers of migrants have been crossing dangerous waters to Europe from North Africa, landing at the Canary Islands, Malta, Italy. Indeed, the island of Lampedusa, 70 miles south of Sicily and close to the coast of Tunisia, has been termed the 'tragic epicentre' of the refugee crisis. The civil war in Libya in 2011, exacerbated by Western military intervention, only increased the flow of refugees and migrants across that Mediterranean strait, since people traffickers flourished in the post-war turmoil and political anarchy in the region. Worldwide, the total number of displaced people reached a staggering 65.3 million, according to the United Nations, a 5.8 million increase on the previous year. There were migrations across the Mexican-US border, escapes into Cameroon from Boko Haram in Nigeria and flights into Uganda from war mainly in South Sudan, but also the Congo, Burundi, Somalia and Rwanda. The countries taking in the largest number of refugees were not actually in Europe or northern America at all but in Asia, the Middle East and Africa: Turkey, 2.9 million; Pakistan, 1.4 million; Lebanon, 1 million; Iran, nearly 1 million; Uganda, 940,800.

Nevertheless, it was the situation in Europe which dominated global news in 2015. The so-called War on Terror and its consequences, in Libya, Iraq and Syria as well as in Afghanistan, produced the greatest forced migration of peoples in Europe since the Second World War, peaking in the summer and autumn of 2015. Lines of people, as far as the eye could see, trudged across Europe through fields and rivers and anything else in their path. When one border closed, with razor wire fences, the migration route would divert through another country. Camps, filled well beyond their original capacity, would be closed down or relocated, only for crowds to gather in railway stations, beside the tracks, beneath bridges. The so-called 'Jungle' camp at Calais, where migrants and refugees collected with the hope of crossing the border channel to the UK, held over 6,000 people by the end of 2015 in terrible, unsanitary conditions. Every day thousands would attempt to smuggle their way past the tough security fences, stowing away in trucks as they waited at the border, stopping vehicles and storming onto lorries, trying to run clandestinely the thirty miles of the tunnel, with sometimes fatal results. And still the leaky boats would come in to Greece and Italy, night after night, relentless in their appeal for help.

Watching this collective act of supplication on a mass scale, reporters found themselves resorting to ancient terms to describe the scene. The exodus was 'biblical'. The capsized boats and drowned families off the island of Lesvos were a 'Greek tragedy'. The 'Jungle' camp at Calais hinted at some more atavistic fears, a projection of primitivism and savagery. It was clear that aid agencies and journalists were struggling to describe the overwhelming nature of the situation, the desperation of the people, the sheer scale of the numbers. Literature, narrative, mythology and tragedy were needed to rise up to the descriptive task and do justice to the phenomenon.

Supplication – the ritual act of appealing humbly for help – in fact lies at the core of Western literature from its earliest beginnings. It is there at the beginning and the end of Homer's *Iliad*. Achilles' mother, the goddess Thetis, kick-starts the epic by begging Zeus to redress the insult her son has suffered and make the Greeks appreciate him. Priam, the king of Troy, ventures to the enemy Achilles' tent as a suppliant at the end of the epic to ask for the body of his dead son Hector to be returned. Supplication is there also in some of the earliest Greek tragedies: Aeschylus's *Suppliant Women*, first performed around 460 BC, where fifty Egyptian women claim asylum in Argos, Greece; Sophocles' *Oedipus at Colonus*, in which the aged, blind, exiled king of Thebes seeks sanctuary in Athens; Euripides' *Suppliant Women*, in which the Argive mothers of warriors killed in war against Thebes beg the Athenians to intervene on their behalf to force the Thebans to return the dead bodies for burial. And, of course, it's there in the biblical story of Exodus, where Moses begs the king of Egypt to let his people go back to the Promised Land, and he leads them through trial, hardship and hostile pursuit to the land supposedly of their ancestors. Significantly, however, that biblical story might begin with supplication and precarious wandering through the wilderness but it concludes with invasion and battle. 'God's people', led this time by Joshua, following the death of Moses, conquer the local inhabitants and take the land of Canaan by force.

In many of these examples, we can see the development of the rules and rituals of supplication and sanctuary, as well as their violation. On an individual basis, the suppliant must touch the feet, knees or chin of the powerful person supplicated, penetrating symbolically – it is thought – to the most vulnerable and closely guarded core of the other and therefore either appealing to what is most liable to compassion or making 'symbolically aggressive, yet unhurtful, contact with what the supplicated most seeks to protect'.[3] So Thetis in *Iliad 1* sat in front of Zeus and 'clasped his knees / with her left hand, and with her right took hold of him beneath his chin'.[4] She does not let go until he has agreed to her request. On a collective basis, suppliants carry olive branches, sometimes wrapped with white wool, signs of their peaceful intention of supplication (the origin of our white flags of surrender?), and they rest in a sacred space of sanctuary, within a temple, beside an altar, within a holy boundary line which ensures their inviolate state. Suppliants bear with them, in equal measure, an abject appeal for compassion and assistance and a veiled threat, often self-destructive, if they are turned away. So, in *Oedipus at Colonus*, the body of the king will bring a blessing to the city that gives him sanctuary and a curse to the city that sends him away. There is, in this ancient tradition of supplication, a combined force of desperation and certainty, an open demonstration of their utter precariousness together, paradoxically, with the god-inspired sense of entitlement in their new world.

Humans are and have always been migratory. The history of civilization is a story of trade and exploration, voyaging and emigration, displacement and exile, and the cross-fertilization of ideas and progress that can arise from this. After all, the origin myth of Europe itself is one of migration and flight. The young princess Europa, playing on the shore of Phoenicia (modern-day Lebanon and Syria) with her friends and gathering flowers, was seduced by Zeus disguised as a white bull. Tossing the young girl on his back, he carried her off over the sea to Crete, where she gave birth to the Minoan dynasty and indirectly to the whole continent. This in itself was but a shadowy iteration of that earlier violated woman and cattle myth, the story of Io, transformed into a cow by the goddess Hera and driven out of Greece across the known world, through Asia, the Caucasus and the Middle East, to finish in Egypt, still pursued by Zeus's desire and now impregnated by his touch to produce the future race of Egyptians. Europa was her great-granddaughter; her flight to Greece, then, a mythical right to return. Ebbing and flowing from Greece to Egypt, the Middle East and North Africa, and crossing the species boundary between human and animal, the Greek myths thought through the complex origins of their civilization.

So, in this respect, we are all migrants. The refugees are just like us, and could indeed have been us if circumstances had been different, if what the artist Ai Weiwei has called the 'human flow' had gone from north to south, from west to east, instead of the other way.[5] Our response, therefore, should recall the Aristotelian classic response of pity and fear (*eleos* and *phobos*), namely that 'pity is felt towards one whose affliction is undeserved, fear towards one who is like ourselves'.[6] Yet often the refugees are feared not in the Aristotelian sense of connection with our own precarity ('one who is like ourselves') but rather as threatening aliens, invading our carefully guarded culture and destabilizing peace and order. On the surface, they disturb the assumptions of Western society, its assurance of continued prosperity and secure sense of identity and belonging. On a deeper, scarcely acknowledged level, they trouble us as a reminder of where we have come from and the havoc we have sown and would rather forget. The decisions that had to be made quickly amid the real crisis in 2015, eliciting a complicated tangle of feelings, of pity, fear, bewilderment and denial, recall, in their urgency and ethical difficulty, the classic tragic dilemmas and dramas that have confronted us for centuries.

Performing the community

O Zeus
God of sanctuary grant us asylum
We are women of Egypt
Neighbours of Syria,
Who dug our toes into the soft sand
At the mouth of the Nile,
And pushed our boat into the sea, to flee.[7]

Aeschylus's chorus, supposedly of fifty Egyptian women, arrive at the Greek seashore, seeking sanctuary at the temple of Zeus, determined, defiant and desperate. They have escaped their homes by the Nile and a forced marriage to their cousins, led and encouraged somewhat paradoxically by their father. The reason for their fear of this marriage is unclear: Is it the inter-familial violation of taboo, cousin to cousin? Is it the rapacious intentions behind it? Is it marriage as an institution and a hatred of all men in general? The confusion accurately speaks to the trauma behind the refugee experience, the conflation of causes reflecting the frequent impossibility of disentangling the personal from the political, economic desperation from military threats. No matter what exactly triggers their flight, the women claim asylum based on a distant kinship connection with Argos; they are sixth generation descendants of Io, the Greek-born woman turned cow who was driven from Argos by Zeus's violent desire and Hera's jealousy. The king of Argos, Pelasgus, after much debate, consultation and threats of various kinds, resolves to protect them. This decision is immediately tested when the fifty cousins arrive to drag the women back to Egypt. But Pelasgus stands up to them and the play concludes with the women safe, for now, and invited to take up residence in the city.

The tragic dilemma of Pelasgus, the king of Argos, arises in part from the tension between the women's strangeness and their alleged kinship. They look different. They are dressed according to foreign custom, in supposedly luxurious, un-Hellenic clothes, and they are dark, like the women of Libya. Their bold manner is more like the Amazons, 'with no husbands, hunting freely / For the pot, catching meat', according to Pelasgus.[8] They do not understand some of the contemporary Greek customs such as democracy and the politics of the state or how decisions are made and guaranteed. Yet they claim to be 'Argive women', descended from Io, and therefore related to Pelasgus. And they know very well the Greek laws and customs regarding sanctuary, which appear to have been adopted as universal. The tension between their Hellenic and un-Hellenic nature captivates and terrifies Pelasgus:

Held in their left hand, suppliant branches.
At least that's Greek. At least there's that.
Who are these women? These strange women.
I could stare all day. Do you think they can speak?[9]

Of course, when the women do speak (fluent Greek, on which more later), they appeal to the notion of αἰδώς (*aidos*), a sense of shame or honour. Zeus is *aidoios* (regarded with respect or reverence: line 192); the women's words are *aidoia* (commanding respect or modestly respecting others: 194); Pelasgus is enjoined to respect or *aidou* the symbolic garlanding of the gods' statues with suppliant branches in the temple (line 345). The terrifying force of *aidos* permeates the drama, whether it is an ethic to be adopted oneself, a common virtue to be shared or an injunction demanded of others. For as the classical scholar John Gould explained, αἰδοιος can mean both feeling shame oneself and also causing another to feel shame. The power dynamics involved are complicated, fluid and ambiguous. 'It seems plausible to suggest that here we have a member of that not inconsiderable class of Greek words where reciprocity of usage implies reciprocity of behaviour and attitude', he commented.[10] The Greek language includes various examples of these strange, paradoxical words. Ξενος (*Zenos*) means both stranger and guest, the doubling of the meaning suggesting the liminal boundary between unfamiliarity and familiarity which is breached by the act of hospitality. Φαρμακος (*Pharmakos*) means both poison and cure, again charting the ambiguity between harm and benefit, and the uncanny connection between the two notions. So αἰδως (*aidos*) means feeling shame and also feeling respect, as well as causing another to feel shame, respect and reverence for oneself and general modesty and compassion. The term suggests a hierarchy of power: the weaker party shows suitable respect or *aidos* for the stronger, while the stronger shows mercy and self-restraint or *aidos* for the weaker. But it also acts as a leveller since all parties are governed by an overall principle of *aidos* or shame before any of the rules and codes of behaviour are violated. Zeus polices these rules, the god of supplication, Zeus ἱκετης (*hiketes*). He is the source of succour and reciprocal respect, which is, of course, given additional irony in this play by the fact that he was also the scourge of Io and the cause of her original flight from Argos to Egypt.[11] Zeus drove her out by his passions and now he prevails over the welcome shown to her returning descendants.

It is against this background of shame, honour and respect that the suppliant women mount their ultimate threat if their plea for asylum is not accepted. They will kill themselves by hanging their bodies from the statues of the gods in the temple. Pelasgus is understandably terrified at the prospect.

Horror, horror, now like a wave
Sweeps me away to a bottomless ocean.
If you die here like that, the name of this city
Will be spoken in whispers of shame forever.
Suicide, the worst stain. We'll never be clean.[12]

The Greeks frequently drew on metaphors of the sea to describe the overwhelming nature of ruin and disaster, so in that sense Pelasgus's speech is not unusual. But here, given the fact that the women have just survived a dangerous sea crossing to Greece and are calling upon the reciprocal force of *aidos* to make their case, his words are striking. Overcome by the terror of not respecting the suppliant and incurring the 'stain' or literally, in the Greek, the μίασμα (*miasma*: pollution) of their deaths under his watch, Pelasgus appears to have taken on their experience, to have become a helpless suppliant himself, swept away to 'a bottomless ocean'.[13] The women have succeeded in wresting power back to themselves through the dramatic impact of their bodies and their vestiges of agency; they have the moral upper hand and Pelasgus is undone by his susceptibility to *aidos*, or reverence to what is right.

So, the king appeals to his people to make the decision about what should be done with the suppliant women. As he puts it starkly, there will be costs whichever option is taken. If he does not give the women asylum, they will kill themselves and the city will be polluted with the dishonour. If he does offer them asylum, the Egyptians will wage war upon his city and Greek lives will be lost. How much are the Greeks prepared to sacrifice to save the lives of fifty women? Though a king, Pelasgus puts the decision to the assembly of the city and the people vote by raising their right hands. To coin a phrase from the Occupy movement, 'this is what democracy looks like' and the Egyptian women's father, Danaus, has to explain the process to them. The decision-making follows closely the contemporary practices of Athens' fledgling democracy in the fifth century BC, with each man accorded one vote. Some other descriptions in Greek literature of the voting procedure in the assembly were far from positive, most notably the critical account given by the messenger in Euripides' *Suppliant Women*, where a demagogue 'finds favour by his gross flattery' and twists the city 'this way and that for his private gain' and one might wonder 'how could the common people correctly govern a city when they can't even correctly assess a speech?'.[14] By 423 BC, when Euripides' play was first performed, the dangers of populism were starting to be experienced. But forty years earlier when Aeschylus was composing his play, the prospects for democracy and particularly the process of collective decision-making, and the ordinary citizen's capacity to think and choose options wisely, were very optimistic. Consequently, in Aeschylus's play, the people vote to protect the asylum seekers, even if that will bring about hard repercussions. So, the women are given the status of μετοικοι (*metics*), resident aliens, and afforded certain rights and security. They are given accommodation, a living, and the reassurance that if anyone tries to evict them or drag them back to their original nation, he will be punished.[15] The women are thus assimilated into Argos and protected by the king when their kinsmen (described repeatedly as filled with *hubris*, the direct opposite of *aidos*) arrive to seize them violently and force them back to Egypt. Through this challenging process, they now form part of the community of Argos.

It was with the intention of exploring the nature of community, which is thrown into question by the refugee crisis, that the touring production of *The Suppliant Women*, in a version by David Greig, was initiated. Drawing its chorus from the local community in each city on the tour (Edinburgh, Belfast, Newcastle, Manchester, Dublin, London and Hong Kong), the director and professional creative team trained them up over a two-month preparation period prior to performance. The purpose was in part to recreate the historical conditions of Greek dramatic performance. In ancient Greece, the chorus was made up of ordinary citizens, determined by lot, undertaking their civic duty by participating in theatrical performance, rather as we might undertake jury duty today. They would be trained by a professional *choregos*, or chorus master, as the Actors Touring Company production did. The production also followed ancient traditions by inviting an important leader in the community (a member of Southwark council when I was in the audience in London in November 2017) to give thanks to the sponsors before the play began and to pour out a libation to the god Dionysus: wine across the front of the stage.[16] But the historical accuracy was sought in order to think about the connections and disconnections between antiquity and now. As the director Ramin Gray noted, 'the Athenians invented theatre and democracy in the same breath'. The intention behind the production was to find, in a play which dramatized the celebration of reciprocal *aidos* through a collective, civic process, the means of reflecting upon and reasserting the importance of community today. 'Given the current crisis of faith in our democratic institutions, in elections and referenda in particular, it's salutary to revisit the moment when these ideas were conceived and in the simplest ways to start to renew our commitment to being together in a shared, civic space.'[17]

Theatre is both a performance and a renewing, healing ritual, a political or ethical response to the καταστροφη of our times.[18] The Actors Touring Company production showed us the connection between them and us, the suppliant and the supplicated, that is and should be at the core of the refugee crisis. Indeed, blurring the boundaries between the precarious and the settled even further, they divided the volunteer chorus into three, so that the community also played the Egyptian pursuers and the local Argive inhabitants who welcome in the suppliant women at the end as well. The divisions between insiders and outsiders, the entitled and not entitled, were explored and tested during the 90-minute performance, as fluidly as the choreographed twists and turns of the chorus across the stage. This was part theatre and part ritual, undertaken with such passion and commitment by the community chorus that a few were in tears by the end, as they took their bow.

A comparison could be made with the production of *Trojan Women* in Jordan in late 2013. Working with Syrian refugee women living in the capital Amman, the director Omar Abu Saada and co-producers Charlotte Eager, Hal Scardino and Itab Azzam workshopped Euripides' tragedy set in post-conflict Troy depicting the women waiting to be shipped off to their new lives as slaves in cities scattered across Greece. Euripides' play explores the anxiety of waiting and the dread of what is to come, as well as the abjection of defeat and exile and the terrors of being severed from one's community. The Syrian project was designed to help in the healing, therapy process for the participating women as well as raising awareness of the refugee experience for outsiders. The women incorporated their own stories of war into the drama.[19] Developed in time into the adapted play 'Queens of Syria', the production toured the UK in 2016, performing in London, Liverpool and Edinburgh. One of the actors, Khaula, explained the benefits and purpose of participating in the production: 'We came to a new society and we were isolated. Doing the play made us break the ice and we started to connect with others and make some friends. It gave us the courage to talk about our problems frankly and clearly.'[20]

These two productions, *Queens of Syria* and *Suppliant Women*, clearly had many differences. In one production, the cast had direct experience of war, exile and the precarious existence of the refugee. The other production included a diverse cast from each local city, whose experience of privilege or vulnerability no doubt varied widely but who were living in the relatively safe and settled environment of Britain. The women's performance of supplication was based upon empathetic imagination for the plight of the desperate, rather than intimate familiarity. So these two productions raise the question of the relationship between an actor and what is being performed. Is theatre-making performance or ritual? And by extension, who has the right to speak for the oppressed and the traumatized, the most marginal and voiceless in our society? Ramin Gray's production was notable in its commitment to the community and the principle of the concerned citizen, regardless of experience or any individual's direct, personal connection to catastrophe. This is a crisis that implicates us all was the message. We must confront it and think seriously about it as a community.

Awareness or alertness

There are limits, however, to the healing capacities of theatre, nor indeed can a sense of community and connectedness to others be enforced. The tragedy of the refugee crisis is much more complicated. How are decisions to be taken? How is the community to be defined and how can it be integrated? What is the extent of collective sympathy, the *aidos* or respect and compassion for others?

The film critic A. O. Scott raised these kinds of questions about the ethics of watching the arrival of refugees and migrants nightly on the shores of Europe:

> There is a type of documentary – one of the most prevalent varieties these days – that earnestly acquaints its audience with a terrible problem and rewards our attention with a gold star of virtue. You know the kind of film I mean. We are presented with a tableau of human misery or global catastrophe that has

been put together with the vague but unarguably noble intention of 'raising awareness,' as if such awareness were itself a kind of solution.[21]

Instead of this 'earnest' type of documentary which prides itself on 'raising awareness', Scott was drawing attention to the work of Italian documentary film-maker Gianfranco Rosi, who had made a film about the Italian island of Lampedusa which, along with Sicily, has received nearly half a million migrants since 2014. The crossing there is the most dangerous of any migrant route in the world, accounting for 88 per cent of all migrant deaths in the Mediterranean. The situation is grim, then, and Rosi, according to Scott, did justice to this:

> I'm not sure that Mr. Rosi is interested in trafficking in hope,which is among his great virtues as a filmmaker. He takes a hard, empathetic look at reality, which contains wonders as well as horrors. He doesn't bear witness – an overused and often presumptuous idea. He observes, with humility and precision. Instead of raising awareness, he cultivates alertness.

What is the distinction here between 'awareness' and 'alertness'? The film that prompted A. O. Scott's reflections was *Fire at Sea*, a documentary, lasting just under two hours, charting the life in a little fishing community on Lampedusa. Each night the Italian coastguard keeps watch, regularly receiving distress calls from overcrowded, sinking boats at sea. The film shows rescue operations, refugees lifted from the boat suffering from dehydration, hunger and shock. Bodies are retrieved and, already tied into bags, lowered carefully into the navy rescue ship. One particularly harrowing shot reveals dead bodies and ordinary debris mingled together in the hold. The men and women in the coastguard work apparently dispassionately and efficiently, dressed in hazmat suits and checking each migrant without conversation or gestures of communication, allocating them shiny gold foil blankets against hypothermia, which add to the strange mechanization of the encounter. The one source of compassion is located in the island's doctor, who is shown conducting a scan for a newly rescued refugee woman pregnant with twins. He describes the injuries he encounters among the fatalities, the burns from fuel oil that spills across the overcrowded hold in rough sea, and confesses that he is haunted by his experience of examining and treating these victims at night in his dreams. 'It makes you think, dream about them. These are the nightmares I relive often, often', he says.

Meanwhile, however, the emotional heart of the film is found in the daily life of a twelve-year-old boy, Samuele Pucillo, who spends his time making and testing out his slingshot, learning how to row a boat and playing pretend soldiers with guns with his friends. He is apparently oblivious to the nightly tragedy of the refugees. He goes out after dark not to watch out for a struggling boat but to find a small bird singing in the bush, even as another villager, also disconnected from the migrant crisis, sets out to dive for sea urchins. The two worlds, the world of the islanders and the world of the refugees and their rescuers, do not connect in the film, but there are undertones of anxiety and melancholy. Samuele confesses to the doctor that he suffers from shortness of breath and a sense of panic, unusual for someone so young. He becomes very seasick when out on a boat with his fisherman father. He needs to practise spending time on the pontoon in the harbour to get his sea legs, his father advises. His grandmother listens to the radio while she is preparing dinner and sighs briefly ('Poor souls') when she hears a report of another case of migrants drowning. The radio DJ looks reflectively into the distance as he plays a requested record, the old song 'Fire at Sea', about the bombing of an Italian warship in the port of Lampedusa. And the skin-diver explores in the dark sea, uncertain what he will find.

The film thus reveals the disconnection between the two worlds and yet latent points of connection and comparison. We see the limits of our capacity to take notice and the different ways in which we are and are not affected by tragedy. The islanders are given names and individual stories; the refugees are merely faces, bodies to be processed. And thus the viewer becomes more emotionally caught up in the lives of the islanders than in those of the refugees. We feel horror at the scenes involving the migrant boats, but we feel a warm compassion when we see Samuele's somewhat lonely effort to grow up in the small fishing community. And so, to go back to Scott's distinctions, do we become 'alert' in the film to the islanders' lack of awareness and by extension to our own? Is non-empathetic 'alertness', rather as practised by the coastguard, more effective than sentimental empathy?

The ambiguous complications of 'alertness' to the refugee crisis are highlighted also in Richard Mosse's award-winning photographic and video works, *Heat Maps* and *Incoming*. Using an infrared thermal surveillance camera designed to detect body heat from a distance of over 30 kilometres, Mosse photographed and filmed refugees arriving in boats or being processed on the shore by the coastguard. He trained the camera on the huge refugee camps at Idomeni in northern Greece or Tempelhof in Berlin, capturing figures waiting in line for food or lying in their shelters or wandering amid the garbage, watched by the guards. Humans appear as black-and-white inverted silhouettes, their faces erased of definition but their gestures, touching their face or reaching out to others, recognizably familiar and intimate. Parents help children, women stoop with exhaustion, guards watch the horizon through binoculars. The camera picks up everything from a great distance with scientific precision and neutrality, detecting humans as heat traces through walls and tent canvases, leaving nowhere to hide. It makes no distinction between migrant and local inhabitant with its de-individualizing, heat-seeking mechanism, other than the fact that the officials wear protective clothing to shield them from the many hazards and the migrants do not. The figures are thus both de-naturalized and yet restored to the essential human vitality which we all share, their hot breath in and out and their beating hearts. As Mosse himself has commented: 'All that's left to them is the biological fact of their birth – a thing foregrounded by the camera, which depicts the human body as a radiant glow of biochemical processes such as respiration, energy production, hypothermia and warmth.'[22]

Mosse's images – which are very large and visually overwhelming – are unsettling.[23] What exactly are we seeing? And with whose gaze? The infrared technology is originally designed for military surveillance and can be connected to missiles. This is a 'weapon of war', in fact already classified as a weapon by the International Traffic in Arms Regulations. The mechanical gaze upon the refugee boats or the internment camps puts the viewer potentially with the defensive guards who police our borders. Yet the technology is rigged up to a camera, not a missile, and these figures are shot in a photograph, not targeted in aggressive fear. Mosse has described the power of 'using technology against itself'. Through the surreal, disorientating, inverted images he produces, we see the scenes of migrants (familiar from news footage) again in a novel way. And we see ourselves seeing this material. We become 'alert' to the act of looking. We look afresh, disturbingly, at the spectral misery normally unattended to at the borders of our daily consciousness.

Egyptian tears in Ionian strains

Although Richard Mosse's pictures were awarded the Pictet Prize for Photography and attracted much admiration and praise, they have also drawn criticism. For a start, the norms of conventional photojournalism are absent in that the camera shoots from such a distance away. The people are unaware that they are being filmed – they do not give their consent. This has implications for issues of power and agency. As one critic has observed, 'The camera operates as any device under power; it provides an advantage that increases the visibility of its object, while removing its own capacity to be seen.'[24] But more specifically, Mosse's work is considered by some critics to turn suffering into spectacle, to exploit the desperate plight of refugees for a work of art that finishes up on a gallery wall. The videos, in particular, which slowed the film down from 60 frames a second to 24, paradoxically lent the grim or harrowing scene a lyrical beauty.

But in drawing attention to the controversial border between ethical attention and aesthetic appreciation, Mosse is situated within an age-old tradition. Tragedy historically thinks about what form it will convey its suffering in or what medium will best shape and communicate the pain. When Aeschylus's suppliant women arrive at Argos, singing their opening choral song of lament and appeal, they acknowledge the metrical prosody they must adopt in order to draw their audience's attention. 'Indulging my sorrow in Ionian musical strains, I tear at my soft cheek warmed by the Nile's sun and my endlessly weeping heart.'[25] The devastating, almost uncontainable grief is Egyptian (Νειλοθερῆ: *Nilothere*, meaning fostered by the Nile or nurtured by the Nile's summer – the Greek word is ambiguous here). But the medium is Greek (Ionian) and pleasingly musical. 'I am picking flowers of lamentation in fearful hope', the women continue, persisting in this aestheticization of their misery for instrumental effect. These suppliants are participating in an act of translation. On a literal level, of course, they are speaking and singing fluent Greek; there is no sense that they have linguistic difficulties of communication. On a cultural level, they must transform Egyptian customs of grief – tearing the cheek or beating the chest excessively – into recognizable Greek customs, adapting to a new life even as they disembark upon the shore. But they also have to convert their feelings to a new medium, to the act of tragic performance which involves drawing attention self-consciously to that process of conversion itself.

> Such piteous suffering I have
> To tell and wail, shrill, heavy, all falling tears!
> Cry grief![26]

Suffering that is wailed: the much more cryptic and effective two words in the Greek – πάθεα μέλεα (*pathea melea*) – can be literally translated as suffering songs or musical sung calamities.[27] This oxymoron, which nevertheless is the traffic of tragedy, cuts to the heart of a viewing audience.

There is a dark paradox, then, when the most abject suffering turns out to be somehow staged or performed in order to communicate itself to us. The suppliant women of Aeschylus do this knowingly, singing their Egyptian grief in Ionian measures. And this happens too in one of the grimmest and greatest dramatic portrayals of displacement and homelessness, *King Lear*. The king has been driven out of his palaces by what he considers is the harsh treatment at the hands of his daughters, who 'reason ... the need' for the symbolic trappings of his kingly identity and plan to strip him of all his retinue.[28] Unhoused literally and spiritually, the king is abandoned to wander the wilderness through a night of terrible storms. At the height of his despair, he comes across a naked, apparently mad, homeless wretch, shivering with cold, who describes himself as 'poor Tom' and has – so he says – been led by a fiend through fire, flame, ford and whirlpool. Lear is transfixed by this vision. 'Is man no more than this?', he cries. 'Thou art the thing itself: unaccommodated man is no more but such a poor, bare, forked animal' (3.4.98–100). The king uses this revelation as a prompt for reflecting upon the savagery at the heart of civilization ('the thing itself'), the beating, unadorned essence of a human being. All the rest of civilization is an 'originary fiction', as the philosopher Giorgio Agamben might say, masking and also shaping the 'bare life' which is foundational for our culture.[29] But the answer to Lear's question 'Is man no more than this?' is actually – yes, he is. For 'poor Tom' is more than he appears. This is really Edgar disguised as a wandering madman, *performing* the role of 'poor Tom'. Indeed, poor Tom is both more and less than he appears: more in that he is far from demonically insane and has qualities of cold calculation and warm compassion in equal measure; less because the motivation for his disguise, or at least its excessive abjectness, is somewhat enigmatic and withheld from the audience.[30] So the 'bareness' of the displaced man turns out to be much more complex in its 'bareness' than at first appears. This is 'bare life' produced by the provocations and projections of courtly intrigue and the power of the state.

On seeing the poor, 'bare' Tom and expressing his profound insight or 'physic' about the basic essence of man, the half-demented Lear famously strips off his clothes, his 'lendings', to join him in poverty and simplicity. This will, he thinks, allow him to understand the suffering of all the abject naked wretches who wander the heath without shelter or asylum. 'Expose thyself to feel what wretches feel', he roars above the storm (3.4.35). The implication is that this radical empathy must paradoxically be cultivated. Both Lear and Edgar have by this stage deliberately undressed and taken on the roles of refugees, driven across the heath seeking shelter. Compassion, in *Lear* at least, is stirred up by the fictional and sentimental performance of utter helplessness.

And so back to the heart-breaking photo of little Alan Kurdi in Bodrum, Turkey, in September 2015. Why did that photo affect the general public around the world in a way that all the other images and reports about the refugees did not? Just about a week before Alan Kurdi's death, another terrible story about migrants hit the news. An abandoned truck had been found at the side of a highway in Austria, filled with the decomposing bodies of seventy-one refugees (from Iraqi Kurdistan, Afghanistan and Syria). At first people had assumed that the refrigerated meat truck, with the slogan 'Honest chicken' on the side, must have broken down or been involved in an accident. But then they noticed blood and other bodily fluids seeping out of the back of the lorry. The bodies of the victims were already so badly decomposed and tightly packed together that it was impossible to identity them all. The international reaction was one of shock and horror, but also one of disgust. Here was no *pathea mathea*, but dishonest chicken, human lives as cheap and disregarded as processed meat. The pictures in the newspapers were of the lorry; there were no images of its victims.

But Alan Kurdi had the individualizing, tender gaze of Turkish photographer Nilüfur Demir's lens. In a couple of her images, the toddler's body was carried gently up the beach by the Turkish aid worker. In the most iconic, he was alone, the soles of his trainers upturned to the viewer. And the arresting poignancy of the image was paradoxically so beautiful and well-composed that it had an impact. Mainstream newspapers published it. And governments took notice. The British prime minister announced that the country would accept 20,000 Syrian refugees over five years (although paradoxically taking and resettling the ones that had stayed put near Syria, in the refugee camps just over the border, while not accepting the ones who, like Alan Kurdi's family, had risked their lives to come across to Europe). France agreed to take 24,000 over two years. Canada, under a new prime minister, began to take in 25,000 refugees. The term 'migrant' started to be replaced with the word 'refugee', reflecting a change in public attitudes and understanding. There was a new wave of compassion for refugees, prompted by the sentimental photo of a little child. You could say, it marked the beginning of an era of *aidos*.

The lost plays of the trilogy

But the *aidos* was short-lived. In summer 2015 Hungary had begun constructing a 4-metre-high fence along its borders with Serbia and Croatia, thus stemming and diverting the stream of refugees across the continent. Macedonia followed suit, erecting a barrier along the border with Greece in November 2015, and Slovenia began a similar razor-wire barrier on its border with Croatia. Hungary – along with the Czech Republic, Poland, Romania and Slovakia – blocked the EU proposal for a compulsory redistribution of migrants among member states according to relative economic prosperity.[31] And then a shocking night of terrorist attacks occurred in Paris on 13 November, in various bars and cafes and notably the Bataclan nightclub, with the loss of 130 lives. Refugees were quickly and unjustifiably blamed.[32] Marine Le Pen, the leader of the far-right Front National party and soon-to-be presidential candidate, immediately made the false connection between the migration crisis and terrorism to whip up public fear. 'The influx of migrants must be stopped', she announced in an interview a fortnight later, and a terrified public lapped it up.[33] The following month, over one thousand women reported being the victims of sexual assault during the New Year's Eve celebrations in Cologne and other cities in Germany. The attacks seem to have been semi-coordinated in that women were encircled and hemmed in by a group of men and then abused. This time, it was subsequently confirmed that most of the perpetrators *were* from North Africa and had been in Germany for less than a year, arriving as asylum seekers or illegal migrants. Attitudes to all migrants began to change, with innocent refugees from Syria or Pakistan being attacked and community tensions mounting. The promises made after Alan Kurdi's death were not all put into effect. A year on from pledging that the UK would accept 20,000 refugees by 2020, so around 5,000 a year, it was revealed that the country had taken in only half that number. Over one thousand were taken in the first month, but in the period afterwards the numbers dwindled to a few hundred. Meanwhile, the so-called Dubs amendment, committing the government to take in 3,000 unaccompanied refugee children, which was passed in May 2016, was scrapped in early 2017.

In Aeschylus's *Suppliant Women*, the king fears the consequences for his city if he takes in the asylum seekers. Either the Egyptian men will seize them and carry them back to the shores of the Nile or they will wage war upon Argos. In that case, the citizens of Argos might turn against the women and against him for harbouring them. Whatever decision he makes, there will be tension and turmoil. Their arrival presages the end of peace and complacency for the community. It is only through his guidance that the city comes to its judgement that the women should be protected and given rights in the city. And it is through his strong leadership that the Egyptian men are warded off and sent back to sea, with a firm warning from the king. The women sing blessings upon their new city of Argos, ready to be fully integrated into the community:

> You people who live in the city of Argos,
> Welcome us kindly.
> No more will you hear of us
> Praising the Nile

Welcome us in. Welcome us in.
Now all our love is for the river Erasinos
Flowing so calm through meadows of Argos,
Filling her fields with all her children.
You people who live in the city of Argos,
Welcome us in.[34]

But there were two subsequent plays in the trilogy, now lost. The second play, probably entitled *Egyptians*, is thought to have dramatized the women being forced to marry their cousins after the men returned to defeat and kill the Argive king Pelasgus in battle. The Argive promise to protect the women was thus only short term. And in *Daughters of Danaus*, the third play, the women have killed their husbands on their wedding night, all that is except one woman, Hypermnestra, who has spared her husband out of love. She is consequently under threat of being killed, possibly by her father Danaus, but the goddess Aphrodite saves her, thus cementing the value of love and the custom of marriage. The texts of these plays have vanished, and the details can only be surmised from ancient descriptions and citations, but the overall impression is clear: the integration of the suppliants ushers in violence and recrimination, fear and punishment, and ultimately the taking of risk and the expression of hope to bring about change. Hypermnestra has the courage to take a different course from the rest of her community and thus to steer the family and city in a different direction, and – we surmise – to reconciliation.

The year 2016 witnessed the dark repercussions of the previous year's so-called refugee crisis. In Britain, the fears about immigration which had been latent for a number of years were exacerbated by the reports of terrorism on the continent and then further encouraged and legitimized by the United Kingdom Independence Party (UKIP) and the campaign to leave the European Union. It was not by chance that a surge in support for leaving the EU noted in a poll in November 2015 coincided with increased unease about migrants and refugees following the media news reports about the numbers over the summer.[35] Conflating the numbers of migrants from within the EU with the legitimate anxiety about the record numbers of refugees arriving in Europe and crossing the continent, the campaigners to leave the EU sowed confusion over the difference between migrants and refugees and a false understanding of international law concerning asylum, resettlement of refugees and arrangements for immigration within the EU.[36] Instead, apocalyptic and deliberately inflammatory language was used to describe the refuge crisis. There was a 'flood', a 'surge', a 'tidal wave'; migrants were 'sweeping' or 'streaming' across Europe. The metaphors of inundation permeated the discourse. The effect was to dehumanize the refugees; they were an unstoppable, sublime force of nature like a tsunami or an earthquake. And in the face of this, the ordinary person was portrayed without agency, overwhelmed by this fearful power. 'Breaking point' declared the controversial UKIP advertising billboard over a picture of an endless line of mostly non-white refugees and migrants, photographed at the Croatian-Slovenian border in the summer of 2015. Responding to a campaign designed to incite racial hatred and anxiety, together with the encouragement to 'take back control', a fearful British public voted to leave the European Union by a slim majority (51.89 per cent to 48.11 per cent) on 23 June 2016.

While the motivations behind the Brexit vote were multiple and complex, it could overall be described as a vote for fearful isolationism over open globalization, for national self-interest over international collaboration and – according to some – for hate over tolerance. Certainly, the immediate effects of the vote were to embolden and provoke expressions of racial animosity and violent attacks on marginalized groups. The murder of the MP Jo Cox, just before the referendum, by a militant right-wing extremist, who shouted 'Put Britain First' as he shot and then stabbed her in the street, was the shocking beginning of this hate-filled hostility. Prejudice, intolerance and aggressive bullying were now given open season. Racist attacks reported to the police in July 2016 were ten times the number reported for the same month the previous year. The common consensus that held together the United Kingdom was fractured by the divisive vote and its rhetoric. Families split apart over politics; the nations and regions of the kingdom (Scotland, Ireland, London) which had voted to remain in the EU questioned what held them together with their compatriots. As Gloucester reflects to his treacherous son Edmund about the broken kingdom in *King Lear*, 'Love cools, friendship falls off, brothers divide: in cities, mutinies; in countries, discord; in palaces, treason; and the bond cracked 'twixt son and father .... We have seen the best of our time. Machinations, hollowness, treachery, and all ruinous disorders, follow us disquietly to our graves.'[37] Such are the divisions and discord triggered by Lear's simple but devastating and unnecessary question, 'Which of you shall we say doth love us most?' (1.1.49).

Bolstered by the Brexit vote in June, and actually assisted by the same social media campaigning algorithms peddling misinformation that had been trialled in the run-up to the British EU referendum, Donald Trump's presidential election drive appealed to similar fears about immigration in America.[38] In his case, this was mainly targeted at migratory arrival from Central America. 'Mexico are sending people that have lots of problems, and they are bringing those problems to us. They are bringing drugs and bringing crime, and they're rapists', he declared as he announced his presidential candidacy in the summer of 2015.[39] But as the election battle wore on and following the terrorist attack in San Bernardino, California, in which fourteen people were killed, he promised that if elected he would introduce a 'total and complete shutdown' or ban on Muslims entering the United States.[40] By the end of the campaign, almost every marginal group had been targeted for hate: Muslims, Mexicans, African Americans, the disabled, women, Liberals. This was the most divisive, hate-filled, rabble-rousing and mendacious election battle in US history, deliberately bringing out the aggressive, frightening and atavistic emotions normally repressed deep in the human heart, and it resulted in the election of a president who has only continued that polarizing, campaigning spirit in office. His inauguration speech, on 20 January 2017, normally designed to bring a nation together in a common endeavour, threw down the gauntlet to his perceived enemies, the elite and their liberal concern for the marginal and oppressed. 'For too long, a small group in our nation's Capital has reaped the rewards of government while the people have borne the cost. Washington flourished – but the people did not share in its wealth', he said, with four former presidents sitting behind him. 'We've defended other nation's borders while refusing to defend our own … From this moment on, it's going to be America First', he went on, repeating his campaign pledge.

Brexit and Trump's victory at the polls in 2016 represent a backlash against the spirit of international co-operation and recognition of mutual interdependence and reciprocity that had prevailed since the Second World War. It was a retreat from the Greek ethos of *aidos*. According to David Miliband, president of the International Refugee Committee, 'the assumptions and institutions that have been fundamental to global progress in the last seventy years are now under challenge in the very countries that helped create that order in the first place ... The treatment of refugees is a weather vane of the character, stability and values of the international system.'[41] As mentioned in the last chapter the challenge to 'global progress', fuelled by racist fears of refugees, has been experienced right across Europe in the period since 2015 with the success at the polls of the Freedom Movement in Austria, the Front National in France, the Party of Freedom, led by Geert Wilders, in the Netherlands and the Alternative für Deutschland (AfD), which has links to neo-Nazi movements. All these parties, which drew ideas and encouragement from each other, promoted explicitly anti-Islam, anti-immigration policies along with a general message of nationalism, isolationism, climate-change denial and intolerance. The 'weather vane' of politics was pointing to the icy blasts of fear, division and *hubris*.

Recently, however, we have witnessed a fight back against this extreme right-wing resurgence. Geert Wilders was defeated in the Dutch election in March 2017, a victory for 'free and tolerant societies in a prosperous Europe' according to Jean-Claude Juncker; Marine Le Pen, the leader of the Front National, lost to Emmanuel Macron in the presidential election in France in May 2017. More people were voting for hope rather than fear and for the European Union collaborative project. Meanwhile in Trump's America, cities and states organized resistance against his new tough anti-immigration laws by declaring 'sanctuary' status. Claiming sanctuary status saved them from having to register and deport undocumented immigrants and allowed them to use local state or city laws to legislate against federal violations of their own powers of government and protection. By the end of 2017, there were over 300 sanctuary cities and counties in the United States. Governor Jerry Brown even signed a bill in October 2017 that made the whole of California a 'sanctuary state'. The Trump administration responded with executive orders and tax legislation aimed at punishing these sanctuaries, with California the particular target of the attack. The fierce legal tussle continues over who has the authority, ultimately, to decide immigration policy and the right to protect or deport some of the most vulnerable people in the country. Statistics which prove that sanctuary status has either no impact on crime figures or actually lowers them have had no effect on Trump's beliefs or those of his supporters. The well-supported claim that helping refugees is beneficial pragmatically as well as morally, since the financial, military and political costs of neglecting the crisis are far greater than any short-term gains, also falls on deaf ears. But lawyers, liberal politicians, activists and ordinary families persist in their efforts to resist the harsh and blinkered policies of fear and hate by hosting refugees, fighting for their rights in Congress and the law courts and putting forward the arguments for sanctuary again and again. As David Miliband has pointed out, helping refugees means ultimately helping ourselves.

> This is a fight for international cooperation over unilateral grandstanding, for the benefits of pluralism over the tyranny of groupthink, and for the enduring importance of universal values over the slicing and dicing of populations and religions in a fake and faulty clash of civilisations. It is a fight for values, insights, and institutions that imperfectly uphold the best of human nature in the face of impulses and arguments that humour the worst.[42]

The end of Aeschylus's *Suppliant Women* might end in hope, with the Egyptian men dispatched back home and the women invited into the city, but there are rumblings of fear and portents of struggles and violence still to come. The local citizens express their anxieties:

> Girls, we're afraid.
> Refugees bring cold winds.
> Evil pains follow, and bloody wars.
> Why did the gods give
> The men who've been chasing you
> Such easy passage from over the sea?
> We don't know the answer. No,
> We can't see what's coming. No,
> The dark mind of Zeus
> Is not ours to know.[43]

What happens next, 'what's coming', is, of course, unknown. The texts of the next two plays are missing, lost to the ravages of history and circumstance, and the mind of Zeus and time's narrative remain 'dark'. But somehow, by some twists and turns of plot now vanished, the trilogy closes with Aphrodite prevailing, her fragmentary speech the one element of the lost trilogy to survive:

> The wide sky aches for sex with earth
> The dark earth yearns for penetration
> Wetness falls from sky's wide fullness
> Rain then impregnates the land.
> The land gives birth to wheat, to barley
> Fruit trees, grass to feed the beasts
> This fecund marriage, moist, eternal
> Brings to flower all things alive.
> The maker of this match is me:
> I'm sex. I'm love. I'm Aphrodite.

Maybe this is not quite the 'pluralism' that David Miliband had in mind. But its vision of harmony and an inclusive, sustainable ecology and its passionate bringing together of opposites chimes with that moral purpose. Somehow the lost plays, the dark turbulent times in which we live, could emerge into that peaceful, cosmopolitan, inclusive love.

7

Hamartia in the Anthropocene

Traditionally tragedies take place over a limited period of time. The protagonist is presented with a dilemma, a temptation. He makes a choice. Terrible consequences rapidly ensue. 'Peace! The charm's wound up', whisper the witches near the opening of *Macbeth*.[1] So swift is the action in the Scottish play that Macbeth and his wife almost want to speed up time, doing the deed 'quickly' (1.7.2), feeling the 'future in the instant' (1.5.56) or willing to 'jump the life to come' (1.7.7). As soon as Macbeth kills the king, he is considered damned and the country is doomed to violent disorder. His drunken porter turns his castle into hell; men report stories of horses eating each other that very same night and further indications of natural abnormalities and cosmic turbulence. Blasphemous transgressions will have immediate and certain repercussions: 'It will have blood, they say. Blood will have blood' (3.5.121). And the play hurtles towards its necessary conclusion, the witches' impossible prophesies coming true with banal neatness.

But the tragedy of environmental disaster, in which we find ourselves facing (or not facing up to) a tragic choice, operates to a different timescale. The bleaching of the coral reefs, the shrinking of the Arctic polar ice each summer, the extreme droughts and floods are just symptoms and portents of decisions and actions already taken but whose full consequences have not yet been felt. Carbon emissions, which cause global warming and climate change, follow a complex but inexorable schedule. According to the Intergovernmental Panel on Climate Change (IPCC), there is a direct correlation between carbon particles in the atmosphere (measured as parts per million, or ppm) and temperature rise, but there is a time lag between the two because of the thermal inertia of the oceans: 350 ppm of carbon means 1 degree of temperature rise above the 1951–80 global average; 400 ppm means 2 degrees. At present, we have reached 410 ppm but not quite 1 degree Celsius of temperature rise.[2] But projecting forward, if we continue at the current rate of emitting 2 ppm more of carbon each year, we will have reached 471 ppm by 2050 which translates as between 3 and 4 degrees of temperature rise. This relentless plot is made more complicated, however, by the terrifying twists that are modelled to occur between 2 and 3 degrees of warming and again between 3 and 4. Between 2 and 3 degrees, the carbon cycle feedback is predicted to kick in, as photosynthesis begins to shut down and stressed plants release carbon rather than absorbing it, thus warming the planet by a further 1.5 degrees. And between 3 and 4 degrees, we could be faced with the Siberian methane feedback, as the Arctic tundra melts and releases tons of methane, pushing temperatures up further.[3] This is what is known as 'runaway climate change', when the consequences of global warming become the causes of further warming and the linear progression of cause and effect is inverted, speeded up and stretched beyond the capacity of exact prediction.

So extended is the plot of the climate's tragic narrative that we are now experiencing the temperature rise caused by carbon emissions released in the 1970s while simultaneously laying down the conditions for global warming forty years from now. One degree of temperature rise means that there are severe droughts currently ravaging Australia and southern and eastern Africa, where 36 million people face hunger as a consequence, and these droughts are predicted to increase in frequency until they become the 'new norm'.[4] It means that glaciers are already retreating rapidly on mountain peaks around the world, affecting river flow into the oceans, interrupting freshwater fish behaviour patterns and reducing drastically the globe's water storage for the future. The melting of the Arctic sea ice might have reached a tipping point. The ice and snow reflect back the sun's rays but the dark ocean, newly exposed by the shrinking of the ice cap, absorbs heat, raising the temperature further and making it more difficult for ice to form in winter. With shorter winters and longer summers, polar bears are threatened with extinction while the warmer Arctic is pulling the jet stream closer to the pole, radically affecting the pattern of the weather in the northern hemisphere. Meanwhile the warming of the oceans further south is increasing the intensity and frequency of hurricanes. In 2005, during Hurricane Katrina, the storm surge broke the protective levees and flooded the city of New Orleans, resulting in 1,245 deaths and huge environmental damage. Accusations followed that the levees broke because they had not been constructed properly in order to save money and that the evacuation and rescue plans were inadequate and too slow, leaving the poorest to suffer the worst of the storm. A few years later, in 2012, Hurricane Sandy, after barrelling across the Caribbean with destructive force, devastated New York and the New Jersey coastline, resulting in 233 deaths and massive damage as homes were washed away by the coastal surge (Figure 5).

These critical events and the yearly loss of habitat, homes and livelihoods – and the lives of the world's poorest – are attributable to the global warming caused by the carbon emitted around the time that I was born. But the amount of carbon that the world is releasing now into the atmosphere has already exceeded the level needed to

FIGURE 5 *A roller coaster that was swept off the pier at Seaside Heights, New Jersey, during Hurricane Sandy. November 2012.* © *Robert Wallis/ Panos Pictures.*

force global temperatures to rise to 2 degrees above the 1951–80 average. So although we may not experience this until 2050, with the time lag, it seems inevitable that we are heading towards the environmental destruction predicted for those conditions, modelled on geological samples from the deep past. The oceans will feel it most. Carbon dioxide dissolving into the water is making the seas more acidic, with huge implications for marine life. First coral reefs are bleached by warming sea waters. Then as the oceans become more acidic, the weakened reefs will be killed off entirely and irrevocably. In the last few years a third of Australia's Great Barrier Reef has died, along with nearly all the coral around the Maldives, Sri Lanka, Kenya and the Seychelles.[5] Meanwhile phytoplankton, which – like land plants – absorb carbon dioxide and form the bottom of the marine food chain, are susceptible to warming and acidification and are predicted to decline in great numbers. If the reefs and plankton die, then the two most important ecosystems of the oceans will be destroyed and much of the world's fish will go with them. Mussels, oysters and other shell fish will have already disappeared, unable to form their shells in the acidic waters. At the other end of the planet, the ice will continue to thaw in the polar regions but at 2 degrees, there is a threat that enough Greenland ice could melt to 'drown coastal cities around the world'.[6] If the consequential sea level rise is around 1 metre by 2100, as the fifth IPCC report suggests, it could wipe out Miami and Boston; if, as James Hansen predicts, it will be closer to 7 metres, it could submerge London.[7]

Scientists make their predictions about the future based partly on geological research into the planet's climactic past. The polar ice or the shrinking glaciers hold information about different global temperatures or changing sea levels in deep time and from this data models can be extended for different conditions in the decades ahead. It's a strange palimpsest of past, present and future. But with the time lag and the continuing carbon emissions, the present is itself a synthesis of past causes and future consequences, a future of inexorable destruction. After all, present emissions should force a temperature rise not of 2 degrees but between 3 and 4 degrees, which will be experienced by the end of the century, but runaway climate change could amplify an exponential temperature rise to 5, 6, or 7 degrees. At that point, vast areas of the planet would be uninhabitable, food supplies would be scarce, floods, droughts and tsunamis more and more likely, and probably the future of humans as a species will be precarious, as we are torn apart by conflict as well as starvation and the struggle for survival.[8] This apocalyptic future is what we are creating now. Trying to think about the tragic plot of climate change is the inverse of looking at stars. The twinkling white pinprick in the night sky is the light emitted by a distant star now already dead. The world around us – the fish, the birds, the forests, human civilization itself – is, if current circumstances continue, already doomed to die. We are the walking dead, wandering between two worlds, the past and the inexorable future.

It might seem, then, as if traditional tragedy has nothing to offer our understanding of the catastrophic environmental tragedy we are witnessing. Aristotle argued that tragic plots should be linear and tightly structured, with a beginning, a middle and an end. They should be finite, unitary, ideally with fixed stages along the way: the tragic mistake or *hamartia*, the fall, the act of recognition. Maybe we do not see the situation of climate change as tragic because the temporal time lag is too long, the gap between decision and consequences too extended, the conclusion too terrifyingly uncertain and apocalyptic. Maybe we cannot see it as a narrative at all, despite the inexorable certainty of the plot as I have been describing. In fact, even traditional tragedies did strange things with time. Despite being Aristotle's prime example of tragedy, *Oedipus* does not really fit his model because it complicates his notion of plot. The events of the story – Oedipus killing his father and marrying his mother – have already happened before the play begins and the drama follows his metaphorical journey to recognition of what he has done. He carries his past within him, literally for the Greeks in the pollution which courses through his veins; his search for the truth becomes a quest into his own origins. Where is Aristotle's moment of *harmartia*? When he tries to escape his fate? When he kills his father at the crossroads? When he marries his mother? When he decides to find out the truth? Even *Macbeth*, my classic example of tight plotting and direct relation between cause and effect, stretches and compresses time. Macbeth might at times want to anticipate and speed up the time to come – 'Present fears / Are less than horrible imaginings' – but he also has a vision of temporal progression as slow and imperceptible as glacial pace: 'Tomorrow and tomorrow and tomorrow, / Creeps in this petty pace from day to day, / To the last syllable of recorded time.'[9]

But there is one tragic drama which explores the difficulty of conceptualizing eternity or rather conceptualizing time not on a human scale but on the planet's or on the gods' level of measurement: *Prometheus Bound*. Indeed, Aeschylus's play should be termed a global warming tragedy, so concerned is it with the relationship between the present and the future, predicted centuries later. On first impression, it appears to be about an unchanging situation, the implacable opposition between Prometheus, who stole fire from the gods to give to man, and Zeus, chief of the immortals, who has chained his opponent to a rock as punishment. As divine beings, neither Prometheus nor Zeus can die but rather they are capable of maintaining their hostility for eternity. The static, defiant resistance of Prometheus – literally unable to move throughout the drama – has been an inspiration to readers over the centuries. '*Prometheus Bound* is the representation of constancy under suffering', according to the influential Romantic critic A.W. Schlegel. Prometheus is 'an image of human nature itself; endowed with an unblessed foresight and riveted to a narrow existence, without a friend or ally, and with nothing to oppose to the combined and inexorable powers of nature, but an unshaken will and the consciousness of [his] own lofty aspirations'.[10] Schlegel and others, like Byron and Percy Bysshe Shelley, drew attention to the contradiction between the freedom of the mind and the imprisonment of the body which symbolically figured the extent to which the tragic hero is bound to his destiny. This implacable conflict lay at the heart of tragedy, they believed.

Yet in fact the conflict between Zeus and Prometheus is not static, nor is it fated to last forever; Prometheus can foresee some change decades, centuries, millennia ahead. He knows two secrets: the cause of Zeus's overthrow years in the future and the figure who is destined to release him from his imprisonment. The latter will be a descendant of Io, victim of Zeus's rapaciousness and cruelty, who stops in her endless flight from her torment to view Prometheus's plight. Prometheus tells her of her destiny and his future saviour, 'one born from the third generation after ten others'. 'This prophecy is becoming hard for me to understand', responds Io.[11] Prometheus tries to clarify things by describing the geographical extent of her wandering, the vastness of the space covered evoking the similarly unfathomable extent of time, and by showing how the certainty of the past suggests that his predictions will be equally reliable: 'These are proofs (σημεια) for you, of how my mind sees rather more than has appeared openly.'[12] The first secret is that he knows that a marriage which Zeus is contemplating will produce a son who is stronger than his father and will overthrow him. This is bound to happen unless he reveals the secret to Zeus so that he can avoid the marriage or else he is himself released. So, the implacable fate of Zeus and Prometheus turns out to be based upon Prometheus's will, upon the brinkmanship between the two. The more Zeus tortures Prometheus to wrench the secret from him, the more obdurate he becomes. Powerful violence intensifies the likelihood of violent destruction to come.

In the superhuman world of *Prometheus Bound*, decisions taken now will have repercussions which continue to be felt centuries down the line. The willpower which Prometheus exerts under the current pressure and the apparently limitless suffering he endures carry within them the source of his eventual release. This apprehension of what appears eternal actually being subject to the progress of history, moving with geological pace, is assisted by the Greek belief that each generation of gods usurped the previous one so that the world was not stable but subject to repeated cosmic change through time. Unlike the Christian idea of God existing eternally and creating the world, the Greeks posited the notion that even the gods were vulnerable and limited, and that the world itself was therefore subject to catastrophe, conquest and destruction. Of course, the generations of the gods lasted longer than the generations of men; the Olympian gods seemed pretty powerful and impregnable. But eventually they too would go. It was partly a question of distinguishing two types of time: *Kairos* and *Chronos*. *Chronos* was the long-term passage of time, the 'three thousand years of sleep-unsheltered hours / And moments', the 'wingless, crawling hours' of suffering, as the 'crawling glaciers pierce me with the spears / Of their moon-freezing chrystals [*sic*]', as described by Shelley in his *Prometheus Unbound*.[13] *Kairos*, on the other hand, was the timely moment, the point of crisis, the event rather than the trend. Those climate-change deniers who deliberately confuse 'weather events' (a sudden cold spell) with long-term climate change (a steady rise in global temperature year on year) would do well to think about the difference between *Kairos* and *Chronos*.

Zeus is a new god, trying to establish his regime, after defeating the old gods. He feels precarious and not a little paranoid about rivals and traitors. And so, equally, his demise and other apocalyptic events are not unfathomable. But the question of what is known or unknown in the play is highly ambiguous. Prometheus himself gave men 'blind hopes' as one of his treacherous gifts to them, stopping them from 'foreseeing their death'. Mortals believe blissfully but falsely that their way of life will last forever. But Prometheus is aware of the irony that while he gave humans every *techne* in civilization, every means to subdue nature and push forward technology, he himself does not know how to escape, he has 'no stratagem to free me from the torment I have now'.[14] Of course, he has his secret which supposedly will free him, something which he appears to know and not know at various points in the play. And surely Zeus knows it too. He sends his messenger Hermes to force Prometheus to 'declare what marriage you are vaunting, by which he is to be thrown from power',[15] but surely all Zeus really needs to do is to avoid all marriages, not force exact names out of his opponent. Is the secret really the fact that Prometheus has a second secret, the alternative narrative of his release through Io's descendant? Or is it that Zeus just wants an excuse to exert his bullying power over Prometheus? Is he repressing his real awareness of his eventual demise with 'blind hopes' like the mortals? Whichever interpretation is correct, what matters is that this is a play in which truth is displaced by distraction and subterfuge, or deferred until centuries later, stretching ahead like the wanderings of Io. Prometheus's decision, not to tell Zeus the truth, results in his personal suffering now and the forecasted change in the cosmic balance of power, centuries in the future. But Zeus's decision, not to acknowledge a truth he must already fathom but instead to divert his efforts into violent oppression for a confused mix of reasons, only ensures more strongly his eventual demise. This complicated plot is tragic in its dramatization of displaced motivation and weakness masquerading as strength, of decisions either taken or shirked and of complex truth telling which is deferred but brings both good and harm and is potentially earth-shattering in its consequences.

Truth telling

The truth, of course, of climate change, that it is occurring and that it is caused by human activity, is not under dispute by scientists. The experts have devoted many years to researching all the evidence available, from the oceans, the polar and glacial ice, the air and the soil, and to creating different computer models based on this data to calculate predictions for the future. They are united in their conclusions that the planet is facing a rise in global temperature which will have destructive effects. The IPCC undertakes a systematic review of published scientific, primarily peer-reviewed research papers and, based on this vast range of literature, produces a report roughly every five to seven years. These reports are analysed and approved by delegates from all participating countries – currently 120 countries – and thus they are the closest to an objective, factual account of the current situation, commanding universal assent, that it is conceivably possible to achieve. This is what global truth looks like. And yet there is a popular belief, still pertaining in much of culture, including in the mainstream media and even among politicians and some governments, that the fact of anthropogenic climate change is under debate. The range of uncertainty among scientists over exactly how many degrees of warming we will experience by 2050 or how many metres the sea level will rise is misinterpreted by an unscientifically trained audience as an uncertainty over the fact of climate change at all. Disagreements are exaggerated into division; discrepancies become occasions for questioning the whole endeavour.[16]

The truth of anthropogenic climate change is based both upon scientific consensus and upon hard, experimental evidence. In other words, it brings together objective facts and collective conviction. In opposition to this, climate-change deniers often use traditional religious beliefs in order to question scientific facts and to urge the burning of fossil fuels as God's plan for his stewards on earth.[17] But some writers have portrayed religious truth and scientific truth interestingly and provocatively as analogous. There is a parallel between science and religion in their interest in revolutionary insight and conversion and in the pressures brought to bear upon unorthodox forms of knowledge and understanding. Richard Bean's satirical play *The Heretic* makes this analogy explicit by its very title. The play features a scientist whose narrowly defined research, measuring sea levels in the Maldives, seems to contradict what is deemed to be the orthodoxy in climate science – namely that global warming will cause sea level rise – and she finds herself bullied and marginalized. The play suggests that the consensus on climate change is politically motivated and that scientists skew the objective truth in order to win large grants which are only awarded for research that confirms the prevailing view on global warming. The play, first performed at London's Royal Court in February 2011, was 'provocative, funny, contrarian and stimulating' according to Michael Billington in the *Guardian* but raised in him some uncomfortable qualms about its apparent climate scepticism. 'Does Bean admire his heroine because of her courageous independence, or because he believes she is right?', mused Billington.[18] The political agenda of the evening was confirmed by the response of the *Telegraph*, a right-wing newspaper: '*The Heretic* is a play on the side of life and optimism, with a faith in humanity that goes markedly against the grain of current thinking.'[19] This 'faith in humanity' would be welcome if it were supported by anything other than wishful delusion and self-deception. But in a culture in which the 'current thinking' in scientific circles is at odds with powerful industrial lobbies and government policy, the provocative celebration of a sceptical climate scientist as a plucky 'heretic' and, by implication, the scientific community as a modern form of the Inquisition, fuelled by 'religiosity', renders this supposed black comedy into a poignant tragedy of misdirected anger and misinformation.

By contrast, Brecht's *Life of Galileo* pits science and religion in opposition. Galileo has reached a scientific discovery (the earth goes around the sun) which is now recognized as objectively true by scientists, but which the church sought back then (successfully) to deny, because it allegedly pushed mankind and their God into the periphery of the universe instead of confirming them at the centre. Galileo is silenced by imprisonment and the threat of torture and cajoled into acquiescence with the religious orthodoxy by the promise of personal comforts. His is a personal tragedy born of the decision to compromise in order to survive. It is revealed, however, that his discovery about the earth and the sun will be disseminated in the underground scientific community and will gradually gather more and more popular assent, even if Galileo will not be able to claim credit for it. In the final scene, his book manuscript, the 'Discorsi', crosses the Italian border in his pupil Andrea's hands while Galileo is still under house arrest. Ultimately the truth will emerge and the religious authorities, so powerful in the play, will be shown to be in the wrong, on the losing side of history. This is an 'optimistic tragedy' about human progress, even while it is pessimistic about individual bravery and heroism.[20] 'Unhappy the land that has no heroes!', says Andrea, disappointed about his master's apparent cowardice. 'No. Unhappy the land where heroes are needed', Galileo corrects him.[21]

Scientific truth comes under sustained political pressure in Ibsen's *An Enemy of the People* in ways which seem increasingly resonant now. In this play, a medical officer, Dr Stockmann, has conducted research at the spa baths he was instrumental in establishing and has discovered the water is contaminated and that the spate of illnesses which have been reported can be attributed to a specific polluting cause. He breaks the news in a report to the town council, believing that, in advocating the closure and urgent repair or relocation of the baths' water supply, he is being of 'some service to [his] home town and fellow citizens'. But the Mayor thinks primarily of the cost of the repair and – even more importantly – the damage to the town's reputation as a new spa resort, with all the consequential economic loss that will ensue, and so he proceeds to repress the publication of the report, to call its scientific basis into question and ultimately to tarnish Dr Stockmann's name. Attention is diverted in the play away from the detail of Stockmann's report and its microscopic analysis of the toxic bacteria (what one sceptical old man describes as 'some little creatures that had got into the water pipes ... and yet nobody can see them')[22] and on to the economic threat to the town's prosperity and the danger that Stockmann poses. In the climactic scene at a public town meeting, Stockmann is prevented from making his case by the Mayor who claims that he is 'saddling the ratepayers with an unnecessary expenditure of several hundred thousand crowns' and by the popular trade union leader, who realizes that jobs are at stake if the baths have to close and who therefore maintains that Stockmann has an 'ulterior motive' and that he is really interested in 'revolution'.[23] The ordinary people of the town, who have not been given access to the raw data of Stockmann's report and are alarmed at these emotive speeches from their leaders, throw him out of the meeting violently as an 'enemy of the people'.

When Ibsen first wrote this play, in 1882, it's arguable that the telling of scientific truth meant something different to what it does today. This was, to be sure, just over twenty years after Darwin published *The Origin of the Species* with all the religious and political controversy which that caused. But Ibsen was interested in the wider implications of telling the truth. Revealing the reality behind the comfortable lies which society told itself could often be destructive. His play *The Wild Duck,* produced two years later, depicted the arrogant, insensitive intrusion of a young man, Gregors, into a family that has muddled along on various forms of deception for years; devastating consequences ensue after he reveals the reality behind the delusion. The cost of truth telling, in this play, seems to outweigh whatever benefits it is supposed to bring. Better to continue telling each other, and believing, the 'life-lie' as one character, Dr Relling, puts it. 'Take the life-lie away from the average man and straight away you take away his happiness.'[24]

Ibsen was also concerned with the political implications of arriving at and pursuing the truth. There was a truth that was arrived at by consensus (a family white lie that all could subscribe to in *The Wild Duck*) and an alternative, ideal truth, objectively factual or transcendent but recklessly unconcerned with the consequences on the community, which was frequently the goal of the individual (the unfeeling, self-satisfied Gregors in *The Wild Duck*). These two sources of authority, the common people and the idealistic expert or messianic figure, often came into conflict. In *An Enemy of the People*, Stockmann is goaded by the lack of appreciation for his efforts and increasing public hostility to his message into castigating his fellow men and becoming provocatively undemocratic. 'The worst enemy of truth and freedom in our society is the compact majority. Yes, the damned, compact, liberal majority', he rages.[25] His original purpose in producing the report, to benefit his fellow man, gets twisted by the silencing of his voice and the hysterical intensity of the debate, until he loses sight of it altogether and is prepared to eradicate the whole town for the sake of winning his argument and asserting his superior perception. 'I love this town so much that I'd rather destroy it than see it prosper on a lie', he cries, seemingly oblivious to the paradox.

Isolated by his community and deciding, like Coriolanus, to 'banish' it before it banishes him, Stockmann is a typical Romantic figure, tortured, misunderstood and ultimately solipsistically creating his own alternative world. He plans to set up a school in which he can choose his own pupils and teach them whatever truth he wants. Unlike contemporary science, which is produced by teams and international collaborations and monitored by peer review, Stockmann's research is conducted in isolation, the Romantic mad scientist in his laboratory. In recent years, the increasingly acute crisis of climate change, as well as distrust of politicians and political spin and the growth of populism, has prompted at least six revivals of this play in Britain in the last dozen years, the last in January 2019.[26] The tenor of many of these productions is to portray Stockmann as a 'wild extremist'[27] or 'dangerous authoritarian'[28] or to suggest that 'campaigning courage can easily turn into self-righteous fanaticism'.[29] Stockmann's claim of intellectual elitism, the 'minority is always right', has played well with an audience increasingly permitted or encouraged to distrust experts and to put more faith in the will of the ordinary people.[30] Stockmann's Christ-like references ('I'm not as sweet-tempered as a certain person I could mention. I'm not saying: "I forgive you, for you know not what you do"') become less about heroic martyrdom and more an indication of his arrogance and insanity.

But if we turn again to the play in the wake of the failure of the Copenhagen climate summit of December 2010, the even darker mood of the latest IPCC report and – most recently – the determination of the new Trump administration in America to withdraw from Obama's commitments to the 2015 UN Paris agreement, not to mention the era of 'post-truth' and 'alternative facts' we are now supposedly entering, then the emphasis and searing tragedy of *An Enemy of the People* seem very different.[31] This is not Stockmann's tragedy and he is not the tragic hero of the piece, nor should we be concerned about the trivial, unattractive flaws in his character. This is the tragedy of the town that does not listen to him, that allows short-term financial gain to silence long-term health and prosperity for the whole community.[32] It is the tragedy of the ordinary people in the town, such as the editor of the local paper, who start out receptive to the scientist's words but allow themselves to be swayed by the politicians. And while Stockmann appears to have his own resources – social, financial and mental – to survive the ostracism of the town, the ordinary people have now been abandoned to the unscrupulous machinations of the town mayor, conned by the promise of a couple of years of prosperity before the toxicity of the baths makes itself apparent. How will they survive financially at that point when some visitors have been struck down by disease, the town is ruined by the scandal of poisonous waters and it is too late to repair the damage? And, now that truth has been replaced by post-truth, who will they trust?

Reading *An Enemy of the People* against the grain of the established Ibsen tradition gets us to the heart of the tragic dilemma facing us: Why not take the action which may be tough now but which will lead to the long-term benefit of the collective community if you know the truth? In decades and centuries to come, when people will look back at the first two decades of the twenty-first century, and see that 97 per cent of scientists knew that irrecoverable damage was happening to our planet and that there were four international reports alerting governments to the human causes of the impending disaster, they will ask why, with access to all this information and all this data, we did nothing. George Steiner argued in his book *The Death of Tragedy* that *An Enemy of the People* is not tragic because something relatively simple could have been done to alleviate the situation. 'Saner economic relations or better plumbing can resolve some of the grave crises in the dramas of Ibsen', he declared. By contrast, he believed that 'in tragedy there are no temporal remedies ... Tragedy speaks not of secular dilemmas which may be resolved by rational innovation, but of the unalterable bias toward inhumanity and destruction in the drift of the world'.[33] But this is to assume that tragedy is always about action: action taken or action thwarted by the implacable gods. But what Steiner does not realize is that there is also the tragedy of inaction, just as there could be irrational evasion. Is it not more devastating, for our sense of ourselves as humans, our sense of responsibility and ethical concern for anything beyond ourselves, to realize that there was something that we could have done which would have prevented the harm and that we even were privy to the knowledge of this, and yet we chose to ignore it and to opt instead for short-term expediency.

What is the connection – or crucial lack of connection – between truth, knowledge and action? Plato believed that a rational man would always act correctly if he knew the truth and therefore one need only either educate the population wisely or persuade them to leave all decisions to their philosopher-king rulers and then virtue would prevail. No sane person would have knowledge of the good course of action and not follow it. For Plato, to fail to do the right thing was illogical and therefore unthinkable. Aristotle, on the other hand, always a more streetwise, pragmatic philosopher, recognized that people sometimes take the less virtuous option even if they intrinsically know the correct answer. Philosophically he explained this with the notion of a false step in reasoning, a slippage in connecting one stage of a logical syllogism with the next, and with different definitions of 'knowledge'.[34] On a literary or dramatic level, he explained it with his theory of *hamartia*, the error in judgement or the crucial mistake which leads the tragic hero to take the wrong action and suffer the consequences. Prometheus's *hamartia* might lie in having given technology and fire to humans and thus angering the gods. Or it might consist in his stubborn resistance of Zeus. Aristotle's theory is never as easily applicable to Greek tragedies as it might initially appear, mainly because of the intractable nature of our human experience.

It is a similar puzzlement which drives contemporary philosophers to wrestle with the ethical problems associated with action or inaction in confronting climate change. According to Stephen Gardiner, we are faced with a 'perfect storm' of intersecting 'serious and mutually reinforcing problems'.[35] The challenge is global, and thus any one country or individual cannot feel that their action or inaction will contribute greatly to the overall problem. The crisis is, as Gardiner puts it, 'intergenerational', so that the present causes will produce consequences that will be experienced a generation or two later (the issue of the time lag I discussed earlier). And the debate, based as it is on future theoretical projection using experiential date from the past and present, is so abstract that its absolute scientific certainty comes under pressure and apparent dispute. These three challenges to the conventional rules of logical reasoning further attenuate the capacity of the individual or nation to make the right decisions and change its behaviour. According to Gardiner, our erroneous thinking about climate change can best be explained by the well-known philosophical problem known as the 'tragedy of the commons'. This can be illustrated by a group's approach to common grazing land. While it would be best if collectively the farmers limited their livestock so that the common grazing land was enough to feed all the animals and could last sustainably into the future for mutual prosperity, on an individual basis it makes sense for each farmer to increase his flock so that he individually makes more profit. 'Each agent accepts that it is *collectively rational* to cooperate but each agent believes that it is *individually rational* not to cooperate', explains Gardiner.[36] Profit on an individual basis means loss of profit for the whole. 'The initial situation drives people by an inexorable process towards an outcome that is worse by their own lights, and away from one that is better. Indeed it is the very same values that make cooperation preferable that drive each agent away from it'.[37]

We are quite familiar in traditional tragic drama with the staged opposition between private self-interest and public harm. Arthur Miller's play *All My Sons*, for example, explores an individual's dilemma between his responsibility for the safety of wider society and his desire to create wealth and security for his own family. The father, Joe Keller, knowingly allowed defective aircraft parts to be shipped out of his factory during the war, because otherwise future orders would dry up, and subsequently twenty-one pilots lost their lives flying faulty planes. He has hushed up the truth for years, allowing his friend and business partner to take the sole blame and jail-time, in order to create a successful business to pass on to his son. But his son forces the truth out of the father by the end, losing his own idealism in the process. The neighbour reassures his mother:

> He'll come back ... These private revolutions always die. The compromise is always made. ... Every man does have a star. The star of one's honesty. ... He probably just wanted to be alone to watch his star go out.[38]

Miller set much store by personal integrity which depends upon standing on the right side of history even if that results in one's individual short-term dishonour or even death.[39] Indeed when he adapted Ibsen's *An Enemy of the People* in 1950, he cut the problematic statements about eugenics articulated by the original Stockmann character and instead portrayed him as a heroic idealist, resisting government hypocrisy and championing the needs of ordinary working people at the expense of his own reputation.[40] His Stockmann is strong. But his other plays, like *All My Sons*, portray weak characters who reveal the private, deceiving and self-deceiving compromises with the truth which many of us make when there is the temptation of individual reward. There is, in the climate-change debate, a similar tragic choice that is made daily on an individual basis, to opt for private short-term profit and comfort at the expense of the collective long-term loss and destruction in the future.

The distortion of the truth when it comes to climate change is also being done on a collective, national and international scale. Public decision-making is made or neglected under the full glare of international attention. To return to Ibsen's *Enemy of the People*: the climax of the play occurs at the town hall meeting, when Stockmann defends himself against the Mayor and gradually the rest of the town. The most artistically successful of the recent revivals, Thomas Ostermeier's at the Barbican, explored the social context of any decision-making and the extent to which 'society privileges economic relations over personal ones'.[41] During the town hall meeting scene, the audience was invited to vote between Stockmann and the Mayor. This involved the audience raising their hands and actively participating in the stage business. They self-consciously performed their own decision-making and reflected upon their own discernment of justice and truth.

Dying thought in the Anthropocene

So far I have been discussing the tragedy of climate change in recognizably human terms, even if this pushes the traditional dimensions of tragedy, such as plot, time, decision-making and truth telling, to their furthest limits. The unthinkability of the environmental crisis, I have been arguing, is due to the time lag between carbon emissions and temperature rise and to the difficulty of reconciling private gain with public loss or short-term individual benefit with long-term collective harm, coupled with the various distortions and misunderstanding of the truth that we face. But while these dilemmas test the structures of conventional thinking, they are not wholly out of step with traditional tragedy, and indeed many canonical tragic dramas confront similar issues and can help us to think through our responses now.

But one effect of environmental catastrophe is that it kills off thought altogether. This is partly due to the strange interdependence of the human and non-human in the current crisis. As Bill McKibben has put it, we have reached 'the end of nature'. There is no wilderness left, few unmanaged forests, no wildlife flourishing in zones unaffected by man.[42] Such is the extent of man's carbon footprint upon the globe that the climate itself is changing with the result that even in areas inhospitable to man, like the Antarctic, the environment has been radically altered. Nature as an independent force has gone. The world beyond the human, the natural sphere against which human activity is measured and grounded, turns out to be corrupted by mankind. There is nothing 'outside the text' of human machination or narrative. As philosophers might say, the objective has become subjective. 'The Earth is no longer "objective"', philosopher Bruno Latour commented recently. 'It cannot be put at a distance and emptied of all Its humans. Human action is visible everywhere – in the construction of knowledge as well as in the production of the phenomena those sciences are called to register.'[43] It is to register this sense that the globe itself has been transformed by human activity that atmospheric scientists have coined a term for the new geological epoch in which we now find ourselves: the Anthropocene.

> The term Anthropocene ... suggests that the Earth has now left its natural geological epoch, the present interglacial state called the Holocene. Human activities have become so pervasive and profound that they rival the great forces of Nature and are pushing the Earth into planetary *terra incognita.*[44]

While scientists debate at what point the Anthropocene supposedly began – With the sudden measurable increase in carbon emissions since 1950? With the industrial revolution starting in the late eighteenth century? With the development of farming and deforestation since the Stone Age? – there is widespread acceptance of this term by writers and scientists alike, as a useful way of thinking and talking about the anthropogenic environment in which we now live.[45]

But the irony is that while nature is irrevocably and universally shaped by human activity, the consequences will overwhelm us beyond anything we can control. We have set in motion a non-human disaster. Drought, floods, storms, sea level rise, mass species die-off, runaway climate change: these are forces that threaten not only individual communities but, in the long-term, the survival of humankind as a species. We have reached the end of Nature, but as a consequence Nature will end us. The term 'Anthropocene' has consequently come to signify, for some environmental or ecocritical thinkers, not only the impact of humans upon the earth but also the extinction of the possibility of human moral thinking, of logical understanding, of human existence itself. How can we think ourselves out of life? For some critics, like Timothy Morton, everything is 'enmeshed' within an interconnected text, human and non-human, with the result there is no 'presence' and no 'present' but only the 'irreducible uncanny futurality of things'.[46] With no objective nature external to human understanding, there is no substantive, external meaning that can ground thought, but, rather, forces or 'hyperobjects' beyond our comprehension which yet participate in and are intimately bound up with our world. 'The Anthropocene is a threshold at which all "our" concepts of horizon, milieu, ethos and polity are voided', writes Claire Colebrook. Philosophy itself is undone by the thought of climate change. One response is to consciously attempt to undo thought, to think destructively or 'deconstructively'.[47]

According to writer and former soldier Roy Scranton, in a brilliant *New York Times* article, the solution is to 'learn how to die in the Anthropocene'.[48] With the time lag of carbon emissions and temperature rise, the failure of current governments and the wider public to do anything to change our current energy use and the prospect – on present behaviour – of being set on the path of runaway climate change, we are already living a doomed existence. Humans as a species will die. And what we have to do, like a samurai warrior going into battle, is to meditate upon our death. By recognizing the situation, facing the facts instead of denying them, we can confront the end with calmness and, effectively, die well. 'We can learn to see each day as the death of what came before, freeing ourselves to deal with whatever problems the present offers without attachment or fear', argues Scranton. The effect is to treat existence as a tragedy to which we are stoically resigned. Or even, that the only response to the threat of human extinction is to detach oneself from the world, like a Buddhist monk, and to become non-human oneself, transcending the particular through meditation. In this case, Western models of tragedy become a less useful tool for thinking than Eastern ones: the sacrificial suicide, death as an ideal to be welcomed, the 'intoxication and superhuman clarity' to be found at the 'privileged moment' of the tragic samurai death, according to Yukio Mishima.[49]

But for us in the West, the relatively easier response is to grapple with the dying of thought as it happens, trying to salvage hope from the imagination's rich capacity to continue to express its own extinction and thereby to resist it on an individual, personal basis. This might be through the exuberance of the philosophers and theorists already mentioned who apparently relish the complex, anarchic, 'intellectually liberating' possibilities of deconstructive thinking and meaninglessness.[50] Or it might be via the biblical cadences of apocalyptic texts such as Cormac McCarthy's *The Road* or Byron's *Darkness*. In McCarthy's novel, a father and son have travelled through a destroyed land, scavenging for food and warding off other desperate migrants in their struggle for survival. Unnamed, they come to take on larger, generic significance; they carry the hope of the species with them. In the final scene, the boy encounters a new family whose origin seems miraculous. They are, the boy thinks, 'one of the good guys'.[51] And they offer to take the boy with them to a new life. This is the ultimate escape fantasy of so many fictional responses to planetary destruction, that there is a future and there might be a world elsewhere. Not learning how to die in the Anthropocene, in this case, but learning how to kid ourselves better.

By contrast, Byron's poem is much bolder, offering ultimate annihilation instead of McCarthy's final gesture of hope. Byron describes the shrouding of the sun with darkness, and the ensuing war, human destruction and death of all life. Alongside this, he enacts the cancelling out of writing and human consciousness itself, the disintegration of the boundary between the subjective and objective:

> I had a dream, which was not all a dream.
> The bright sun was extinguish'd, and the stars
> Did wander darkling in the eternal space,
> Rayless, and pathless, and the icy earth
> Swung blind and blackening in the moonless air.[52]

This is a poem that undoes itself, a tragic poem that loses all frame of reference including the definitions of tragedy or epic. It culminates, without hope, in apocalyptic bleakness and negation:

> The waves were dead; the tides were in their grave,
> The moon their mistress had expired before;

The winds were withered in the stagnant air,
And the clouds perish'd; Darkness had no need
Of aid from them – she was the universe.[53]

It is the loss of generic definition alongside the extinction of human thought, and indeed human existence, which puts into jeopardy the very possibility and notion of tragedy in the Anthropocene. If there is nothing 'outside of the text' or 'no outside-text' ('*il n'y a pas de hors-texte*', according to Derrida), there is no way to measure traditional notions of tragic loss or fall; there is nothing at stake, nothing to matter.[54] Beckett's plays offer us something of this vision, a world in which it is not clear whether anything exists beyond the play and the stage, whether there is any external referent.[55] In *Endgame*, one character cannot stand up or see, another cannot sit down or leave and two further older characters are stuck in dustbins. All are held fast in some unexplained form of paralysis as the environment seems to diminish to nothing around them. 'Finished, it's finished, nearly finished, it must be nearly finished', says Clov in his opening speech. 'Grain upon grain, one by one, and one day, suddenly there's a heap, a little heap, the impossible heap.'[56] But while Clov might cheer himself with the thought that eventually the narrative will end, the play seems always in process, ending rather than ended. Neither the final point nor the starting point is legible for the protagonists: 'I say to myself that the earth is extinguished, though I never saw it lit', Clov observes.[57] Similarly, in this absurd atmosphere, another character Nell (in her dustbin) cannot distinguish between comedy and tragedy: 'It's always the same thing. Yes, it's like the funny story we have heard too often, we still find it funny, but we don't laugh any more.'[58]

For many years Caryl Churchill has also been exploring the surreal possibilities of theatre to articulate the menacing unthinkability of catastrophe. Using humour as well as violence, brutality and destruction, her plays defy logical interpretation, portraying a world in which rationality and understanding seem to be breaking down, even if ordinary human acts of communication and care persist. Her play *Far Away*, for example, first performed at London's Royal Court in 2000, opened with a quasi-realistic scene of vicious battery and bloodshed, which is hushed up. It finished with a vision of the whole planet in conflict: humans, animals and even the climate and elements. This cosmic war is apocalyptic and absurd, confusing in its bizarreness. The elephants have gone over to the Dutch and the weather is on the side of the Japanese.[59] As Lyn Gardner wrote in her review of the revived version of the play at the Young Vic in 2014, 'this twisted fairytale clearly demonstrates that if you declare war on the world, the world will declare war on you.'[60] The brutality and blindness of the first act morphs in some undefined way into the chaos of the third act; human control and intervention result in the terrifying loss of human control. An earlier Churchill play, *The Skriker*, which has also been revived again recently, portrays a similarly catastrophic and confusing world, across whose ruined landscape two desperate young women, one pregnant and the other suffering maybe from post-natal depression, struggle to survive, supported and mocked by a mysterious 'shapeshifter and death portent, ancient and damaged', the Skriker. The play is as difficult to pin down as *Far Away*, but here the destruction is evident not only in the cosmic order and the drama's rationality but in the language of the Skriker herself. Words and well-known phrases are wrenched out of their expected forms or meanings so that the end transforms the beginning and the middle. The narrative arc of the play, which circles back on itself like the carbon feedback loop and climate time lag, is mirrored by the swiveling, jumbled mishmash of language which denies its listeners a stable perspective and overview:

> Lily appeared like a ghastly, made their hair stand on endless night, their blood run fast. 'Am I in fairylanded?' she wandered. 'No,' said the old crony, 'this is the real world' whirl whir wh wh what is this? Lily was solid flash. If she was back on earth where on earth where was the rockabye baby gone the treetop? Lost and gone for everybody was dead years and tears ago.[61]

These apocalyptic, climate-change dramas invoke the strange unthinkability of environmental catastrophe with surrealism and darkly comic absurdity. Fear, paranoia and unexplained threats are pervasive but so is humour and farce and comic excess. Tragedy and comedy blur their boundaries under the existential disintegration of meaning that accompanies species extinction. To a certain extent the anarchy might release some carnivalesque revelry in destruction, as we see, for example, in some of J.G. Ballard's gloriously subversive and post-apocalyptic novels: *The Drowned World* or *High Rise*, for example.[62] Or we might discern a human resilience and even love in the face of the bewilderingly inhuman. *Far Away* closes with the main character Joan describing what she went through in order to be with her husband: 'I'll go on to the end after this. It wasn't so much the birds I was frightened of, it was the weather.'[63] But in other respects, the latent violence in Churchill makes her bizarre alliances of militarized animals, humans and other forms of nature in *Far Away* just a temporary, nervous release of laughter in an otherwise menacing, desolate and emptied world.

All this begs the question: Is tragedy necessarily a human form? Can we only measure what is tragic in human terms? Once we start to think about the planet dying along with mankind, can we no longer think or speak of this as tragedy? The attempt to think about and respond to the Anthropocene, and the death of human thought, results, it seems, in generic confusion, in comic absurdity as much as tragedy, in surrealism or Zen-like detachment as much as Aristotelian *hamartia*. To mourn the planet, to lament the coral reefs or the Arctic ice or the wonders of human civilization, might be to impose a human perspective upon the world. After all, the earth will continue spinning without humans, without one half of the animal and plant species existing today which are predicted to become extinct in the next hundred years.[64] Is tragedy too anthropocentric? Are we reducing the world to our narrative, our emotions, our capacity to explain and narrate events?

In this respect, we might turn to the biblical Book of Job in which God reprimands the mortal Job for seeking explanations for how the world works and expecting justice to operate in human terms. Job has been gradually stripped of everything: animals, servants, fortune, children, health and all sources of comfort. On a microcosmic scale, his is a tale of environmental collapse, of a world coming to an end. His friends come to visit him in his misery and seek to impose some explanation for what has happened. This must be punishment for some wrongdoing, they say; Job must be sinful since God never betrays the innocent. Job resists this easy explanation. He has done nothing wrong. But still he seeks to question God, to rail at his suffering. Finally, God's voice comes out of the whirlwind: 'Where were you when I laid the foundation of the earth?'.[65] This is, on the one hand, an example of ecological theology. God reminds humans that the world existed long before they did, that it is far larger than they are, has its own 'independent meaning' and could equally continue beyond their lifespan.[66] 'I have uttered what I did not understand, things too wonderful for me, which I did not know', says the chastened Job after God's lengthy speech from the whirlwind (42.3). The forces of cosmic or divine justice are too immense for mortals to comprehend. But on the other hand, God lets Job and humankind off the hook. Only he is responsible for the oceans and the sunrise and the well-ordered ecological food chain of his animals. Mortals have no effect. But in the Anthropocene, we cannot shirk this culpability so easily. While God in Job might have 'shut in the sea with doors when it burst out from the womb' (38.8), now it is we who have caused the cracks in those doors by our insatiable demand for energy and fossil fuels. The injustice is human; the horrible justice is inhuman and beyond human control or comprehension, unstoppable and greater than anything we can imagine.

The death of animals

Of course, before humankind dies as a species, vast numbers of animals will vanish from the earth because of anthropogenic climate change. Biologists estimate that one-fifth of the plant and animal species currently existing will die in the next thirty years and that half the current total will be extinct within a hundred years. We are witnessing the sixth mass extinction that the Earth has experienced, and this time it is as a direct result of human activity. Can we call this a tragedy? As we watch film footage of the last polar bears struggling to survive the ever-longer Arctic summers or the few remaining snow leopards driven further out of their usual habitats in the hunt for food, the potential loss of such natural beauty seems, by definition, tragic. But what about the less obviously beautiful wildlife, the extinct golden toad of Costa Rica, the rat-like rodent recently vanished from an island off Australia, the critically endangered wood bitter-vetch or Texas wild rice, which have a less clear-cut appeal to our compassion? Does climate change only matter because of its implication for the human race? Or is the loss of the planet's biodiversity tragically significant for its own sake? It is not even clear what it means to say that. Is there such a concept as the tragedy of animals, or non-human tragedy?

Animals have traditionally featured in tragedies as touchstones of innocence. The horses are said to have eaten each other in *Macbeth* because of the unnatural turmoil the hero unleashed by murdering the king. 'If I were your father's dog, you should not use me so', Kent protests to Regan in *King Lear* (2.2.139–40). Michael Morpurgo's *War Horse* derives its searing emotional poignancy from the unmerited suffering of the horse in a war for which he bore no responsibility and was powerless to stop. In these cases, animals are the blameless victims in a world corrupted by mortals. They become the moral standard of goodness by which to measure human iniquity; we see them as metaphors for our own lost innocence. As Marjorie Garber notes in her book on dogs, it is not only that 'how we treat animals becomes a litmus test for "humanness"' but also that they become analogies or simpler substitutes for more complicated human relationships: 'The dog becomes the repository of those model human properties that we have cynically ceased to find among humans.'[67] The greater simplicity of our love for animals than for humans means that the suffering of animals often has a greater impact upon the public imagination than that of humans. Think, for example, about the public outrage in Britain in 1995 over intensive veal farming and lorries delivering young calves in crates to France and Holland, even while the same numbers did not protest in the streets over the massacre in Srebrenica which happened the very same year.[68] There might be an element here of sentimental distraction or evasion rather than a coherent response to tragedy.

In other cases, the tragedies of animals anthropomorphize them within their own narratives, often primarily intended for children. So, for example, *Watership Down* tells the epic story of a colony of rabbits who, warned by a dream of the future destruction of their warren, choose to leave it and seek new burrows. As in classical epics like the *Aeneid* or the *Odyssey* to which the book has been compared, there are tragic episodes of fearful foreboding, betrayal and death within the larger epic narrative.[69] Fiver, the prophetic rabbit, anticipates bloodshed like Cassandra; Hazel, the leader, must take difficult decisions like Aeneas to trust the hospitality of unknown and perfidious warrens; Bigwig, the warrior rabbit, Ajax-like risks his life on a number of occasions to save the group.

These examples treat animals allegorically. If their stories are tragic, it is because, ultimately, they tell us something about ourselves as humans. But in recent years, scientists have been discovering more and more about how animals actually think and – more importantly – how they feel. As a way of measuring whether animals are capable of feeling love, Barbara King considers 'how animals grieve'. From elephants, dogs and cats down to chickens, goats and rabbits, she uncovers tales of animal loyalty and bereavement, urging her readers to rethink their preconceptions about non-human emotions. 'Bunnies', she observes at one point, 'are the tip of the iceberg because they point us toward a future time, maybe not too long from now, when the fact of animal mourning across diverse species will be taken as common knowledge'.[70] If we take King's book and other similar ones seriously, then the destruction of the environment and species extinction will be felt acutely by the animals affected. The death of animals, and the depletion of their family groups caused by drought, food scarcity and pollution, which is already happening, might provoke the pity, fear and at least grief which could be described as tragic emotions.

However, this is to project a human template upon the environmental crisis in the animal kingdom. We believe that the death, and more widely the extinction, of animals is tragic because we anthropomorphize them in various ways. By contrast, we could equally zoomorphize humans, treating them as animals especially given the extent to which the Anthropocene virtually negates human, rational, traditional thinking as already discussed. The boundary between human and non-human animals, interrogated so provocatively by Darwin in the nineteenth century, is becoming increasingly blurred, producing new taxonomies both theoretically within philosophical, literary circles and more widely in the agribusiness, technological world.[71] Farming always engineered the close proximity and interdependence of man and animal, since wild aurochs were domesticated to become the 'man-made' cow between 6000 and 4000 BC.[72] But now modern intensive farming methods have reduced cows to objects or machines, pumping them with hormones and antibiotics or artificially inseminating them to increase production and lower costs. And conversely certain classes of humans are treated like expendable commodities under capitalism, herded and dispensed with like metaphorical cattle.[73] This is certainly the case with the Belgian tragic film *Bullhead* (2011), in which the hero, Jacky, and his cattle are both pumped up, abused and pushed around by the multimillion-euro meat industry.[74]

Injecting himself with testosterone like the bulls he farms, Jacky is at the mercy of his hormones, and of his circumstances, brutalized by his past and the environment of the criminal agricultural underworld. Beefed up and brutish, but also sensitive and lonely, Jacky's is the tragic story of a modern minotaur, half human and half animal, in the harsh world of agribusiness.[75]

The sixth extinction will also probably include man in its mass cull of life on Earth. Given the wonder of human civilization, and the fact that we are human and so feel our own demise most acutely, that would seem to be a tragic prospect. According to Barbara King, although animals grieve, the human species is unique in our capacity to anticipate the inevitability of death, to 'look far ahead with dread, or relief, or a mix of the two, aware that death is coming'. And, while animals might make sounds of lament, only we can shed tears. Most importantly, 'alone of all species, we may pour our lamentations into art'.[76] While the death of animals might be *tragic*, it is we humans who can express that loss – through our artistic skills – as *tragedy*. However, as the planet warms up and the delicate ecosystems, built up over millennia, go out of kilter, destroying the perfect balance of plants, animals and humans in their co-dependency, we get a renewed appreciation of just how good it was when we witness it disappear. Ecology acquires an ethical force, as opposed to a neutral substratum, as we realize how imbricated it was with human activity and how corrupted it has become by our neglect and exploitation. In this case, the equilibrium of the seasons, the climate, the animal kingdom, the tides of the ocean, the rivers and forests are valuable and precious in themselves. And to allow all this to be destroyed, both within and then without our control, is tragic in all senses: human, non-human, cosmic and divine.

Coda: Figuring Tragedy

The experiences and tragic dilemmas that I have been discussing in this book are, in many ways, unthinkable, un-representable, incomprehensible. They range from the trauma of 9/11, to the hidden atrocities of the wars in Iraq and Afghanistan, to the revolutionary sublime rupture of 2011, to the fearful power of mass movements – whether of refugees or hysterical populism – and ultimately to the catastrophic prospect of climate change. They are hard to fathom partly because they are so recent; they have scarcely had time to settle from event into narrative, from experience into knowledge. They also often have the shattering effect of removing individuals from the picture. They might not seem understandable on a human scale, particularly in the case of the tragedy of climate change, as I've been discussing. These crises, we might say, disfigure our imaginations. They remove the individual figures that make empathy or compassion possible.

Yet, throughout the critical two decades that I have been discussing, and the apocalyptic future we are now facing, human figures are put back by the popular imagination into the void. Through the act of mourning and lament after 9/11, through the choices taken and patterns exposed by the symmetries of revenge in the Iraq War, through the various moments of recognition and the intimacy of pity and fear, love and hate we witness in the tumultuous years of conflict, revolution and counter-revolution, we project the human scale with all its particularities and feelings back into the inhuman disaster. We can even endeavour to shape the unthinkable catastrophe of global warming through some human dramatic plots and animal perspectives. Thinking about our contemporary world, in other words, involves a tussle between figural interpretation and disfiguration.[1] Individual fortunes and feelings are negated in the chaotic roller coaster of history only for them to return repeatedly in our news stories and private experiences as prompts for grief or anger or fear.

According to the literary critic Erich Auerbach, 'figural interpretation establishes a connection between two events or persons, the first of which signifies not only itself but also the second, while the second encompasses or fulfils the first'.[2] His primary illustration of this was the connection between the Old and New Testaments, and the Christian belief that the New Testament was a transformation and fulfilment of the Old. But we could equally suggest that tragedy is another such figurative and figuring way of seeing, both in the sense of reminding us of the figure in history, with his or her own feelings, desires and decisions, and also in the Auerbach sense of reading one historical event in light of another. 'Thus history, with all its concrete force, remains forever a figure, cloaked and needful of interpretation', continues Auerbach. 'In this light the history of no epoch ever has the practical self-sufficiency which, from the standpoint both of primitive man and of modern science, resides in the accomplished fact; all history, rather, remains open and questionable, points to something still concealed.'[3]

If tragic events are open to being read in the light of previous events or, indeed, in the light of a long canonical tradition of tragic drama and philosophy, this is because there is something generic about human error, anger, cruelty and suffering. The tendency among commentators and critics recently has been to push back against the notion of genre and to describe the transformation of an experience into something generic as regrettable and politically problematic.[4] The conventional thesis is that the generic empties out politics and makes sorrow bland. But the argument of this book has been, by contrast, to find value in the generic and to recuperate the genre of tragedy as a powerful hermeneutic tool for our times. Setting individual stories into a wider, traditional pattern of narrative or theatre has the merit of making intelligible what seems particular. It makes it recognizable and therefore grievable. It allows us to 'read' the world out of joint. This is not to say that such figural, tragic interpretation smooths out the difficulties or empties out the content. Traditionally, tragic dramas make us see each text and each performance as unique to *that* place, *that* moment, *that* body – and this is frequently the unexpected and devastating *punctum*, as Roland Barthes put it, in any performance.[5] But tragedies also figure that moment of witness in a wider context too; they make it readable within a tradition.

It should be clear from this book, too, that classical tragedy is itself not orderly. Despite Aristotle's analysis in the *Poetics*, tragic dramas are not strictly and successfully patterned; they do not offer 'the God's eye view'.[6] Classical tragedy acknowledges its own blind spots and resistances and frequently does not conform to, or confine itself within, the pattern. It registers unruliness.[7] So reading events now, *figuring* them again, in the tradition of tragedy is by no means to order them. And it is certainly (I'm afraid) not to come up with a solution or a recipe for organizing the world in a better way. *Pace* Hamlet, it is not possible to 'set it right'.

But it is to pay attention to the wider narratives of our times and to think about the attempts to make week-to-week events intelligible through that patterning. We can then try to think seriously about the relationship between history, politics and culture, the 'longue durée' of collective progress, and the historically contingent nature of the stories we tell about our world and the rituals we employ to make it bearable or even register our lack of understanding.[8] This might be the start of action, informing and revising the structures of feelings and ideas of tragedy that respond to social disorder and recuperating a sense of what we all share, what we hold generically in common.[9] Might we then, collectively and gradually, hope to bend that flawed and fragile arc of the moral universe steadfastly towards justice?

NOTES

Chapter 1

1 Tony Blair, 'Labour Party Conference Speech', *The Guardian*, 2 October 2001.

2 Martha Nussbaum, 'Compassion and Terror', *Daedalus*, Winter 2003, p. 11.

3 Judith Butler, *Precarious Life: The Power of Mourning and Violence* (London: Verso, 2004), p. 22.

4 Slavoj Žižek, *Welcome to the Desert of the Real* (London: Verso, 2002), p. 18.

5 The latest contribution to this long tradition of separating tragedy in the theatre or literary world from 'everyday tragedy' is Hans-Thies Lehmann, *Tragedy and Dramatic Theatre*, translated by Erik Butler (London: Routledge, 2016), p. 9, and *passim*.

6 Raymond Williams, *Modern Tragedy* (London: Hogarth Press, 1966), p. 47.

7 Adrian Poole, '*Macbeth* and the Third Person', *Proceedings of the British Academy*, 105 (2000), p. 79.

8 For the complicated pressures of complicity in Shakespeare (for both characters and 'observers'), see Harry Berger, *Making Trifles of Terror: Redistributing Complicities in Shakespeare* (Stanford, CA: Stanford University Press, 1997), pp. 26–7; Poole, '*Macbeth* and the Third Person', pp. 90–1.

9 Aristotle, *Poetics*, translated by Stephen Halliwell (London: Duckworth, 1987), chapter 7, p. 39.

10 Hegel, *Hegel's Aesthetics: Lectures on Fine Art*, translated by T. M. Knox, vol. 2 (Oxford: Clarendon Press, 1975), p. 1198.

11 Aristotle, *Poetics*, Loeb edition (Cambridge, MA: Harvard University Press, 1932), chapter 6, p. 22. The Greek phrase τῶν … παθημάτων κάθαρσιν (*Ton pathematon katharsin*) is ambiguous here and can be interpreted either way, depending on the translation of *katharsis* as

purgation or purification and on the relation between *pathematon* and *katharsin*. According to Stephen Halliwell, katharsis 'entails both an expenditure of emotion, and an amelioration of the underlying emotional disposition': Stephen Halliwell, *Aristotle's Poetics*, 2nd edn (London: Duckworth, 1998), p. 198.

12 It's in line with this interpretation of Aristotle that tragedy has been criticized for being a politically conservative form, coercing the citizens into conformity or complacency and suggesting that they must accept their inexorable fate: see Augusto Boal, 'Aristotle's Coercive System of Tragedy', in *Theatre of the Oppressed*, translated by A. Charles and Maria-Odilia Leal McBride (London: Pluto Press, 1979), pp. 1–52; and Brecht, 'On the Use of Music in an Epic Theatre', in *Brecht on Theatre: The Development of an Aesthetic*, translated and edited by John Willett, 2nd edn (London: Methuen, 1974), p. 87.

13 Pity, according to Martha Nussbaum, has acquired 'connotations of condescension and superiority', whereas compassion entails 'fellow-feeling': see Martha Nussbaum, *Political Emotions: Why Love Matters for Justice* (Cambridge, MA: Harvard University Press, 2013), p. 416, n.7.

14 Nussbaum, *Political Emotions*, p. 142.

15 For Iago as a 'supremely empathetic villain', see Rowan Williams, *The Tragic Imagination* (Oxford: Oxford University Press, 2016), pp. 45–6.

16 Paul Bloom, *Against Empathy: The Case for Rational Compassion* (New York: Harper Collins, 2016), p. 5.

17 Nussbaum, *Political Emotions*, p. 157.

18 George Eliot, *Middlemarch*, edited by W. J. Harvey (London: Penguin, 1965), Book 2, chapter 21, p. 243. Eliot's novel rethought the genre of tragedy for the purposes of nineteenth-century fiction.

19 This understanding of recognition gets its best articulation by Charles Taylor, 'The Politics of Recognition', in *Multiculturalism: Examining the Politics of Recognition*, edited by Amy Gutmann (Princeton, NJ: Princeton University Press, 1994), pp. 25–73.

20 For further analysis of the significance of 'acknowledgement' rather than 'recognition', see Stanley Cavell, 'Knowing and Acknowledging', in *Must We Mean What We Say?* (Cambridge: Cambridge University Press, 1976), pp. 220–45; Stanley Cavell, 'The Avoidance of Love', in *Disowning Knowledge, in Seven Plays of Shakespeare*, 2nd edn (Cambridge: Cambridge University Press, 2003), pp. 39–124; Patchen Markell, *Bound by Recognition* (Princeton, NJ: Princeton University Press, 2003), pp. 7; 32–8.

21 Aeschylus, *Oresteia*, Loeb critical edition (Cambridge, MA: Harvard University Press, 1926), line 177 [my translation].

22 Aristotle, *Rhetoric*, translated by Lane Cooper (New York: D. Appleton, 1931; reprinted 1960), p. 107; section 2.5.

23 Pankaj Mishra has identified the prevailing '*climate* of ideas, a structure of feeling' as one of anger: *Age of Anger: A History of the Present* (London: Penguin, 2017), p. 28. There is a debate among scholars as to whether Aristotle does limit the tragic emotions to only two (pity and fear) or whether he implies and acknowledges other ones in the *Poetics*: see Halliwell, *Aristotle's Poetics*, p. 200, n.44.

24 Indeed Donald Trump reversed President Obama's policy of closing down the prison at Guantanamo and signed an executive order to keep the detention centre open: 'Donald Trump Signs Executive Order to Keep Guantanamo Bay Open', *The Guardian*, 31 January 2018.

25 Arnold J. Toynbee, 'Law and Freedom in History', in *A Study of History*, Abridgement of vols. 7–10 (Oxford: Oxford University Press, 1957), p. 265.

26 Percy Bysshe Shelley, Preface to *The Revolt of Islam* (1818), in *Shelley: Complete Poetical Works*, edited by Thomas Hutchinson and G. M. Matthews, 2nd rev. edn (Oxford: Oxford University Press, 1971), p. 33.

27 Jennifer Wallace, 'Shifting Ground in the Holy Land', *Smithsonian Magazine*, May 2006, pp. 58–66.

28 Helene Foley, *Ritual Irony: Poetry and Sacrifice in Euripides* (Ithaca, NY: Cornell University Press, 1985).

29 For more detail on tragic sacrifice in the War on Terror and in *Iphigenia in Aulis*, see Jennifer Wallace, 'Tragic Sacrifice and Faith: Abraham and Agamemnon Again', in *Christian Theology and Tragedy: Theologians, Tragic Literature and Tragic Theory*, edited by Kevin Taylor and Giles Waller (London: Ashgate, 2011), pp. 35–51.

30 Different ways of viewing and responding to conflict were explored in the Tate Modern exhibition and catalogue: *Conflict, Time, Photography*, edited by Simon Baker (London: Tate Publishing, 2014).

31 The anxiety about writing in Greek tragedy, and especially at this moment in *Hippolytus*, is described in Simon Goldhill, *Reading Greek Tragedy* (Cambridge: Cambridge University Press, 1986), pp. 135–6. In the Renaissance period, rhetoric was also a source of both admiration and fear.

32 Emma Graham-Harrison and Carole Cadwalladr, 'Cambridge Analytica Execs Boast of Role in Getting Donald Trump Elected', *The Guardian*, 21 March 2018.

33 The philosopher Gillian Rose anticipated the threat to political action which arose from what she termed the 'phantasy life'. The solution, she argued, was to be alert to the situation, to read the distortion for what it was: 'To see the built forms themselves as ciphers of the unjust city has political consequences: it perpetuates endless dying and endless tyranny, and it ruins the possibility of political action.' See Gillian Rose, *Mourning Becomes the Law: Philosophy and Representation* (Cambridge: Cambridge University Press, 1996), p. 26.

34 Jean Baudrillard, 'No Reprieve for Sarajevo', *CTheory.net*, January 1994.

35 'To Sarajevo, Writer Brings Good Will and "Godot"', *New York Times*, 19 August 1993.

Chapter 2

1 Cathy Caruth, *Unclaimed Experience: Trauma, Narrative and History* (Baltimore and London: The Johns Hopkins University Press, 1996), p. 91.

2 Freud, 'Remembering, Repeating and Working Through', in *Beyond the Pleasure Principle and Other Writings*, translated by John Reddick (London: Penguin Books, 2003), pp. 33–42; *Beyond the Pleasure Principle*, p. 55. Freud strikingly draws on the analogy with theatre here in *Beyond the Pleasure Principle*.

3 Dominick LaCapra, *Representing the Holocaust: History, Theory, Trauma* (Ithaca, NY: Cornell University Press, 1994), p. 209.

4 Ann Kaplan points out the difficulty of distinguishing private and collective trauma in the case of 9/11, or indeed 'vicarious trauma'. Her account of the 'working through' of trauma through art and collective 'witnessing' sounds very like an account of the task of tragedy, though she never uses this term: Ann Kaplan, *Trauma Culture: The Politics of Terror and Loss in Media and Literature* (New Brunswick, NJ: Rutgers University Press, 2005), pp. 1–2, 19, 135.

5 See my *The Cambridge Introduction to Tragedy* (Cambridge: Cambridge University Press, 2007), pp. 176–81. Dominick LaCapra writes of oscillation between 'acting-out' and 'working-through': LaCapra, *Representing the Holocaust*, p. 205.

6 Slavoj Žižek, *Event* (London: Penguin, 2014), p. 3.

7 The concept of the event as rupture which opens up the possibility of rethinking reality is foundational to Alain Badiou's philosophy:

Being and Event, translated by Oliver Feltham (London: Continuum, 2006); and *The Logics of Worlds: Being and Event 2*, translated by Alberto Toscano (London: Continuum, 2009).

8 Jean Baudrillard, *The Spirit of Terrorism and Requiem for the Twin Towers*, translated by Chris Turner (London: Verso, 2002), p. 4.

9 According to Kristiaan Versluys, 'September 11 – for all the physicality of planes impacting on giant skyscrapers and for all the suffering caused to victims and their near and dear – is ultimately a semiotic event, involving the total breakdown of all meaning-making systems': *Out of the Blue: September 11th and the Novel* (New York: Columbia University Press, 2009), p. 2.

10 The intentions of al-Qaeda were 'apocalyptic, not political': see Michael Ignatieff, *The Lesser Evil: Political Ethics in an Age of Terror* (Edinburgh: Edinburgh University Press, 2004), p. 99.

11 Baudrillard, *The Spirit of Terrorism*, p. 57.

12 Paul Ricoeur, *Time and Narrative, volume 3*, translated by Kathleen Blamey and David Pellauer (Chicago: University of Chicago Press, 1988), p. 103. Ricoeur's time is 'aporetic' (or sublimely impossible to grasp) because it is really just a series of moments, a succession of events, only apprehensible when structured into a narrative pattern.

13 Arundhati Roy, 'The Algebra of Infinite Justice', *The Guardian*, 29 September 2001. See also Noam Chomsky, *9–11* (New York: Seven Stories Press, 2001), pp. 59–62.

14 I visited the viewing platform at the top of the World Trade Center in 1998 and was struck then by how hard it was, looking down, to comprehend that one was still on land. For the implication of the 'God's eye view' which the towers afforded, and the 'illusion of abstract, distant, visual mastery', see Una Chaudhuri's contribution to 'A Forum on Theatre and Tragedy: A Response to September 11, 2001', *Theatre Journal*, 54.1 (2002), p. 97.

15 Alex Houen, 'Novel Spaces and Taking Place(s) in the Wake of September 11', *Studies in the Novel*, 36.3 (Fall 2004), p. 419.

16 Horatio's words in *Hamlet*, 4.5.7–9. All references to Shakespeare's plays in this book are taken from *The Norton Shakespeare*, edited by Stephen Greenblatt (New York: Norton, 1997).

17 *Hamlet*, 4.5.29–30. Ophelia's grief conforms to a stereotypical performance of mourning and madness, according to Early Modern theatrical expectation.

18 The poet Alice Oswald followed the example of Homer's simple elegies for dead warriors in her long poem *Memorial*. Beginning with

just a list of the names of Homer's dead, like the columns of names carved on a war memorial, she continues with a brief description of each death accompanied by the haunting natural similes which underpin Homer's epic. This confrontation with death is for Oswald the main, scarcely bearable point of the *Iliad*; she strips the epic back to reveal this tragic, lamentable core: Alice Oswald, *Memorial: An Excavation of the Iliad* (London: Faber and Faber, 2011).

19 Thomas W. Laqueur, *The Work of the Dead: A Cultural History of Mortal Remains* (Princeton and Oxford: Princeton University Press, 2015), p. 437.

20 Ibid., p. 365.

21 Auster quoted in Janny Scott, 'A Nation Challenged: The Portraits, Closing a Scrapbook Full of Life and Sorrow', *New York Times*, 31 December 2001.

22 'Jose Cardona: The Good Things', *New York Times*, 9 December 2001.

23 'Laura Rockefeller: Her World a Stage', *New York Times*, 8 January 2002.

24 Nancy K. Miller, 'Portraits of Grief: Telling Details and the New Genres of Testimony', in *Literature After 9/11*, edited by Ann Keniston and Jeanne Follansbee Quinn (New York and Abingdon: Routledge, 2008), pp. 27–8.

25 Euripides, *The Trojan Women*, translated by James Morwood (Oxford: Oxford University Press, 2000), p. 51, lines 473–5.

26 Ibid., p. 44, lines 199–207; pp. 52–3, lines 512–22.

27 Ibid., p. 57, lines 684–5.

28 Ibid., p. 43, lines 187–9.

29 *Portraits 9/11/01: The Collected Portraits of Grief from the New York Times*, introduction by Janny Scott (New York: Times Books/ Henry Holt and co., 2002), p. ix.

30 Bruce Weber, 'Standing in for New Yorkers: Expressions of Grief over Sept. 11' [Review of *The Guys*], *New York Times*, 28 January 2002.

31 Nelson, *The Guys* (New York: Random House, 2002), p. 63.

32 Hecuba's words could be considered cynical here: 'We need to suffer so that men have a subject for their tragic literature in the future.' This is, needless to say, not the point of the comparison I am intending here, but rather the alternative interpretation of the line: 'We suffered but at least we are not forgotten for song memorializes and compensates for loss.'

33 Eric Lipton and James Glanz, 'In Last Piles of Rubble, Fresh Pangs of Loss', *New York Times*, 17 March 2002.

34 Hamlet's 'solid flesh' in the Folio version of the play is 'sullied flesh' in John Dover Wilson's amended edition of the Quarto version. Wilson's 'sullied' has its interesting merits too. For more on Renaissance concerns with the decomposition of the body and their dramatization in *Hamlet*, see Michael Neill, *Issues of Death: Mortality and Identity in English Renaissance Tragedy* (Oxford: Oxford University Press, 1997).

35 *Hamlet*, 4.3.30-31, 27–8.

36 Ibid., 5.1.151, 174–5.

37 Keith J. Dillon, quoted in Lipton and Glanz, 'In Last Piles of Rubble'.

38 See Richard Seaford (ed.), *Euripides' Bacchae* (Liverpool: University of Liverpool Press, 1996), l. 1300–1 n., pp. 249–50.

39 *The Bacchae*. Directed by James Macdonald, Almeida Theatre, London, 2015.

40 David Simpson, *9/11: The Culture of Commemoration* (Chicago: University of Chicago Press, 2006), p. 46.

41 Ibid., p. 23.

42 See Margaret Alexiou, *The Ritual Lament in Greek Tradition* (Cambridge: Cambridge University Press, 1974), pp. 4–7 and passim.

43 Alexiou, *Ritual Lament*, p. 12. While the tradition of professional mourners has been lost in Western Europe and the United States, it still persists in other parts of the world where 'the bereaved solicit the authority of professional mourners to occupy, negotiate and shape their loss' (Taryn Simon). Taryn Simon's art performance piece *An Occupation of Loss* (Islington, London, April 2018) brought together professional mourners from Mongolia to Albania to Burkina Faso to pour out their laments simultaneously in a vast underground urban cavern.

44 Alexiou, *Ritual Lament*, pp. 131–2.

45 Aeschylus, *Seven against Thebes*, translated by Christopher Collard (Oxford: Oxford University Press, 2008), pp. 60–1, lines 966–70.

46 Homer, *The Iliad*, translated by Caroline Alexander (London: Vintage Penguin, 2015), p. 527: book 24, lines 509–12.

47 Alexiou, *Ritual Lament*, pp. 131–50.

48 Nicole Loraux, *The Mourning Voice: An Essay on Greek Tragedy*, translated by Elizabeth Trapnell Rawlings (Ithaca, NY: Cornell University Press, 2002), p. 35.

49 Pig Iron Theatre, *Love Unpunished* (Philadelphia, 2006). See https://vimeo.com/121787637.

50 Cited in Steven McElroy, 'A Philadelphia Theater, Set in Its Free-form Ways', *New York Times*, 6 September 2006.

51 Indeed, Richard Gray criticizes the novel for offering only traumatic 'symptom rather than diagnosis' but I consider that to be its merits. See Richard Gray, *After the Fall: American Literature since 9/11* (Hoboken, NJ: Wiley-Blackwell, 2011), p. 28.

52 Don DeLillo, *Falling Man* (London: Picador, 2007), pp. 32, 46, 137.

53 Ibid., p. 49.

54 Jasper Johns, 'Farley Breaks Down (After Larry Burroughs)'. Matthew Marks Gallery, New York, 2014.

55 For an excellent detailed account of the rebuilding project, and the tussle between Silverstein and Libeskind, see Elizabeth Greenspan, *The Battle for Ground Zero: Inside the Political Struggle to Rebuild the World Trade Center* (London: Palgrave Macmillan, 2013).

56 'WTC Memorial Jury Statement for Winning Design', 13 January 2004: https://www.911memorial.org/sites/default/files/WTC%20 Memorial%20Jury%20Statement%20for%20Winning%20Design.pdf

57 Pindar, 'Pythian Ode' 8, *Pindar's Victory Songs*, translated by Frank J. Nisetich (Baltimore: Johns Hopkins University Press, 1980), p. 205, lines 95–6.

58 Spencer Finch, 'Trying to Remember the Color of the Sky on That September Morning', National September 11 Memorial Museum, New York, 2014.

59 Freud, *Beyond the Pleasure Principle*, pp. 45–73.

60 Patricia Cohen, 'At Museum on 9/11, Talking through an Identity Crisis', *New York Times*, 2 June 2012.

61 Caroline Alexander, 'Out of Context', *New York Times*, 6 April 2011.

62 Nelson, *The Guys*, p. 79.

Chapter 3

1 The relationship between tragedy and ritual is ancient but also complicated. Tragedies draw on ritual practices in their plots and also have served a ritual function over the centuries. Indeed, in his recent book, Rowan Williams refers to tragedies and tragic performance as

'liturgical': Williams, *The Tragic Imagination*, pp. 8–11. However, tragedies might also be said to interrogate and subvert the reassurance of ritual.

2 Williams, *The Tragic Imagination*, pp. 15, 27.

3 Rowan Williams, *Writing in the Dust: Reflections on 11th September and Its Aftermath* (London: Hodder and Stoughton, 2002), p. 64.

4 Ibid., p. 63.

5 There were 3,407 coalition deaths in Afghanistan between 2001 and 2015. The number of Afghan soldiers and civilians killed up until 2016 is 111,000; the number of civilians killed in 2017 were 1,662. In Iraq, 4,486 US soldiers and 179 British soldiers were killed. The fact that the precise number of Iraqi casualties is unknown has been the subject of much controversy and debate. In 2013, it was announced that probably the Iraqi casualty figures were around 500,000. It has been estimated that a further 19,000 civilians have died in the years since 2014 and well over 30,000 combatants.

6 Nussbaum, 'Compassion and Terror', p. 11.

7 Butler, *Precarious Life*, p. xii.

8 See Shoshana Felman, *The Juridical Unconscious: Trials and Traumas in the Twentieth Century* (Cambridge, MA: Harvard University Press, 2002), pp. 2–3.

9 Aeschylus, *Oresteia*, translated by Christopher Collard (Oxford: Oxford University Press, 2002), p. 8, lines 205–17.

10 Aeschylus, *Oresteia*, A New Adaptation by Robert Icke (London: Oberon Books, 2015), p. 16. Icke's *Oresteia* ran at London's Almeida Theatre May–July 2015 and later transferred to the West End.

11 Euripides, *Iphigenia in Aulis*, translated by James Morwood (Oxford: Oxford University Press, 2000), pp. 97, line 450; 121, line 1264.

12 Aeschylus, *Oresteia*, A New Adaptation by Robert Icke, p. 22.

13 Aeschylus, *Oresteia*, Loeb critical edition, p. 23, lines 222–3.

14 'Transcript: Sen. Barack Obama's Speech against the Iraq War', Chicago, 2 October 2002. National Public Radio.

15 'Obama Defends Strategy in Afghanistan', *New York Times*, 17 August 2009.

16 Richard Haase, *War of Necessity, War of Choice: A Memoir of Two Iraq Wars* (London: Simon & Schuster, 2009), p. 10.

17 Ibid.

18 Steve Coll, *Ghost Wars: The Secret History of the CIA, Afghanistan and Bin Laden, From the Soviet Invasion to September 10 2001* (New York and London: Penguin Books, 2004), pp. 311–13, 364–6.

19 Jean-Charles Brisard and Guillaume Dasquié, *Forbidden Truth: U.S.-Taliban Secret Oil Diplomacy and the Failed Hunt for Bin Laden*, translated by Lucy Rounds (New York: Thunder's Mouth Press/Nation Books, 2002), p. 35.

20 Ibid., pp. 43–6.

21 Homer, *The Iliad*, translated by Caroline Alexander, p. 179: Book 9, lines 316–20.

22 Richard Haase, 'In Afghanistan, the Choice Is Ours', *New York Times*, 20 August 2009.

23 Clarke quoted in Seymour Hersh, *Chain of Command: The Road from 9/11 to Abu Ghraib* (New York: Harper Collins, 2004), p. 146.

24 George W. Bush, 'Address before a Joint Session of the Congress on the State of the Union,' 29 January 2002. Online by Gerhard Peters and John T. Woolley, *The American Presidency Project*: http://www.presidency.ucsb.edu/ws/?pid=29644.

25 Dick Cheney, 'Meet the Press', 9 December 2001. NBC: http://www.washingtonpost.com/wp-srv/nation/specials/attacked/transcripts/cheneytext_120901.html

26 George W. Bush, 'Speech to the UN General Assembly', *The Guardian*, 12 September 2002: https://www.theguardian.com/world/2002/sep/12/iraq.usa3

27 *Hamlet*, 1.5.75–6; 1.5.25.

28 Ibid., 1.5.42–3; 1.5.99–100.

29 Ibid., 1.5.189–90.

30 'Full text of Tony Blair's Statement to Parliament on Iraq', *The Guardian*, 24 September 2002: https://www.theguardian.com/politics/2002/sep/24/foreignpolicy.houseofcommons

31 See Sir John Chilcot's public statement prefacing the publication of his report, 6 July 2016. *The National Archives*: http://webarchive.nationalarchives.gov.uk/20171123124608/http://www.iraqinquiry.org.uk/the-inquiry/sir-john-chilcots-public-statement/.

32 Aeschylus, *Oresteia*, translated by Christopher Collard, p. 40, lines 1431–4.

33 Ibid., p. 62, lines 400–1.

34 Ibid., p. 64, line 461.

35   John Kerrigan, *Revenge Tragedy: Aeschylus to Armageddon* (Oxford: Oxford University Press, 1996), p. 6.

36   Bush's 'Mission Accomplished' speech explicitly linked Iraq and 9/11: 'The battle of Iraq is one victory in a war on terror that began on 11th September 2001, and still goes on…. The liberation of Iraq is a crucial advance in the campaign against terror. We have removed an ally of Al-Qaeda, and cut off a source of terrorist funding.'

37   Gregory Burke, *The National Theatre of Scotland's Black Watch* (London: Faber and Faber, 2007; revised edition, 2010). *Black Watch* premiered at Edinburgh's Festival Fringe in August 2006 and subsequently toured internationally.

38   The deployment of the Black Watch was controversial, as it was widely considered to serve a political purpose rather than a military one. The Americans needed to say that not only US troops were involved in confronting the insurgency in the run-up to the November 2004 presidential election but the Black Watch was deployed in an extremely dangerous zone. See Richard Norton-Taylor, 'Black Watch Troops Move into Position', *The Guardian*, 28 October 2004.

39   *Battle for Haditha*. Directed by Nick Broomfield. London: HanWay Films, 2007. The effect of mingling fact and fiction is to allow for the different versions of the events of 19 November 2005 and the inevitable areas of uncertainty and speculation.

40   The cover-up report declared that fifteen civilians were killed by the IED and eight insurgents were subsequently killed when the Marines returned fire.

41   In the film, after the twenty-four Iraqi civilians have been brutally shot dead, the Marine commander calls together his men to congratulate them: 'We lost a great young warrior today but the battle was won. Please give the United States marine corps the courage and ability to destroy the enemy who hide like cowards amongst civilians.'

42   By June 2008, the year after Broomfield's film was released, six of the eight Marines responsible for the Haditha killings had had their court cases dropped and a seventh was found not guilty. The eighth, Frank Wuterich, was finally convicted in 2012 simply of 'dereliction of duty', with all charges of murder dropped. He was demoted in rank but avoided jail: 'Haditha Residents Outraged as Marine Avoids Jail', *The Telegraph*, 25 January 2012.

43   Anonymous [Thomas Middleton or Cyril Tourneur], *The Revenger's Tragedy* (1607), in *Four Revenge Tragedies*, edited by Katharine

Eisaman Maus (Oxford: Oxford University Press, 1995), 3.5.30. On the performative aspect of the Abu Ghraib pictures as trophies, see Susan Sontag, 'Regarding the Torture of Others', *New York Times*, 23 May 2004.

44 Anthony Lewis, 'Introduction', in *The Torture Papers: The Road to Abu Ghraib*, edited by Karen J. Greenberg and Joshua L. Dratel (Cambridge: Cambridge University Press, 2005), p. xiii.

45 Joshua L. Dratel, 'The Legal Narrative', in *The Torture Papers*, p. xxii.

46 Alette Smeulers and Sander van Niekerk, 'Abu Ghraib and the War on Terror – a Case against Donald Rumsfeld?' *Crime Law Social Change*, 51 (2009), pp. 327–49.

47 Jay S. Bybee, 'Standards of Conduct for Interrogation', 1 August 2002, Memo 14, in *The Torture Papers*, p. 172.

48 Colin Powell, Memorandum to Counsel to the President, 26 January 2002. Memo 8, in *The Torture Papers*, p. 123.

49 Lewis, 'Introduction', in *The Torture Papers*, p. xvi.

50 Powell, Memorandum to Counsel to the President, pp. 122–3.

51 See John Yoo and Robert Delabunty, 'Application of Treaties and Laws to al Qaeda and Taliban Detainees', 9 January 2002, in *The Torture Papers*, Memo 4, pp. 38–9.

52 Alberto Gonzales, 'Decision re application of the Geneva Convention on Prisoners of War to the Conflict with al Qaeda and the Taliban', 25 January 2002, Memo 7, in *The Torture Papers*, p. 119.

53 As Karen Greenberg points out, the rulings about the 'failed state' of Afghanistan did not apply to Iraq, and yet prisoners arrested during the 'battle for Iraq' were also detained without trial at Guantanamo: in *The Torture Papers*, p. xviii.

54 Agamben declares that the prison or concentration camp, 'as the pure, absolute and impassable biopolitical space (insofar as it is founded solely on the state of exception)', is 'the hidden paradigm of the political space of modernity': *Homer Sacer: Sovereign Power and Bare Life*, translated by Daniel Heller-Roaxen (Stanford, CA: Stanford University Press, 1998), p. 123.

55 Alfred McCoy, quoted in Derek Gregory, 'The Black Flag: Guantanamo Bay and the Space of Exception', *Geografisker Annaler, Series B, Human Geography*, 88.4 (2006), p. 418. One of the consequences of the Arab Spring in 2011 was that, for a year or two at least, America no longer had a useful ally in Mubarek's Egypt to which it could outsource its torture. The situation, under the presidency of Al-Sisi, has now returned to 'normal'.

56 Agamben, *The State of Exception*, translated by Kevin Attell (Chicago: University of Chicago Press, 2005), p. 4: 'The state of exception is not a special kind of law.... rather insofar as it is a suspension of the juridical order itself, it defines law's threshold or limit concept.'

57 Butler, *Precarious Life*, p. 57.

58 Thomas Kyd, *The Spanish Tragedy* (1587), in *Four Revenge Tragedies*, 4.4.166–73.

59 Anonymous, *The Revenger's Tragedy*, in *Four Revenge* Tragedies, 5.1.132.

60 *Hamlet*, 1.4.67; 5.1.151.

61 Ibid., 2.2.557–8, 563.

62 Mohamedou Ould Slahi, *Guantanamo Diary*, The Fully Restored Text, edited by Larry Siems (Edinburgh: Canongate, 2017), p. xxxiv.

63 Ibid., p. xxxv.

64 Ibid., pp. 40–1.

65 Kerrigan, *Revenge Tragedy*, p. 6.

66 Bush, 'Address before a Joint Session of the Congress on the State of the Union'.

67 According to Katharine Eisamen Maus, 'quit' is the word (meaning both vengeance and 'have done with') which is most often used in Jacobean revenge tragedy. It 'suggests a welcome finality to the revenger's action'. But 'in revenge tragedy visions of restored equilibrium almost always turn out to be mirages': *Four Revenge Tragedies*, p. x.

68 *Hamlet*, 4.7.100.

69 *Restrepo* (2010), directed by Sebastian Junger and Tim Hetherington, was awarded the Grand Jury Prize for best documentary at the 2010 Sundance Film Festival and nominated for the 2010 Academy Award for Best Documentary. Tim Hetherington bled to death in Misrata, Libya, in 2011 while covering the civil war.

70 *Hamlet*, 4.4.18–19.

71 Ibid., 4.4.53–65.

72 Jonathan Shay, *Achilles in Vietnam: Combat Trauma and the Undoing of Character* (New York: Scribner, 1994), p. 20.

73 Eugene O'Neill, 'The Haunted', Act 4, in *Mourning Becomes Electra* (London: Nick Hern Books, 1992), p. 161.

74 Aeschylus, *Oresteia*, A New Adaptation by Robert Icke, p. 128.

Chapter 4

1 Lucy Madison, 'Clinton on Situation Room Photo', *cbsnews.com*, 5 May 2011.

2 In this respect, professional embedded photographers are very different from amateur photographers – citizens, other soldiers – who are likely to be immersed in the situation. For Judith Butler to term those who took the photographs in Abu Ghraib 'embedded reporters' is therefore to conflate and confuse two very different situations and to misrepresent the work of serious, professional photographers. See Judith Butler, *Frames of War: When Is Life Grievable?* (London: Verso, 2009), p. 83.

3 Tim Hetherington, *Infidel* (London: Chris Boot, 2010). Hetherington's book accompanied his Academy Award–nominated documentary film *Restrepo*, directed by Tim Hetherington and Sebastian Junger, Washington, DC/National Geographic Entertainment (2010).

4 See Rob Sharp, 'Combat Fatigue: Tim Hetherington's Intimate Portraits of US Soldiers at Rest Reveal the Other Side of Afghanistan', *The Independent*, 10 September 2010.

5 Peter van Agtmael, *2nd Tour Hope I Don't Die* (Portland: Photolucida, 2009).

6 Aristotle, *Poetics*, translated by Stephen Halliwell, chapter 16, p. 49.

7 Ibid., chapter 16, pp. 48–9.

8 Sophocles, *Oedipus the King*, translated by H.D.F. Kitto (Oxford: Oxford University Press, 1994), p. 89, lines 1184–5.

9 Sophocles, *Antigone*, translated by F. Storr, Loeb edition (Cambridge, MA: Harvard University Press, 1912), p. 417: line 1322. Storr's translation captures the pile-up of negatives in the original Greek here better than most translations.

10 Two notable exceptions to this convention are Aeschylus's *Eumenides*, line 235, when the stage business moves from Delphi to Athens, and Sophocles' *Ajax*, lines 815–65, when Ajax commits suicide without any witnesses besides the audience.

11 Aristotle, *Poetics*, translated by Stephen Halliwell, chapter 9, p. 42: 'Since, tragic mimesis portrays not just a whole action, but events which are fearful and pitiful, this can best be achieved when things occur contrary to expectation yet still on account of one another.' See Terence Cave, *Recognitions: A Study in Poetics* (Oxford: Oxford University Press,1990), p. 31: 'Commentators oscillate between

views of peripeteia as an abrupt change of fortune, a reversal of the characters' intentions.... and a reversal of the audience's expectations.'

12 Williams, *The Tragic Imagination*, p. 7.

13 Ibid., p. 16.

14 For the classic account of these two parallel practices, see Taylor, 'The Politics of Recognition'.

15 Butler, *Precarious Life*, pp. 30, 134.

16 Kelly Oliver, *Witnessing: Beyond Recognition* (Minneapolis: University of Minnesota Press, 2001), p. 15: 'Moving from recognition to witnessing provides alternative notions of ethical, social, and political responsibility entailed by this conception of subjectivity. Our conceptions of ourselves as subjects, our subjective identities, along with our conceptions of others, hang in the balance.'

17 Aristotle, *Poetics*, translated by Stephen Halliwell, chapter 11, p. 43.

18 Markell, *Bound by Recognition*, pp. 1–2.

19 Sontag, *On Photography* (New York: Farrar, Straus and Giroux, 1977), pp. 109–10. For a more specifically political critique of the photograph's capacity to 'violently' remove the underlying context behind a photographed 'moment', see John Berger, *About Looking* (New York: Pantheon, 1980), p. 40.

20 Sontag, *On Photography*, p. 3.

21 Luc Santé, 'Introduction' to James Nachtwey, *Inferno* (London: Phaidon, 1999), p. 9.

22 Susan Sontag, *Regarding the Pain of Others* (New York: Farrar, Straus and Giroux, 2003), p. 115.

23 Susie Linfield, *The Cruel Radiance: Photography and Political Violence* (Chicago and London: University of Chicago Press, 2010), p. xv. Linfield positions her argument in opposition to Sontag, but in fact her opinions on empathy and moral activism echo Sontag's own, as expressed in *Regarding the Pain of Others*: see Frances Richard, 'The Thin Artifact: On Photography and Suffering', *The Nation*, 13 December 2010.

24 Linfield, *Cruel Radiance*, pp. xv–xvi.

25 Margaret Olin, *Touching Photographs* (Chicago and London: University of Chicago Press, 2012), p. 17.

26 See the interesting discussion in Ariella Azoulay, *Civil Imagination: A Political Ontology of Photography*, translated by Louise Bethlehem (London: Verso, 2012).

27 Ariella Azoulay, *The Civil Contract of Photography* (Brooklyn, NY: Zone Books, 2008), p. 93.

28 Markell, *Bound by Recognition*, p. 7.

29 Nina Berman, *Purple Hearts: Back From Iraq* (London: Trolley Books, 2004). Other remarkable photographic work on the coalition allies' perspective includes Yuri Kozyrev, 'The Things They Carry', *Time Magazine*, November 2006; Robert Nickelsberg, *Afghanistan: A Distant War* (Munich, London, New York: Prestel, 2013); Peter van Agtmael, *Disco Night September 11th* (Brooklyn, NY: Red Hook Editions, 2014)

30 W. J. T. Mitchell, *Cloning Terror: The War of Images, 9/11 to the Present* (Chicago: University of Chicago Press, 2011), pp. 93–4.

31 'Mark Owen' with Kevin Maurer, *No Easy Day: The Autobiography of a Navy Seal. The Firsthand Account of the Mission that Killed Osama bin Laden* (New York: Dutton, 2012), pp. 241–2; 242; 244; 265. The Navy Seal's name was changed to Mark Owen for his security.

32 Ibid., p. 248.

33 Ibid., p. 241.

34 See esp. Sontag, 'Regarding the Torture of Others'; Slavoj Žižek, 'Between Two Deaths', *London Review of Books*, 3 June 2004, p. 19; Nicholas Mirzoeff, 'Invisible Empire: Visual Culture, Embodied Spectacle, and Abu Ghraib', *Radical History Review*, 95 (Spring 2006), pp. 21–44; Butler, *Frames of War*, pp. 63–100; Mitchell, *Cloning Terror*, pp. 99–159; and Katarzyna Beilin, '"The Split-Screen Syndrome": Structuring (Non)Seeing in Two Plays on Abu Ghraib', *Comparative Drama*, 46.4 (2012), pp. 427–50.

35 Sontag, 'Regarding the Torture of Others'.

36 Sophocles, *Antigone*, translated by Robert Fagles (London and New York: Penguin Books, 1982), p. 124, lines 1395–6.

37 Simon Goldhill, *Sophocles and the Language of Tragedy* (Oxford: Oxford University Press, 2012), p. 235.

38 Sophocles, *Antigone*, Loeb edition, lines 37–8. (Line numbers of Greek text hereafter in my text.)

39 Sophocles, *Antigone*, translated by Robert Fagles, p. 100, lines 870–4.

40 Creon's wish to avoid 'defilement' is, of course, ironic, given the fact that Polyneices's body is about to be revealed as polluting the whole city.

41 *Antigone*, directed by Greg Taubman and performed by Extant Arts Company, Columbia Stages, Riverside Theatre, New York, 17–20 October 2012.

42 *The Persians*, performed by the Berliner Ensemble, with translation by Andreas Spätauf, in 1983. For details, see Aeschylus, *The Persians*, edited and translated by Edith Hall (Warminster, Wiltshire: Aris and Phillips, 1996), Introduction, p. 3.

43 Sellars quoted in Mark Pappenheim, 'The Greeks Have a Word for It: Read the Signs in the Work of Peter Sellars and You'll See Actions Speak Louder than Words', *The Independent*, 16 August 1993.

44 Sellars quoted in John Lahr, 'Inventing the Enemy' (review of Persians, dir. Peter Sellars), *The New Yorker*, 18 October 1993, p. 103. Xerxes, however, was depicted less sympathetically as a megalomaniacal Saddam Hussein figure: see Helene Foley, *Reimagining Greek Tragedy on the American Stage* (Berkeley and Los Angeles: University of California Press, 2012), pp. 140–1.

45 Roland Barthes, *Image-Music-Text*, translated by Stephen Heath (New York: Hill and Wang, 1977), p. 31.

46 Peggy Phelan, *Unmarked: The Politics of Performance* (New York and London: Routledge, 1993), p. 6.

47 Hannah Arendt, *The Promise of Politics*, edited by Jerome Kohn (New York: Schocken, 2005), p. 109.

48 Arendt, *The Human Condition* (Chicago: University of Chicago Press, 1958), p. 6. See Jonathan Schell, 'Hannah Arendt and the Atomic Bomb', in *Politics in Dark Times: Encounters with Hannah Arendt*, edited by Seyla Benhabib (Cambridge: Cambridge University Press, 2010), pp. 247–58.

49 Sontag, *On Photography*, pp. 14–5.

50 See, for example, Greg Marinovich and Joao Silva, *The Bang-Bang Club: Snapshots from a Hidden War* (London: William Heinemann, 2000).

51 It was the transmission of the war in Iraq in 1990 on television, replaying the military screen footage of air strikes, which prompted the notorious series of essays by Jean Baudrillard, *The Gulf War Did Not Take Place* (Bloomington: Indiana University Press, 1995).

52 Clive Stafford Smith, 'Who's Getting Killed Today?' *TLS*, 28 June 2017.

53 Ibid. The estimate was produced by Reprieve, the international human rights organization founded by Clive Stafford Smith in 1999, and published in its report of 2016.

54 Grégoire Chamayou, *Drone Theory*, translated by Janet Lloyd (London: Penguin, 2015), p. 46. See also Derek Gregory on the 'Special Kind of Intimacy that Consistently Privileges the View of the Hunter-Killer: "From a View to a Kill: Drones and Late Modern War"', *Theory, Culture & Society*, 28.7–8 (December 2011), p. 193.

55 Chamayou, *Drone Theory*, p. 72.

56 Derek Gregory, 'The Everywhere War', *Geographical Journal*, 177.3 (2011).

57 *Coriolanus*, 4.5.105–112, 114–7.

58 Wilfred Owen, 'Strange Meeting', in *The Poems of Wilfred Owen*, edited by Jon Stallworthy (London: Chatto and Windus, 1990), lines 7, 40. Of course, Owen's poem's 'piteous recognition' occurs in a nocturnal nightmare but is supposedly provoked by the 'real' combat in the trenches the previous day.

59 Joseph Pugliese, *State Violence and the Execution of Law* (London: Routledge, 2013), p. 193.

60 Ibid., pp. 203, 204.

61 Oliver, *Witnessing*, p. 19. Oliver's illustrative example of false witnessing is the complaint by white students of suffering from 'reverse discrimination' as a result of affirmative action.

62 Chamayou, *Drone Theory*, p. 105.

63 *Grounded*, directed by Julie Taylor. Public Theater, New York. 25 April–23 May 2015.

64 George Brant, *Grounded* (London: Oberon Books, 2013), p. 44.

65 *Eye in the Sky*. Directed by Gavin Hood. Toronto: Entertainment One/Glasgow: Raindog Films (2015).

66 Elaine Scarry, *The Body in Pain: The Making and Unmaking of the World* (Oxford: Oxford University Press, 1985), p. 78.

67 Brant, *Grounded*, p. 51.

68 Ibid., p. 56.

69 Berger, *About Looking*, p. 38. Berger was referring to the war photographer Don McCullin here.

70 Tony Harrison, 'Facing Up to the Muses', in *Tony Harrison*, edited by N. Astley (Newcastle-upon-Tyne: Bloodaxe Books, 1991), p. 440.

71 See Adrian Poole, *Tragedy: Shakespeare and the Greek Example* (Oxford: Blackwell, 1987), p. 11: 'tragedy represents the critical moments at which words fail'; and Tony Harrison's response: Harrison, 'Facing Up to the Muses', p. 441.

72 Sophocles, *Oedipus the King*, p. 92, lines 1303–6.

Chapter 5

1 No matter whether or not uprisings are religiously motivated or indeed are even anti-clerical or atheist, revolutionary rhetoric both looks back to the Garden from which corrupt governments have made us fall (Wordsworth's comment on the French Revolution that 'Bliss was it in that dawn to be alive / But to be young was very heaven': *The Prelude,* Book X, 696–7) and forward prophetically to a new Jerusalem, a New Age ('In Jerusalem you will be free': Caryl Churchill's play about the English Civil War, *Light Shining in Buckinghamshire* (1978; London: Nick Hern Books, 2015), p. 8; 'It will be a New Age and there will not have been a bloodbath': Brecht's *The Days of the Commune,* translated by David Constantine, *Collected Plays,* vol. 8 (London: Methuen, 2003), scene 4, p. 79). This double movement – backwards and forwards – is implied in the word's etymology: re-volution or 'turning back' – progress achieved via changing things back to how they once were in the Golden Age before we 'fell'.

2 Hamid Dabashi, *The Arab Spring: The End of Postcolonialism* (London and New York: Zed Books, 2012), p. 3.

3 Ahdaf Soueif, *Cairo: Memoir of a City Transformed* (London: Bloomsbury, 2012; rev edn, 2014), pp. 150, xv.

4 Nathan Schneider, *Thank You Anarchy: Notes from the Occupy Apocalypse* (Oakland, CA: University of California Press, 2013), pp. 5, 31.

5 Indeed, the army crushed a sit-in protest by Morsi supporters at a mosque in Cairo in August 2013, killing at least 817 people which an investigative report by Human Rights Watch declared 'one of the world's largest killings of demonstrators in a single day in recent history'.

6 *Julius Caesar,* 3.1.78.

7 Georg Buchner, *Danton's Death*, in a new version by Howard Brenton (London: Bloomsbury, 2010), Act 3, scene 5, p. 48.

8 *Julius Caesar,* 4.273–6. Brutus's revolutionary 'virtue' becomes a watchword in later political tragedies, notably *Danton's Death.*

9 Williams, *Modern Tragedy,* pp. 80–1.

10 Buchner, *Danton's Death,* Act 2, scene 6, p. 36.

11 Ibid., pp. 36–7; Georg Lukacs, *German Realists in the Nineteenth Century,* translated by J. Gaines and P. Keast (Cambridge, MA: The MIT Press, 1993), p. 84.

12 Hegel, *Aesthetics: Lectures on Fine Arts*, vol. II, p. 1215.

13 Hegel, *Reason in History*, quoted in Walter Kaufmann, *Hegel: Reinterpretation, Texts and Commentary* (New York: Doubleday, 1965), p. 256.

14 Brecht, *Mother Courage*, translated by John Willett, *Collected Plays*, vol. 5 (London: Methuen, 1995), Scene 11, pp. 182–4; *The Days of the Commune*, scene 13, pp. 123–5.

15 Dabashi, *The Arab Spring*, p. xviii.

16 'Tawakkol Karman – Nobel Lecture: In the name of God the Compassionate the Merciful', *Nobelprize.org*. Nobel Media AB 2014. Web. Accessed 6 September 2017: http://www.nobelprize.org/nobel_prizes/peace/laureates/2011/karman-lecture_en.html

17 Marc Lynch, *The Arab Uprising: The Unfinished Revolutions of the Middle East* (2012; new edn, 2013), pp. 245, 9.

18 Andy Kroll, 'How Occupy Wall Street Really Got Started', in *This Changes Everything: Occupy Wall Street and the 99% Movement*, edited by Sarah van Gelder (San Francisco: Berrett-Koehler Publishers, 2011), p. 16.

19 Gelder (ed.), *This Changes Everything*, p. 11.

20 The conflict in Libya is not really a sectarian one, in the way that it is in Syria, Yemen and Iraq. It is more a question of a failure of governance, caused in part by the legacy of the harsh regime of Gaddafi and the nature of his ousting: see Alia Brahimi, 'Why Libya Is Still a Global Terror Threat', *The Guardian*, 25 May 2017.

21 Marc Lynch, *The New Arab Wars: Uprisings and Anarchy in the Middle East* (New York: Public Affairs, 2016). Kindle edition. Location 86.

22 For the claim about the overriding importance of structures rather than agents in the Arab uprisings, see Jason Brownlee, Tarek Masoud and Andrew Reynolds, *The Arab Spring: Pathways of Repression and Reform* (Oxford: Oxford University Press, 2015), p. 213.

23 *Julius Caesar*, 1.2.141–2.

24 Ibid., 5.3.66–8.

25 Ibid., 1.2.307–9.

26 Ibid., 2.1.63–9.

27 M. Cherif Bassiouni, 'Egypt's Unfinished Revolution', in *Civil Resistance in the Arab Spring: Triumphs and Disasters*, edited by Adam Roberts (Oxford: Oxford University Press, 2016), p. 66.

28 Ibid., pp. 68–9.

29 *Julius Caesar*, 3.2.222; 3.2.244.

30 Mohammad Rabie, *Otared*, translated by Robin Moger (Cairo and New York: Hoopoe, 2016), p. 65.

31 Ibid., p. 72.

32 Ibid., p. 341.

33 Basma Abdel Aziz, *The Queue*, translated by Elizabeth Jaquette (Brooklyn and London: Melville House Publishing, 2016). Kindle edition. Location 386.

34 See also Nael Eltoukhy, *Women of Karentina*, translated by Roger Moger (Cairo: The American University in Cairo Press, 2014). Dystopian and surrealist novels are now proliferating in Egypt: see Alexandra Alter, 'Middle Eastern Writers Find Refuge in the Dystopian Novel', *New York Times*, 29 May 2016.

35 George Gordon, Lord Byron, *Childe Harold's Pilgrimage* IV, cviii, lines 965–7: in *Byron's Poetical Works*, edited by F. Page and corrected by J. Jump (Oxford: Oxford University Press, 1970).

36 Walter Benjamin, 'Theses on the Philosophy of History', in *Illuminations*, edited by Hannah Arendt (London: Fontana Press, 1992), p. 249.

37 Shelley, *Prometheus Unbound*, IV, lines 570–4: *Shelley's Poetry and Prose*, edited by Donald H. Reiman and Neil Fraistat (New York and London: Norton, 2002), pp. 285–6. This poetic drama is one of the few dramatizations of a successful revolution in literature.

38 Shelley also writes very perceptively about the French Revolution and the difficulties for ordinary people of 'listening to the plea of reason' after 'groaning under the calamities of a social state according to the provisions of which one man riots in luxury whilst another famishes for want of bread' in the 'Preface' to his epic of doomed revolution, *The Revolt of Islam: Shelley: Poetical Works*, edited by Thomas Hutchinson, p. 33.

39 Karl Marx, *The Eighteenth Brumaire of Louis Bonaparte*, translated by Eden and Cedar Paul (London: George Allen & Unwin Ltd, 1926), p. 23.

40 Slavoj Žižek, *The Year of Dreaming Dangerously* (London: Verso, 2012), p. 128.

41 Emily Wilson has written powerfully about the tragedy of prolonged or deferred endings: *Mocked with Death: Tragic Overliving from Sophocles to Milton* (Baltimore, MD: Johns Hopkins University Press, 2004).

42 Arendt, *On Revolution* (London: Faber and Faber, 1963), p. 46.

43 Anne Applebaum, *Washington Post*, 11 October 2011.

44 Slavoj Žižek points out the contradictions in Applebaum's own arguments about democracy and global capitalism: *The Year of Dreaming Dangerously*, pp. 84–6.

45 'Declaration of the Occupation of New York City', in Gelder (ed.), *This Changes Everything*, p. 36.

46 Guy Standing, *The Precariat: The New Dangerous Class* (2011; new edn, London: Bloomsbury, 2016), Preface.

47 Ibsen's *Emperor and Galilean* (1864–73) was given its English language premiere in a new version by Ben Power at London's National Theatre, June 2011. In overturning the Emperor Constantine's religious tyranny, the Emperor Julian wishes to bring about the 'freedom of faith for all' but ends up imposing harsh pagan rule and cruelly crushing any Christian dissent.

48 Sarah van Gelder, 'How Occupy Wall Street Changes Everything', in Gelder (ed.), *This Changes Everything*, p. 8. The experiment in egalitarian living in the 1871 Paris Commune – very similar to the Occupy movement – was dramatized in Brecht's *The Days of the Commune*, especially scene 7, pp. 92–7.

49 David Graeber, 'Enacting the Impossible: Making Decisions by Consensus', in Gelder (ed.), *This Changes Everything*, p. 23.

50 Lara Shalson, *Theatre and Protest* (London: Palgrave Macmillan, 2017).

51 *Julius Caesar*, 3.1.111–16.

52 I mean this in the sense of festivals as unifying, celebratory and anarchic within licensed parameters. Compare the much darker interpretation in Mona Ozouf, *Festivals and the French Revolution*, translated by Alan Sheridan (Cambridge, MA: Harvard University Press, 1988).

53 H. Samy Alim, 'What If We Occupied Language?' in *Occupy the Future!* edited by David Grusky, Doug McAdam, Rob Reich, Debra Satz (Cambridge, MA: MIT Press, 2013), p. 225.

54 Shalson, *Theatre and Protest*, p. 76.

55 Judith Butler, *Notes towards a Performative Theory of Assembly* (Cambridge, MA: Harvard University Press, 2015), p. 8. The collective, pluralistic, actively embodied and relational aspects of public assembly make them potentially revolutionary or at least can create change. See also Terry Lovell, 'Resisting with Authority: Historical Specificity, Agency and the Performative Self', *Theory,*

Culture and Society, 20 (2003), pp. 1–17; Lois Ruskai Melina, 'Being the Change: Protest as Performative Discourse in the Occupy Portland Encampment', *Global Discourse*, 4.2–3 (2014), pp. 308–22.

56 Brecht, *Mother Courage*, scene 12, p. 186.

57 Judith Butler, *Antigone's Claim: Kinship between Life and Death* (New York: Columbia University Press, 2000), pp. 6–11.

58 Bonnie Honig, *Antigone, Interrupted* (Cambridge: Cambridge University Press, 2013). According to her interpretation, Antigone and Ismene are 'plotters and conspirators who act ethically and politically' (153), demonstrating 'sororal solidarity' (154) and 'calling into ... question ... the heroic, ruptural notion of action' (154).

59 Žižek, *The Year of Dreaming Dangerously*, p. 83.

60 Schneider, *Thank You, Anarchy*, p. 6.

61 *Julius Caesar*, 3.1.259–62, 270–5.

62 http://www.kormany.hu/en/the-prime-minister/the-prime-minister-s-speeches/prime-minister-viktor-orban-s-speech-at-the-25th-balvanyos-summer-free-university-and-student-camp (accessed 18 October 2017).

63 Thomas Frank addresses the same constituency of forgotten poor white voters in America, from the perspective of the Left and the Democratic Party, in *Listen Liberal, or Whatever Happened to the Party of the People?* (Melbourne and London: Scribe, 2016).

64 'Remarks of President Donald J. Trump – as prepared for delivery. Inaugural Address, Friday, 20 January 2017, Washington, D.C.' WhiteHouse.gov: https://www.whitehouse.gov/briefings-statements/the-inaugural-address/

65 Jesse Green, 'Review: Can Trump Survive in Caesar's Palace?' *New York Times*, 9 June 2017.

66 Fox News, 11 June 2017.

67 Michael Billington, review of *Julius Caesar*, directed by Nicholas Hytner, The Bridge Theatre, *The Guardian*, 30 January 2018.

68 Byron, *Marino Faliero, Doge of Venice* (1821) in *Byron: Poetical Works*, pp. 407–53; Percy Bysshe Shelley, *The Cenci* (1819) in *Shelley's Poetry and Prose*, pp. 138–202; Buchner, *Danton's Death*; Henrik Ibsen, *Emperor and Galilean* (1873) in a new version by Ben Power (London: Nick Hern Books, 2011).

69 Vassilis Lambropoulos: 'Tragedy stages the drama of the Greek *arche* in its double meaning of beginning and rule, and asks whether self-

rule may control itself, whether radical autonomy may limit itself.' In Vassilis Lambropoulos, 'Introduction to the Site', *The Tragedy of Revolution: Revolution as Hubris in Modern Tragedy*. Blog. Department of Comparative Literature, University of Michigan: https://tragedy-of-revolution.complit.lsa.umich.edu/overview/ (accessed 16 May 2018).

Chapter 6

1 Refugees Operational Data Portal, UNHCR: http://data2.unhcr.org/en/situations/mediterranean

2 'Angela Merkel Calls for European Unity to Address Migrant Influx', *New York Times*, 31 August 2015; 'The Real Merkel Finally Stands Up', *Spiegel International*, 16 September 2015: http://www.spiegel.de/international/germany/merkel-refuses-to-apologize-for-welcoming-refugees-a-1053253.html

3 John Gould, 'Hiketeia', *JHS*, 93 (1973), p. 97.

4 Homer, *The Iliad*, translated by Caroline Alexander, p. 17: Book 1, lines 500–1.

5 *Human Flow*. Directed by Ai Weiwei. Los Angeles: AC Films/Participant Media, 2017. DVD

6 Aristotle, *The Poetics*, translated by Stephen Halliwell, chapter 13, p. 44.

7 Aeschylus, *The Suppliant Women*, in a version by David Greig (London: Faber and Faber, 2017), p. 11.

8 Ibid., p. 19.

9 Ibid., p. 18.

10 Gould, 'Hiketeia', p. 87.

11 At the end of her flight to Egypt, chased by Zeus's desire and Hera's gadfly, Io lets fall a sorrowful shame of tears (δακρύων δ᾽ ἀπο- / στάζει πένθιμον αἰδῶ): Aeschylus, *Suppliant Women*, Loeb edition, (Cambridge, MA: Harvard University Press, 1922), lines 578–9.

12 *The Suppliant Women*, in a version by David Greig, p. 26.

13 'ἄτης δ᾽ ἄβυσσον πέλαγος' (*ates d'abusson pelagos*) or a 'bottomless ocean of ruin': Aeschylus, *Suppliant Women*, Loeb edition, line 470 (my translation).

14 Euripides, *Suppliant Women*, translated by Robin Waterfield (Oxford: Oxford University Press, 2001), p. 150, lines 412–14, 418–20.

15 For more details on the play's invocation of the laws protecting *metics* in fifth-century Athens, see Geoffrey Bakewell, 'Metoikia in the *Supplices* of Aeschylus', *Classical Antiquity*, 16 (1997), pp. 209–28.

16 *The Suppliant Women*, directed by Ramin Gray, Young Vic Theatre (14 November 2017).

17 *The Suppliant Women*, in a version by David Greig, Director's Note.

18 The Greek word for 'catastrophe' is used by King Pelasgus at line 442.

19 Charlotte Eager, 'Syrian Refugees Stage Euripides' "The Trojan Women"', *Financial Times*, 3 January 2014.

20 Khaula quoted in Mark Tran, 'Adaptation of Trojan Women Starring Syrian Refugees Set for UK Tour', *The Guardian*, 20 April 2016.

21 A. O. Scott, '*Fire at Sea* Is Not the Documentary You'd Expect about the Migrant Crisis. It's Better', *New York Times*, 20 October, 2016

22 Richard Mosse quoted in *The Guardian*, 4 May 2017.

23 Richard Mosse, *Heat Maps* (New York: Jack Shainman Gallery, 2017). Prints varied between 12 × 20 inches and 50 × 289 inches; *Incoming* (2017). London: Barbican. Fifty-two-minute video. Projected across three screens in The Curve, on giant scale.

24 Duncan Wooldridge, review of *Incoming, 1000 Words*, http://www.1000wordsmag.com/richard-mosse/

25 *Aeschylus, Suppliant Women*, Loeb edition, lines 68–72: my translation.

26 Aeschylus, *Suppliants*, translated by Christopher Collard (Oxford: Oxford University Press, 2008), p. 70, lines 111–13.

27 "pathea melea" in Aeschylus, *Suppliant Women*, Loeb edition, line 112.

28 Lear says to his daughters, 'O, reason not the need! Our basest beggars / Are in the poorest things superfluous / Allow not nature more than nature needs, / Man's life's as cheap as beast's': *King Lear*, 2.4.259–62.

29 Agamben, *Homo Sacer*, p. 131: 'If refugees ... represent such a disquieting element in the order of the nation-state, this is above all because by breaking the continuity between man and citizen, nativity and nationality, they put the originary fiction of modern sovereignty in crisis. Bringing to light the difference between birth and nation, the refugee causes the secret presupposition of the political domain – bare life – to appear for an instant within that domain.' Agamben's (translated) language is staggeringly inadequate to the experience

here (refugees as a 'disquieting element'?), but the point about the precarious 'fiction' of our assumptions about civilization and the nation state and the suppression of 'bareness' beneath and within that fiction is well made and echoed – far more vividly and emotionally – in *King Lear*.

30 Simon Palfrey, *Poor Tom: Living* King Lear (Chicago: University of Chicago Press, 2014), p. 107.

31 The UK already had an opt-out of EU asylum policy and was exempt from the scheme.

32 Only two of the eleven attackers were not French or Belgium citizens and are thought to have entered Europe with Syrian refugees in the Greek island of Leros.

33 Lisa Mayer, 'France's National Front Leader Calls Canada's Refugee Plan "Madness"', CBC News. CBC/Radio Canada, 27 November 2015.

34 *Suppliant Women*, in a version by David Greig, p. 45.

35 Survation poll, November 2015: http://survation.com/latest-eu-referendum-polling/.

36 Ed Miliband: 'The real danger in the UK is that the debate about migration is, deliberately or otherwise, confused with the debate about refugees.' Quoted in Laura Devine, '"Refugees", "Migrants", and the Brexit vote', *The Law Society Gazette*, 16 November 2015: https://www.lawgazette.co.uk/legal-updates/refugees-migrants-and-the-brexit-vote/5052157.article.

37 *King Lear*, 1.2.99–101, 104–6.

38 The work of Cambridge Analytica for both the Brexit and Trump campaigns – and the direct connection between them – has been the subject of committed, lengthy investigation by the journalist Carole Cadwalladr. See, for example, her article, 'The Great British Brexit Robbery: How Our Democracy Was Hijacked', *The Observer*, 7 May 2017.

39 'Donald Trump Announces US Presidential Run with Eccentric Speech', *The Guardian*, 16 June 2015.

40 'Donald Trump: Ban All Muslims Entering US', *The Guardian*, 8 December 2015.

41 David Miliband, *Rescue: Refugees and the Political Crisis of Our Time* (New York: Simon & Schuster, 2017), p. 115.

42 Ibid., p. 119.

43 *Suppliant Women*, in a version by David Greig, p. 46.

Chapter 7

1 *Macbeth*, 1.3.35.

2 'Global Climate Change: Vital Signs of the Planet', NASA website, 'Vital Signs': Carbon Dioxide, Latest Measurement: January 2019; and Global Temperature, 'Latest Annual Average Anomaly: 2018'. https:// climate.nasa.gov/vital-signs/carbon-dioxide/ (Accessed 9 February 2019).

3 Mark Lynas, *Six Degrees: Our Future on a Hotter Planet*, 2nd edn (London: Harper Collins, 2008), pp. 186–90.

4 Beatrice Mwangi, quoted in Lucy Lamble and Emma Graham-Harrison, 'Drought and Rising Temperatures Leave 36m People across Africa Facing Hunger', *The Guardian*, 16 March 2016.

5 Terry P. Hughes (and others), 'Global Warming Transforms Coral Reef Assemblages', *Nature*, 556 (April 2018), pp. 492–6.

6 James Hansen (and others), 'Ice Melt, Sea Level Rise and Superstorms', *Atmospheric Chemistry and Physics*, 16.6 (22 March 2016), pp. 3761–812.

7 Ibid. See also Oliver Milman, 'Climate Guru James Hansen Warns of Much Worse Than Expected Sea Level Rise', *The Guardian*, 22 March 2016; David Archer, *The Long Thaw: How Humans Are Changing the Next 100,000 Years of Earth's Climate* (Princeton, NJ: Princeton University Press, 2008), pp. 160–1.

8 Lynas, *Six Degrees*, pp. 217–41.

9 *Macbeth*, 1.3.136–7; 5.5.18–20. See Rebecca Bushnell, *Tragic Time in Drama, Film and Videogames: The Future in the Instant* (London: Palgrave, Macmillan, 2016), pp. 12–16.

10 A.W. Schlegel, *A Course of Lectures on Dramatic Art and Literature*, translated by John Black (1815; revised edn, London: H.G. Bohn, 1846), p. 93.

11 *Prometheus Bound*, translated by Christopher Collard (Oxford: Oxford University Press, 2008), p. 121, lines 774–5.

12 Ibid., p. 123, lines 841–2.

13 Shelley, *Prometheus Unbound*, I, lines 12–13; 48; 31–2: *Shelley's Poetry and Prose*, pp. 210, 211.

14 *Prometheus Bound*, translated by Christopher Collard, p. 113, lines 470–1.

15 Ibid., p. 125, lines 946–7.

16 Forty-eight per cent of Americans believe that global climate change is occurring because of human activity while 51 per cent believe that either it is happening because of natural causes or that there is no evidence for it happening at all. By contrast, 97 per cent of scientists believe that climate change is human-induced. 'The Politics of Climate' survey, 10 May–6 June 2016. Pew Research Center. http://www.pewinternet.org/2016/10/04/public-views-on-climate-change-and-climate-scientists/ (accessed 2 February 2017).

17 Calvin Beisner, founder of the Cornwall Alliance, and Bryan Fischer, American Family Association, are two of the main spokesmen for this position. See George Marshall, *Don't Even Think about It: Why Our Brains Are Wired to Ignore Climate Change* (London: Bloomsbury, 2014), p. 213. Of course, one of the other chief motivations is our dependence on fossil fuels and the lobbying power of oil and mining companies. For the influence of oil companies upon climate-change scepticism in America, see Elizabeth Kolbert, *Field Notes from a Catastrophe: Man, Nature and Climate Change* (New York: Bloomsbury, 2006; new edn 2015), pp. 162–72.

18 Michael Billington, *The Guardian*, 11 February 2011.

19 Charles Spencer, *The Telegraph*, 11 February 2011.

20 John Willett and Ralph Manheim, 'Introduction', in *Brecht: Collected Plays*, vol. 5 (London: Methuen, 1995), p. xxvi.

21 Brecht, *Life of Galileo*, translated by John Willett, *Collected Plays*, vol. 5, Scene 13, p. 91. In this exchange, a new concept of the tragic is framed. The production of the play at London's National Theatre, directed by Howard Davies (July–October 2006), in modern dress, highlighted its contemporary relevance in an era of climate-change denial.

22 Ibsen, *An Enemy of the People*, translated by James Walter McFarlane (Oxford: Oxford University Press, 1971), Act 2, pp. 23, 24.

23 Ibid., Act 4, p. 71.

24 *The Wild Duck*, translated by James Walter Mcfarlane (Oxford: Oxford University Press, 1971), Act 5, p. 205.

25 Ibsen, *An Enemy of the People*, Act 4, p. 76.

26 Arcola Theatre, directed by Mehmet Ergen, April 2008; Sheffield Crucible, directed by Daniel Evans, February 2010; Young Vic, directed by Richard Jones, May 2013; Barbican, directed by Thomas Ostermeier, September 2014; Chichester Festival Theatre, directed by Howard Davies, May 2016; Union Theatre, London, directed by Phil Willmott, January 2019.

27 Michael Billington on Anthony Sher at the Sheffield Crucible, *The Guardian*, 18 February 2010.

28 Susannah Clapp on Anthony Sher at the Sheffield Crucible, *The Observer*, 21 February 2010.

29 Michael Billington on Greg Hicks at the Arcola Theatre, *The Guardian*, 7 April 2008.

30 See David Harrower's version of the play: Ibsen, *Public Enemy*, in a version by David Harrower (London: Faber and Faber, 2013). This version was performed at the Young Vic theatre, directed by Richard Jones, in May 2013.

31 Obama signed the agreement of the United Nations Framework Convention on Climate Change on 22 April 2016 to hold global temperature rise to within 2 degrees above the pre-industrial average. Trump announced on 1 June 2017 that he would withdraw the United States from the agreement.

32 The most artistically successful of the recent revivals, Thomas Ostermeier's at the Barbican offered an interpretation closest to this vision, whereby the social context was explored and the extent to which 'society privileges economic relations over personal ones': Simon McBurney, *The Guardian*, 24 September 2014.

33 George Steiner, *The Death of Tragedy* (London: Faber and Faber, 1961), pp. 8, 291.

34 Aristotle explained the 'slippage', 'knowing' and 'not knowing' with his theory of *akrasia* or 'unrestraint'. See his *Nicomachean Ethics* Book 7, especially chapter 3: *Nicomachean Ethics*, translated by H. Rackham (London: William Heinemann, 1926), pp. 385–95.

35 Stephen Gardiner, *A Perfect Moral Storm: The Ethical Tragedy of Climate Change* (Oxford: Oxford University Press, 2011), p. 7.

36 Ibid., p. 28.

37 Ibid., p. 27.

38 Arthur Miller, *All My Sons*, in *Plays: One* (London: Methuen, 1988), Act 3, p. 118.

39 Think also of the end of Miller's *The Crucible* and John Proctor's cry: 'Because it is my name. Because I cannot have another in my life! … How may I live without my name?': *The Crucible* in *The Portable Arthur Miller*, edited by Christopher Bigsby (London: Penguin, 2003), Act 4, p. 250.

40 Arthur Miller, *An Enemy of the People: An Adaptation of the Play by Henrik Ibsen* (London: Penguin, 1915). *An Enemy of the People*, directed by Robert Lewis, opened at Broadhurst Theatre, New York, on 28 December 1950.

41 Simon McBurney's review: *The Guardian*, 24 September 2014.

42 Bill McKibben, *The End of Nature: Humanity, Climate Change and the End of the World*, 2nd edn (London: Bloomsbury, 2003).

43 Bruno Latour, 'Agency at the Time of the Anthropocene', *New Literary History*, 45 (2014), p. 6.

44 Will Steffen, Paul J. Crutzen and John R. McNeill, 'The Anthropocene: Are Humans Now Overwhelming the Great Forces of Nature?' *Ambio*, 38 (2007), p. 614.

45 See Wolfgang Behringer, *A Cultural History of Climate*, translated by Patrick Camiller (Cambridge: Polity Press, 2010), pp. 209–11.

46 Timothy Morton, 'Ecology without the Present', *The Oxford Literary Review*, 34.2 (2012), p. 236.

47 Claire Colebrook, 'Not Symbiosis, Not Now: Why Anthropogenic Change Is Not Really Human', *The Oxford Literary Review*, 34.2 (2012), p. 189.

48 Roy Scranton, 'Learning How to Die in the Anthropocene', *New York Times*, 10 November 2013.

49 Yukio Mishima, *Sun and Steel*, translated by John Bester (London: Secker and Warburg, 1971), pp. 12–13. Mishima's ideas about traditional Japanese tragedy and samurai culture were based more upon his own romanticized version of the past than upon historical accuracy. Indeed, samurai culture or *bushido* has been distorted by modern mythologization: see Karl Friday, 'Bushido or Bull? A Medieval Historian's Perspective on the Imperial Army and the Japanese Warrior Tradition', *History Teacher*, 27.3 (1994), pp. 339–49.

50 Timothy Clark, *Ecocriticism on the Edge: The Anthropocene as a Threshold Concept* (London: Bloomsbury, 2015), p. xi.

51 Cormac McCarthy, *The Road* (London: Picador, 2006), p. 237.

52 Byron, 'Darkness', in *Byron: Oxford Authors*, edited by Jerome J. McGann (Oxford: Oxford University Press, 1986), p. 272, lines 1–5.

53 Ibid., p. 273, lines 78–82.

54 Derrida, *Of Grammatology*, translated by Gayatri Chakravorty Spivak (Baltimore and London: John Hopkins University Press, 1976; corrected edn, 1997), p. 158.

55 Kirsten Shepherd-Barr argues that Beckett's theatre 'dramatises the process of ecocide; there is "no way out of denuded nature – just an endlessly denatured void"', in *Theatre and Evolution from Ibsen to Beckett* (New York: Columbia University Press, 2015), p. 240.

56 Beckett, *Endgame*, in *The Complete Dramatic Works* (London: Faber and Faber, 1986), p. 93.

57 Ibid., p. 132.

58 Ibid., p. 101.

59 Churchill, *Far Away: Caryl Churchill: Plays: 4* (London: Nick Hern Books, 2008), p. 159.

60 Lyn Gardner, *The Guardian*, 16 November 2014.

61 *The Skriker, Caryl Churchill: Plays 3* (London: Nick Hern Books, 1998), p. 290. We can compare also the female chatter which mingles 'fantasy intricately wired into current politics' in Churchill's recent play *Escaped Alone* (2016): Susannah Clapp, 'Escaped Alone Review – Small Talk and Everyday Terror from Caryl Churchill', *The Observer*, 31 January 2016. See Sheila Rabillard, 'On Churchill's Ecological Drama', in *The Cambridge Companion to Churchill*, edited by Elaine Aston and Elin Diamond (Cambridge: Cambridge University Press, 2009), pp. 88–104.

62 J.G. Ballard, *The Drowned World* (New York: Berkley Books, 1962); *High Rise* (London: Jonathan Cape, 1975).

63 Churchill, *Far Away*, p. 158.

64 Richard E. Leakey and Roger Lewin, *The Sixth Extinction: Biodiversity and Its Survival* (1995; London: Weidenfeld and Nicholson, 1996).

65 *The Book of Job*, 38.4.

66 Bill McKibben, *The Comforting Whirlwind: God, Job and the Scale of Creation* (Grand Rapids, MI: Eerdmans, 1994), p. 36.

67 Marjorie Garber, *Dog Love* (London: Hamish Hamilton, 1996). p. 15.

68 Hannah Velten, *Cow* (London: Reaktion Books, 2007), p. 168.

69 Richard Adams, *Watership Down* (London: Puffin Books, 1973). See Kenneth P. Kitchell, Jr., 'The Shrinking of the Epic Hero: From Homer to Richard Adams' Watership Down', *Classical and Modern Literature*, 7 (1986), pp. 13–30.

70 Barbara King, *How Animals Grieve* (Chicago: University of Chicago Press, 2013), p. 51.

71 Philip Armstrong and Laurence Simmons, 'Bestiary: An Introduction', in *Knowing Animals*, edited by L. Simmons and P. Armstrong (Leiden: Brill, 2007), pp. 1–24.

72 Velten, *Cow*, pp. 7; 21–5.

73 Ibid., p. 176.

74 *Bullhead*. Directed by Michael R. Roskam, Brussels: Savage Films, 2011. DVD.

75 *Bullhead* can be compared with Buchner's unfinished tragic drama *Woyzzeck*, in which a man is similarly experimented on, given life-changing drugs and then punished when he reacts with violence. Both *Bullhead* and *Woyzzeck* are interested in the tragically brutalizing effects of modernity and the man/animal/machine interface.

76 King, *How Animals Grieve*, p. 152.

Coda

1 Martin Harries analyses the tension between the figure and disfiguration following September 11 in his fascinating account of 'destructive spectatorship': Martin Harries, *Forgetting Lot's Wife* (New York: Fordham University Press, 2007), pp. 103–14.

2 Erich Auerbach, 'Figura', in *Scenes from the Drama of European Literature: Six Essays* (London: Meridian Books, 1959; reprinted 1973), p. 53.

3 Ibid., p. 58.

4 For example, Simpson, *9/11*, p. 46; Harries, *Forgetting Lot's Wife*, p. 114.

5 Roland Barthes, *Camera Lucida: Reflections on Photography*, translated by Richard Howard (New York: Farrar, Straus and Giroux, 1981), p. 27 and pp. 32ff.

6 Chaudhuri, 'A Forum on Theatre and Tragedy', p. 97. See also Diana Taylor's contribution to that Forum, p. 95: 'Tragedy delivers the devastation in a miniaturized and complete package, neatly organized with a beginning, a middle, and an end.' I am clearly resisting both these definitions in my account of classical tragedy.

7 For one of the best accounts of the capacity of tragedy to surpass or subvert its limits, see Wilson, *Mocked with Death*.

8 Terry Eagleton, *Sweet Violence: The Idea of the Tragic* (Oxford: Blackwell, 2003), p. xii.

9 Williams, *Modern Tragedy*, pp. 62–6.

ACKNOWLEDGEMENTS

I wish to acknowledge the institutional support that helped the writing of this book. The Cambridge Newton Trust Foundation awarded me a grant which allowed me to take a year's sabbatical leave to complete the book. The University of Cambridge's Faculty of English and the college of Peterhouse provided assistance, both financial and in other less tangible ways, in my explorations of tragedy.

While focused writing has taken me the last eighteen months, the research for this book began when those planes flew into the World Trade Center. I have tested out my ideas in talks and in publications and have been grateful for the feedback. In particular I have learned from the responses I received from audiences at the Hay-on-Wye Book Festival; the Free University of Berlin; IASH in the University of Edinburgh; the Institute of Literature in Tbilisi, Georgia; the Almeida Theatre in London; the University of Canterbury in Christchurch, New Zealand; the University of Cambridge; and the Department of Classics in the University of Michigan. Chapter 2 contains some material first published in my article '"We Can't Make More Dirt": Tragedy and the Excavated Body', *Cambridge Quarterly*, 32.3 (2003), pp. 103–11. A brief extract from 'Tragic Remembrance in the Era of Fake News', *Modern Theology*, 34.2 (2018), pp. 267–72, appears at the start of Chapter 3. Chapter 4 draws on material first explored in 'Tragedy, Photography and Osama bin Laden: Looking at the Enemy', *Critical Quarterly*, 57.2 (2015), pp. 17–35.

I've had many conversations about tragedy and our contemporary world with friends and colleagues over the years, which have helped to clarify my ideas. In particular I wish to acknowledge Ben Gibson, Ben Hayes, Gloria McLean, Ramona Mosse, Peter Popham, Yopie Prins, Jan Schramm, Matthew Shores, Christine Twite and Giles Waller. Olivia Scott-Berry first got me thinking about the tragedy of animals. Rosemary Newhardt hosted me in New York and talked movingly about the experience of living through 9/11. And there have been numerous interlocutors I have encountered at drinks parties and dinners who have told me confidently what the definition and rules of tragedy really are!

I am enormously grateful to Vassilis Lambropoulos who generously took the time to read the complete draft book and offered detailed and insightful comment. I am also greatly indebted to Sunita Sharma-Gibson and to Ben Gibson for their advice on sourcing the images, both within the book and for the cover. Mark Dudgeon and Lara Bateman at Bloomsbury and production manager Kumaresh Vaidhyanadhaswamy have also been supportive through the process of bringing this book to the light.

Above all I want to acknowledge the help of my husband, Robert Wallis, who read each draft chapter as it was produced and offered advice on politics, photography and navigating the publishing industry. His simultaneous encouragement and questioning scepticism continue to be a much-needed tonic in these difficult times.

INDEX